OF ITS TIME AND OF ITS PLACE
THE WORK OF RICHARD MURPHY ARCHITECTS

Frontispiece: DCA, Dundee
Front cover: British High Commission, Sri Lanka
Back cover: Galeri Theatre, Caernarfon

OF ITS TIME AND OF ITS PLACE

THE WORK OF RICHARD MURPHY ARCHITECTS

In memory of Isi Metzstein

Artifice
books on architecture

CONTENTS

The Breakfast Mission, Edinburgh, home of Richard Murphy Architects since 2001.

ACKNOWLEDGEMENTS

In publishing a new book on the work of our practice we considered the idea of a sequel to our previous book *Richard Murphy Architects; Ten Years of Practice* published in 2001. That book, now out of print, showed a number of projects which at that time were either in design or under construction. All of these are now complete and needed to be re-illustrated. In any event, in order to understand the later work we thought it was important to see how current ideas had developed from the very beginning. We therefore decided to publish a completely new survey starting once again in 1991. This is also much fuller—in 2001, 39 buildings and projects featured—that number has now grown to 107.

The consequent ambition of the new book has been very high and the bulk of the burden of its preparation has been placed on Stephen Leonard assisted by Alex Thurman, James Falconer, Piotr Kmiotczyk, Laura Wardrop, Graeme Armet, Gareth Jones, Brian Tobin, Peter Hunt, Daryl Robbins, David McPeak, Kris Grant, James Cockburn, Paul Pattinson Tersius Maass and Klas Hyllen from the practice. Dave Morris did much of the early research. Over the years the practice has varied in size from two to 35. Everything illustrated here represents the product of a team effort and we are, and have been, privileged to have talented and dedicated colleagues with whom to share the practice. The preparation of the book has put a considerable burden on the office and I would like to thank my fellow directors Bill Black, Matt Bremner and James Mason for their support throughout this long period of gestation.

As I have said on many occasions it is impossible to construct a successful building without a good client and we continue to have some wonderfully supportive clients. Much more than a client has been Carol Grigor (nee Colburn) who has been a particularly steadfast supporter not just in commissioning two houses but in helping to fund feasibility studies and in contributing financially to a number of completed projects illustrated in this book. Murray Grigor has also been a great supporter, and his films about several of our completed buildings have featured in our exhibitions and can be seen on our website. In 2001 we invited four clients to contribute to the book as we thought that this was an important insight into the whole picture of how a building comes into being. We have again extended similar invitations and are delighted that Mike and Julie Lambert, Brian and Lesley Knox, Neil and Marion Thomson, Andrew Burrell, Rob Joiner, Dennis O'Keeffe, Professor Mike Thorne and Gwyn Roberts have all contributed their memories of the client's side of the design and building experience. Similarly we are also very grateful to two building users, Dr Peter Hayes, former British High Commissioner in Colombo, and Clive Gillman, the current Director of Dundee Contemporary Arts. They both have contributed their thoughts on inheriting and using their respective buildings. And, in what may be a publishing first, we invited our favourite contractor, Steve Evans of Inscape Joinery, to reflect on his 21 year association with the practice. I personally was very moved by his contribution.

I am thrilled that my one time employer and long standing friend and mentor, Sir Richard MacCormac, former President of the RIBA and founder partner of MacCormac Jamieson Pritchard Architects has written a scholarly analysis of the practice's work. He no doubt recognises many of his own ideas reworked, somewhat inadequately, by his former employee. I would also like to thank Stephen Briggs who provided the perfect Tuscan Casa Paradisa in which to write the bulk of the script and Kathy Jowett who subsequently laboured at the word processor. I would also like to thank Duncan McCorquodale and Laura Varzgalyte at Artifice books on architecture for their assistance, advice and forbearance.

The book will feature as part of an exhibition at the RIBA in the Autumn of 2012 and in a Festival exhibition at the Royal Scottish Academy in Edinburgh in 2013.

And finally, I am delighted that Dany Metzstein has agreed for us to dedicate the book to the memory of the late Professor Isi Metzstein (1928–2012). Isi has been a friend, advisor, inspiration, mentor, critic and frequent visitor to the office and is sorely missed.

Richard Murphy
April 2012

SIR RICHARD MACCORMAC REFLECTS ON
21 YEARS OF RICHARD MURPHY ARCHITECTS

Writing about the work of Richard Murphy feels like the continuation of a conversation which began when Richard worked in my practice in the 1980s. So I get a sense of recognition of an architectural culture of shared ideas and values; the geometric strategies that maximise floor space, windows as 'aedicules', and the open corner, for example. This is not to take credit, the geometry comes from Leslie Martin and Lionel March and from understanding the Georgian lessons of Edinburgh and Bloomsbury; windows as little houses from Sir John Summerson's essay "Heavenly Mansions", the open corner from Frank Lloyd Wright (1) (via a shared struggle to achieve such effects in our residential scheme for Fitzwilliam College Cambridge (2)).

Richard Murphy shares a DNA with me, and other British practitioners, notably Ted Cullinan and Sir Colin Stansfield Smith (both RIBA Gold medalists). The evolution of this architecture comes through the Arts and Crafts Movement. It is about making things which are beautiful and useful, perhaps beautiful because they are useful. The seeds sown by Pugin and Ruskin grew in the workshops of Morris and found expression in the architecture of Mackintosh, Baillie Scott and Voysey, and gave us a sense of architecture, not as spectacle but as an experience rooted in its making and its purposes. This is finally an ethical standpoint and one which I believe drives the work of Richard Murphy and his colleagues.

To start at the beginning is not just a chronological convenience but a way of setting out an unfolding narrative of architectural ideas implicit in the early projects, such as the Fruitmarket Gallery and the house extensions, which provided the first opportunities to practice architecture. One might also add that being in back gardens, and out of sight, the house extensions avoided obstruction from a certain kind of planning officer intent on imitation, unaware of the origins of SPAB in Ruskin's assertion that the new should never be confused with the old. Where these projects grow out of the remnants of stone outhouses (or "ruins" as Richard Murphy has called them) a deliberate contrast is created between two kinds of space—traditional masonry enclosure—and the spatial ambiguity and open/closed possibilities of lightweight structures. This may also be seen as a neat metaphor for the direction of the practice's work and its relationship with history, a grounded understanding and appreciation of traditional structures, an outstanding example being the Harrison House with its barrel vault and Soanian lighting, and an ability to recognise in such structures the springing points for innovation. (3)

The first of these extensions, the Blythman House, initiates many ideas which find their subsequent development in the practice's work; (4) the constructional contrast between the masonry base and emerging glazed structures above, though never formulaic, finds itself in the dense urban fabric of Old Fishmarket Close, with its nod towards such contrasts in the Mediaeval buildings of the Old Town, in the sophisticated 'bookend' form of the architects own house in Hart Street and in the houses built in open landscape, such as the Stoneman House where the rainscreen of dry stone walling contrasts with the emergence of glass and timber at first floor level.

These early extensions, like the Blythman and the Francis House also establish an idea about roofs—whether flat or pitched—which are manifestly independent, a separation from the existing structure, achieved by roof-lights which backlight the interior. This is the beginning of an architecture which like that of Soane uses light to articulate space. (5) The important structural idea here, which continues into the projects for long houses, such as the Stewart House, is that the steel frame which supports the roof is structurally independent. In both the Blythman and Francis houses, the roof is supported on slender steelwork separate from the architecture of enclosure of timber joinery and glass. What is interesting here is the Kahnian sense of the building envelope having the status of furniture and a continuity with internal screens and alcoves to draw space from inside to outside. (6) A special example of this is Morrison House where the kitchen worktop is part of the external envelope. Below a horizontal pivoting window, the kitchen is enabled to stand in the garden in summer, an extraordinary redefinition of the conventional elements of domestic architecture. (7)

The Edinburgh Mews conversions are projects which explore the constraints and possibilities of existing stone buildings of about five metres frontage and varying depths. The original ground floor heights, marked by enormous stone lintels to accommodate carriages, with the reduced ceiling height of hay lofts above, have been generally reversed on the mews side to create a higher living room over a garage. In Colburn House 1, the new living room floor level, (under a concrete beam that has replaced stone lintels) is represented by a structural steel channel which also acts as the track for the sliding garage door. (8) The resulting horizontal slot becomes something of a signature in the mews houses and an ordering idea which is developed to create horizontal slots to disengage parts of facades, roofs from walls and furniture from floors, particularly in the highly complex section of the architect's own house in Hart Street. In the mews houses such as Colburn House 1 and 2, this horizontal disengagement is used internally to mark slight changes of level between bedroom and living area and kitchen and living area respectively, the steps in the latter being formed as Scarpa like platforms, with the kitchen itself as a floating platform above the bedroom. These relationships achieve the most subtle kinds of enclosure, the upper levels slightly overlooking and the lower levels gently contained, these distinctions reinforced by roof-lights and sectional changes to expand and compress volume.

In the architect's designs for his own house in both the project for Bakehouse Close and the scheme to be realised in Hart Street, these sectional tricks make for extraordinary interiors full of surprises, intimacy and explorable complexity combined with environmental strategies which can insulate in winter, store solar gain for night time use and naturally vent excess heat in summer.

The filmmaker Murray Grigor has suggested that the mews houses are Richard Murphy's "string quartets". If the house extensions can be included in that analogy we see the development of a distinct and recognisable language which, like musical composition, is a way of thinking, not just an architectural outcome. There is nothing repetitious about; this like Wright's Usonian houses, these are variations on a theme.

Private houses in landscape settings offered opportunities to develop three residential types; long houses, walled garden houses and towers. Amongst the long houses, the Stoneman House is characteristically organised with bedrooms at the ends and double-height living in the middle contained within a continuous dominant roof above dry stone walling. (9) It sits comfortably amongst the local cottages. Contrast this with the MacKinnon/Briongos House, another long house of comparable organisation, but with an entirely different response to its location on an airfield. (10) Rather than grounded in stonework, it is clad in mill-finished aluminium and seems almost poised for takeoff. The Stewart House represents another long house variant with all habitable rooms facing south. The section recalls the Palmer House extension with the roof-light at the back of the plan, to separate and distinguish between living spaces and service rooms. Here the light steel frame is capped by a transom, below which timber windows and sliding shutters contrast the scale of the interior with the floating oversailing roof, an architectural proposition first explored in the Palmer House extension. In the long houses and in many future projects the transom becomes a powerful ordering device to establish the scale defined by windows, partitions and furniture within the greater scale defined by storey heights and by roofs.

Proposing innovative houses within landscapes where planning policies have promoted suburban bungalows as being "in keeping" (with other bungalows!) has been deeply frustrating for practices like Richard Murphy's. Proposals for tower houses have all been refused, even though they draw on an ancient Scottish tradition and offer a respect for landscape with their minimal and isolated footprint. To overcome such objections the practice has developed what it calls a "stealth strategy", inward looking walled enclosures buried in the landscape. One such proposal is the Younger House, surrounded by woodland, its circular footprint, partly inhabited and partly a walled garden, suggests the ruin of a "broch"; while the play between the circle and the orthogonal and the inference that the roof is on upper ground level suggests an architectural projection of a Ben Nicholson relief.

It is testimony to the practice's capabilities that these beautiful and innovative interpretations of the family house in the landscape run in parallel with an equal commitment to urban living and the form and character of the historic city. What is important about the projects in the Old and New Towns of Edinburgh and their contribution to their historic setting is that they accept and repair the unique urban structure and meet its extraordinarily high residential density.

Old Fishmarket Close reinterprets the dense linear patterns of the "Kipperbone" organisation of the Old Town with a double-banked corridor building skilfully expressed as two tall narrow offset blocks. (11) The gables contain double-height living rooms and recall the Mediaeval timber framed and gabled roofed rooms, which appear as little buildings embedded in the silhouette of the Old Town. The characteristically sloping site allows offices and a restaurant to be introduced at the lower level to contribute to the urbanity of the project. The architecture of the Fishmarket Close and the adjacent Cowgate development have similar objectives, with rendered volumes out of which roofscape emerges. The gable timber roof and linked monopitch towers fit snugly into their highly exacting context.

At Dean Bank Lane, a private development makes an equally scaled response to the bank of the river stepping down from three storeys on the lane frontage to six storeys on the river bank. This architecture with its horizontal channels, rails and sliding windows convincingly transfers the language of channels and transoms, which originated in the houses, to a multi-storey elevation.

The competition-winning project for the houses and offices at Whitehaven on the Cumbrian coast seems to draw on early work in another way, if one interprets the original house extensions as being themselves little houses facing into back gardens. (12) While with MJP, Richard Murphy worked on the Fitzwilliam College New Court Student residences and was party to a discussion of Sir John Summerson's essay "Heavenly Mansions" in which Summerson considers the aedicule (from the Latin for little house, room or niche) as places for the gods in classical architecture and suggests how the idea can be transferred to windows and their representations of human presence. So one can say that the occupants of the Whitehaven apartments are represented by the outlook of the bays, 'little houses', commanding the maritime prospect. These contribute to an exceptionally animated interlocking elevational composition, which is further articulated by voids at the lower level through which the office accommodation gains views of the harbour. The liveliness of the scheme is further enhanced by giving the lower maisonettes external stairs with direct access to the quay.

External access stairs become an important device in a series of projects for housing, or, as the practice puts it, for "making housing sociable". In Edinburgh there is a precedent for external stairs in the so-called "colony" houses built for artisans at the edge of the New Town, where first floor flats are accessed by stairs at right angles to the terrace, in one of which Richard Murphy lived for 15 years. Visible external stairs overcome the obvious disadvantages of internal tenement stairs as insecure, unventilated and unhygienic, but Richard Murphy has also recognised the social possibilities of stairs which give access to shared spaces at ground level, reinforcing the sense of local community. The competition-winning scheme for the backland site behind Dublin Street recognised that this was the location of the pre-New Town village of Broughton by building on the footprint of the original buildings and using external stairs to animate the spaces between them. (13)

Residents have described the development as "living in a secret village". Not many housing projects can have elicited such a response.

Perhaps the clearest expression of the external staircase and its social role was realised in the Moore Street Houses for Molindinar Housing Association in Glasgow. (14, 17) This is a dramatic piece of urban design making use of an existing classical arch to signal access to the centre of the site, developed by Richard Murphy's team and three other practices. The RMA scheme focuses diagonal external stairs on to a secure central court which belongs to the tenants and is animated by their coming and going. This is a real contribution to medium-density housing, fully recognised, in this case, by a thoughtful and appreciative client who understood the potential of this architectural proposition. Further development of the idea for a combination of social housing and accommodation for the Salvation Army in Aberdeen will not be realised.

It is curious that the ideology for twentieth century Modern architecture in Britain was unable or unwilling (with certain exceptions such as Span housing by Eric Lyons) to address the issue of suburbia, perhaps as an expression of distaste on the part of the urban avant-garde for the bourgeois aspirations of the middle class. The fact is that most people in the UK live in suburbia. It is where people aspire to be and where the most pressing issues of sustainability can be addressed strategically. The context for suburban development is changing. Higher land values and affordability are raising densities and challenging developers. Ever increasing oil prices undermine assumptions about car ownership and concepts of shared space, and "home zones" prompt fresh ideas about the kind of place that suburbia should be. Richard Murphy, inspired by Utzon's marvellous housing projects in Denmark and Peter Aldington's similar approach to the courtyard form, developed a version of a single-storey long house for the RIAS House of the Future competition, setting it in a suburban context. With the houses at right angles to a lane to minimise vehicular space and eliminating front gardens, the layout maximises private open space in the form of walled courtyards.

These principles are realised in a private development at Cramond, northwest of Edinburgh, where a range of house types combine to form courtyard gardens and face directly out onto shared paved surfaces with planted areas, but no front gardens. Projecting semi-circular stairs common to all the house types suggest an informality and special identity to what is a rigorously planned and quite formal layout. This really does look like a new kind of suburbia. The practice had a further opportunity to develop comparable ideas in the exemplary Newhall development by the Moen brothers in Harlow. (15) Here the tighter grain of the master plan led to smaller houses than at Cramond in a combination of terraces and a two-storey version of the RIAS competition long house with secluded courtyard gardens. (16) With a sense of continuity achieved with brick garden walls, paved shared surfaces and

a deliberately limited vocabulary of detail under a dominant theme of steep roof pitches, this scheme, like that at Cramond, makes an important contribution to an idea of suburbia which makes places out of the public realm, simple to construct house types and large gardens at a relatively high-density. It must surely be a matter of time before house buyers recognise the poor value offered by the "traditional" suburban house sitting in the middle of its largely unusable plot.

It is to the credit of the practice that its reputation for integrating new architecture into sensitive urban contexts should have attracted clients wanting to find new uses for important historic buildings. One senses a degree of frustration at finding that a dramatic building such as the Edinburgh Royal Infirmary doesn't readily convert into a hotel, and Donaldson School is equally difficult to convert into apartments. At the time of writing, the school designed by William Playfair and modelled on the Elizabethan Burghley House is being considered as a country house hotel, surrounded by crescents of rooms under formal gardens leading to a lake—a boldly Elizabethan inspiration.

In several respects hotels and student housing are similar in content with repetitive bedrooms and shared facilities. As colleges seek revenue from summer schools there are increasing expectations of high standards. More specific to student accommodation has been the realisation that shared kitchens, particularly if they overlook or are overlooked by staircases, engender sociability, a perception first considered in David Roberts' 1965 residential scheme for Jesus College and further developed in MJP's competition entry for Robinson College, 1974. (18) These schemes were based on the traditional Oxbridge staircase model, in which staircases and kitchens alternate with pairs of rooms around courts with the potential for a rhythmical elevation, expressive of their content. Richard Murphy's competition entry for Jesus College Cambridge, consisting of three open-sided courts with groups of six student rooms sharing a half level kitchen, was a beautiful interpretation of this idea, sadly unrealised. (19)

Another competition entry for 500 student rooms for Warwick University tested this at a larger scale with clusters of three flats per floor consisting of eight student rooms around small open courts containing stairs and overlooked by the three kitchens associated with the flats. This proposal had some important properties; it aggregates enough rooms to achieve an economical distribution of lifts without recourse to corridors, it associates each kitchen with eight students, not too many, but locates them so that they overlook each other—a highly convivial arrangement. This is another scheme that deserved to have been realised.

The shortly to be completed scheme for Queens University, Belfast, consisting of flats will make a similar commitment to sociability, not with shared kitchens but with external staircases derived from the successful strategy for the Moore Street housing association in Edinburgh. (20)

The first Maggie's Centre in Edinburgh pointed a direction for patient care deliberately distinct from the kind of sanitised, rationalised and clinical environments typical of hospitals and their waiting areas. This little building, partly the conversion of a stable block, has been called a "home from home" and "a place apart", and succeeds in creating an atmosphere which is gentle and domestic and centred around a big table and associated kitchen. (21) With a separate meeting room and staff accommodation, Maggie's Edinburgh set a pattern for subsequent centres. The interior is intimate and complex with its own language of sliding timber screens and corner windows within a steel frame, which emerge out of the stonework of the existing building—the legacy of those early mews conversions such as the Colburn Houses.

The practice's range of health projects are all imbued with a deep intuitive sense of the needs of the end user. They are, as Dennis O'Keeffe, NHS Fife's Projects Director, has remarked, the product of "a human centred architecture". The double-sided corridor is banished and circulation, generally day-lit, is usually combined with another function, so that at the Conan Doyle Medical Centre in Edinburgh, circulation and waiting area are wrapped around and, in a sense, become part of a courtyard garden. The same courtyard principle generates the plan of Old See House in Belfast, where pairs of consulting rooms on the outside look into little courts and the eight short stay bedrooms are each expressed as glazed roof bays.

Similar principles are applied to two projects for dementia patients at the rural mental hospital at Stratheden, where the courtyard gardens are accessible to patients, one with the sound of running water. The roofs of each room, pitched in one building and flat in the other, create a lively identity. (22) One could say that each room is an "aedicule", evidence of the development of an architectural language sensitive to these special and delicate situations. These projects show an exceptional empathy for the special needs of their occupants and the skill and experience to respond architecturally. So it is shocking to find that the government procurement system for schools makes it virtually impossible for practices like RMA, which have yet to build a school, to be commissioned to design a new one, an ossifying bureaucratic policy which is likely to prohibit fresh thinking. The practice's nursery school for the private Edinburgh Academy, with its delightful responses to the miniature world of small children, demonstrates what the public sector is being denied.

Whereas the buildings designed for healthcare can be seen to share some of the organisational characteristics of residential projects, particularly student projects, reflecting the iterative content of small rooms, the practice's projects for higher education engage with new kinds of educational briefs which have generated distinctively new and inventive typologies. The developments in learning and teaching which have influenced these projects are the ubiquitous use of computers and laptops and the consequent transformation of libraries into 24-hour access resource centres. Richard Murphy has also observed that the rapid and ad hoc expansion of new universities without master plans has often resulted in dislocated accretions which challenge architects to try and restore to campuses the sense of unified identity of which students and staff can be proud.

The new patterns of open learning have generated two distinctly different but architecturally powerful buildings. The Kirkintilloch Adult Learning Centre takes up a narrow string of land by the Forth Clyde Canal and consists of continuous linear space looking through trees down to the canal. (23) The cranked roof canopy over this space is supported by branching tree-like columns and is back-lit by a continuous roof-light which separates it from the range of classrooms behind. This is a wonderfully eloquent section.

The other major project with an open learning brief, for Edinburgh Napier University, is equally dramatic and uses daylighting and level changes to achieve an interior of extraordinary quality. Entirely enclosed and with no outlook, this very large space could have been monotonous and claustrophobic, but instead it has been made into a kind of landscape, gently changing level under a luminous canopy of uplight barrel vaults, using reflected sunlight without compromising the legibility of computer screens. This interior has been compared to Kahn's Kimbell Art Gallery in Texas. The lighting strategy here is equally original and the effect equally serene.

In London the practice's most extensive higher education project has been to master plan and design new buildings for the University of East London's Stratford campus. (24) Behind the magnificent former Edwardian Workers' Education Institute, now University House, was the kind of chaotic accumulation of buildings and vestigial spaces which result from rapid expansion without a master plan. Like some of the interventions in Edinburgh which Richard Murphy has termed "urban repair", the initiatives in the Stratford campus are the outcome of a decade of consistent master planning and the realisation of buildings which are not only exceptional in themselves but have together created a coherent campus, transformed into a place with which students can identify.

New buildings for Cambridge colleges can involve a particular kind of conflict, almost a paradox, between the sense of inviolable history and the imperative to maintain intellectual leadership by building in response to new requirements. Jesus College's approach to Richard Murphy, ten years after his 1998 competition entry for student housing, involved an exceptionally complex brief which included an auditorium, music practice rooms and a hotel with further phases including a studio theatre/gym and a small research institute. (25) What distinguishes this project from the two twentieth century additions to the college, David Roberts' residential court and Shalev/Evans' library, is that the site is not contiguous with the college's historic pattern of open ended courts revolving around original cloistered core. This separation across an open landscape and through trees invites an

architecture with a strong identity. Richard Murphy's proposal achieves this while responding to the pattern of the college with an open-sided court, which looks back towards the historic core. The diagonal geometry of ventilation chimneys recalls the diagonal planning of David Roberts' residential scheme but is fundamentally more resolved. This is a powerful scheme with beautiful ideas, which if it is eventually developed will be a major contribution to the architecture of collegiate Cambridge.

It is testimony to the urban design experience, pragmatism and ability to master a wide range of typologies that the practice has been engaged in the commercial world, where it has encountered all the frustrations that characterise it. Richard Murphy's first attempt to break out of the formulaic mystique of the speculative office with a round building (taboo, as he points out, until Foster's Swiss Re) in a competition entry for Edinburgh's business park was unsuccessful.

The practice's entry for the new headquarters for Scottish National Heritage, a bespoke building for a marvellous site on the River Ness backed by woodland, offered a special opportunity to make the architectural quality of the place of work a priority, not simply its efficiency. This characteristically inventive and humane proposal was sadly unsuccessful.

An exemplary exercise in creating a piece of city has been realised on Justice Mill Lane, Aberdeen, but not without a false start; after winning the competition it was found that the housing component in the brief was uneconomical. However, the final scheme has produced, for Park Inn, their most successful European Hotel, and the offices have achieved Scotland's highest recorded rents, a result that goes against the myth that good architects are uncommercial. (26, 27)

The practice's involvement with a highly complex site and very ambitious master plan brief on the western edge of the New Town by the Haymarket demonstrated so many of the characteristic problems encountered in the development of industrial sites, in this case railway marshalling yards adjacent to an appallingly planned traffic intersection backing onto the diminutive scale of the artisan colony houses and, almost literally, undermined by railway tunnels. (28) The objectives for the development of such ambiguous sites are driven by commercial ambition and constrained by the ever changing attitudes of conservationists and planning committees. So the first proposal, which focused on a 17-storey hotel was defeated by public inquiry. A new more modest but real urban contribution knitting together this part of the city has now gained consent.

The practice ventured into China with a startlingly beautiful competition proposal for the headquarters of a whisky distillery company, the form of the building recalling the zigzag bridges found in traditional Chinese gardens.

This sense of traditional form and its opportunities for modern interpretation is one of the defining attributes of Richard Murphy's practice and underpins the design of the British High Commission in Sri Lanka, a conceptually simple single-storey linear plan with a series of wings on each side delivers a range of courtyards of the greatest subtlety, each different, and each containing water treated in a different way. (29) Thermal chimneys, like continuous glass lanterns, induce ventilation and by reflections under the soffit bring daylight into the centre of the plan. In combination of local materials, granite, coconut wood and terracotta tiles, they give the building a unique character, at once deeply engaged with its locality and yet clearly innovative and modern. To quote the High Commissioner, Peter Hayes, at the opening of the building, "The use of water and local materials are all characteristically Sri Lankan. Yet the building is quite unlike anything else on the island and retains an air of British practicality and functionality without being austere."

The final chapters on building for the arts and building for performance bring together a number of interrelated themes and a reminder of the practice's inception with the Fruitmarket Gallery, in many ways the seminal starting point for the practice's remarkable trajectory. (30) Here is the Scarpa-like idea of reviving a building both as a kind of archaeological "ruin" and through the intervention of new structures, seemingly layered into the existing masonry with a language of steelwork, metal and glazed panels, some of which slide, and all of which look as though they might. The language is wonderfully elaborated in the building for Dundee Contemporary Arts where the new structure of steel windows and copper panels is set into and against the eroded brickwork of the former warehouse. (31) In the conversion into a theatre of the Grade A Tolbooth in Stirling, such contrasts between the new and existing create astonishing almost implausible juxtapositions, most surprisingly where part of the original slate roof finds itself in the new interior under glass. (32)

The Fruitmarket Gallery initiated a quest to make arts and performance buildings open and sociable rather than exclusive. Bar and cafe facilities which can be seen from outside are an invitation to experience these buildings and their cultural offering as part of the public life of a city. To achieve this, the side elevation of the Peebles United Free Church, converted into the Eastgate Theatre, has been removed to open the building to a busy side street while retaining the ecclesiastical image on the other flank.

Such ideas work internally as well. In the elegant and entirely new construction of the creative Enterprise Centre or "Galeri", in Caernarfon in North Wales, the performance spaces are combined with office facilities for young Welsh speaking creative companies around an atrium and bar at the heart of the building which links all the activities and users together. The Dundee Contemporary Arts Centre not only relates strongly to its urban setting but brings together many kinds of visual art—galleries, cinemas, print workshops and research facilities—around a central social space to achieve,

in terms of visitor numbers, the most successful arts venue in Scotland. This is architecture working as social and cultural catalyst integrated into the city.

It is usual for architectural practices to make their reputation with a building type, such as housing, and the specialist knowledge and expertise which it entails. What is formidable about the achievements of RMA is the range of building types which the practice has mastered. It is a reminder that, contrary to preconceptions about procurement in the public sector, good design is a skill and aptitude which is highly transferable and thrives on the cross-fertilising of ideas.

Design thought of in this way is less likely to be bound by obsolete conventions and unchallenged precedents and to be more open to the input of clients. It is evident that the practice's ability to rethink the scope and significance of projects reflects such lateral thinking. An outstanding example is the building for the British High Commission in Sri Lanka that superseded the previous five-storey office building which, in its time, probably represented what a building for the High Commission should be like. (33) Although the design of the new building owes much to indigenous tradition, the courtyard idea strongly recalls Richard Murphy's entry for the RIAS House for the Future competition, with its gables built into courtyard walls, while the section recalls the concrete vaults of Kahn's Kimbell Art Museum developed into a passive environmental system. The consequence is that the building redefines the quality, not just the efficiency of the place of work, and its relationship with the users, by making it flexible, pleasurable, environmentally responsible and recognisably part of local culture. By thinking beyond the obvious functional requirements of an office building, not only are the users open to a new experience, but there is a change in the perception of what a building for a High Commission should be: "Embassies are more than bricks and mortar (and concrete, steel and glass), they are more than a functional place of work. They are, in a very physical sense our representatives abroad", notes Peter Hayes, High Commissioner, Sri Lanka.

The Edinburgh Maggie's Centre involved an equivalent kind of reconsideration by thinking outside the objectifying standards of the National Health Service. It defies conventional medical criteria; a little house, it is domestic, comforting, intimate and sociable. Other RMA buildings for Health similarly rethink what hospitals should be like to create a sense of individuality, privacy and intimacy for patients in buildings which are responsive to their landscape settings.

Such re-evaluations were also initiated with the inside-outside house extensions and the subsequent private commissions which develop the idea of houses being like large pieces of furniture—a way of thinking which translated into the joinery box that forms the interior of the John Muir Birthplace Trust Visitor Centre.

The subject of suburbia, largely overlooked by architects is seen to be the character of place, not just the house. In the entirely different context of the city, public venues such as Dundee Contemporary Arts, are not thought of simply as buildings but as complex urban fragments able to provide special kinds of social focus, the development of the idea which started with the Fruitmarket Gallery. In the conventions of a Nolli plan, they would appear as hollowed out extensions of the public space of the city.

All this is a reminder that the language of architecture and the sense of style developed here with such tectonic virtuosity, is in RMA's work a continuous medium of thought ranging from the subtle spatial distinctions compressed into the little mews houses to the large-scale projects which catalyse and redefine the institutional and social purposes of the city. This is an architect and practice at the height of their powers.

Sir Richard MacCormac
18 April 2012

Lambert House, Northumberland

House Extensions

BACKGARDEN SUBVERSIONS

Architects in the USA, Australia, or similar young countries where individual private house design is a common aspiration, frequently start their career with just such a project. In the UK, opportunities for a completely new house tend to be reserved for the rich, the eccentric or the very adventurous. The typical equivalent is to design a conversion or extension to an existing home. In the early 90s a combination of recession and an extremely conservative regime in Edinburgh City Council Planning Department prevented anything obviously contemporary from being constructed in the city centre. Indeed, the practice had personal experience of advice from a senior planner that the recently constructed faux-Mediaeval Scandic Crown Hotel on the High Street was the exemplar of how to develop in a conservation area (sic). (2) Consequently, the practice's beginnings were confined to back gardens, extending middle class Edwardian houses out of sight of the public realm; only there was any kind of experiment allowed.

Middle class Victorian/Edwardian houses in Edinburgh follow a tradition of placing all their formal rooms at the front, sometimes on the first floor. The rear was reserved for less important spaces and often there is a "build-out"—an extension usually consisting of a maid's scullery, coal store, etc., sometimes with domestic accommodation upstairs. The rear gardens were used for clothes drying and sometimes vegetable cultivation whilst the front garden was often formal and ornamental. Life today has changed totally. Internally most families now aspire to a generous kitchen-dining space as the cockpit of the home. Externally it is the rear garden that affords necessary privacy, and ideally these two spaces, internal and external, should be connected. While almost all these houses are already large in comparison to contemporary equivalents, on each occasion (with the exception of the Harrison House) an extension was required to allow them to adapt properly to modern family life.

The practice invariably thinks about alterations or extensions to existing building as a process of 'ruination'. (7) Richard Murphy jokes that he spends his time "ruining clients' houses". Stone walls up to 600 mm thick assist this concept and, as the Craigleith quarry from where most of Edinburgh's stone originated is now defunct, it is often necessary to rearrange the existing stone to avoid introducing new. The concept of semi-demolishing was introduced with these extensions, although obviously the inspiration comes from Carlo Scarpa, and particularly his "creative demolitions" at the Castelvecchio in Verona.

BLYTHEMAN HOUSE
Edinburgh; completed 1991

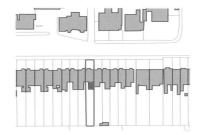

The first project, the Blytheman House, started from the idea of a heavy stone base. (4–10) The original brief of a garden room was completely subverted to be relocated at first floor from where not only is there a view of the garden, but also a spectacular vista of the Edinburgh skyline. (9) With roof removed and walls partially demolished, a steel structure was applied to the exterior, and a new flat roof was then arranged to fly over the existing building. The roof floats above the heavy base. In between, where the enclosure now no longer needs to perform any structural function, is placed that emblem of the modern movement, the 'disappearing' corner window, originating with Frank Lloyd Wright's destruction of the box and expressed so beautifully by Rietveldt in his Schröder-Schräder house in Utrecht. (3)

FIRST

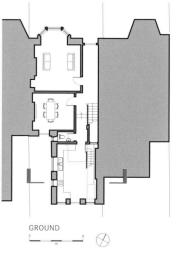

GROUND

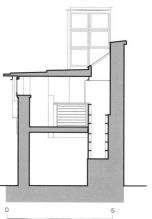

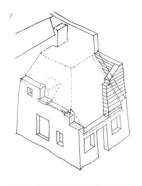
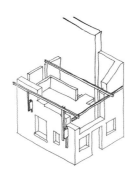
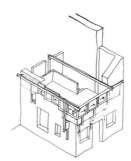
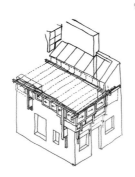

It is a theme common to many projects, although unlike Utrecht, here they all slide rather than pivot. Traditional Japanese houses have been cited as the inspiration although in reality it is only with a sliding mechanism that the windows, when located on the exterior, are able to completely disappear from the interior. A transformation from enclosed space to continuous ambiguous inside/outside space, another emblem of the twentieth century, is thus achieved.

For weathering purposes, the roof flies beyond the footprint of the original walls, but this reduces light so a roof-light is located along the inner boundary of the plan and a secret stair to the kitchen is placed under it. (10) The roof-light, hidden from sight from the main space, gives a hidden source of light (an idea lifted from Soane's Breakfast Room). (11)

Its termination affords the opportunity for an expressive cut into the original stair connecting the main circulation to this little space and making it pivotal to the house. (10) And, finally, between windows and stone 'ruin' is placed a timber window seat as a 'stick-on-stick' expression of construction. When the windows are fully slid back, the seat sits like a belevedere in the foreground against the distant landscape. (9)

FRANCIS HOUSE
Edinburgh; completed 1994

Marion Blythman introduced Richard Murphy to Eileen and John Francis, and the second house extension, the Francis House, this time a kitchen, took shape. (12–19) Replacing a scullery on a plinth above a small garden to the rear, the plinth was 'hollowed out' to form a study and the remainder of the stone work rearranged/ruined in the now familiar pattern. Once again, an external flying structure, new flat roof and extensive roof-light between old and new were employed. New walls of Douglas fir cladding form panels 'offered up' to the old stone so that the new tectonic additions become legible in three dimensions. A sliding corner window gives a new view of Arthur's Seat but the focus of the room becomes a disappearing corner of two sliding glazed doors which open to a steel and wooden seat suspended from the new structure.

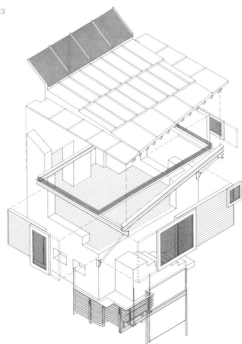

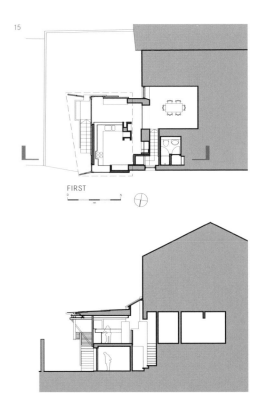

FIRST

PALMER HOUSE

Edinburgh; completed 1996

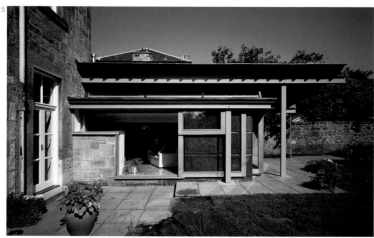

The third extension, the Palmer House, is a combination of the previous two. (20–29) Kitchen, family and garden rooms are combined to sit on the lawn, rearranging stone from a demolished washhouse and semi-demolished kitchen. Again, the familiar elements of an expressed external steel structure, floating roofs (this time monopitch), a hidden source of light over the kitchen and applied tectonic new walls, here clad in lead, were all employed. New, however, is the idea of an inner layer of plywood-clad insulated shutters to doors and roof-lights. (27) Now not only can the space be completely opened to the garden in summer, it can also be totally closed and cocooned in the winter. Of particular interest are the ceiling panels which close clerestorey and roof-lights and are operated by ship's winches. Not only do they provide enclosure and insulation but also they change the section. In such a way the skin of the building (including the roof) has three manifestations: glazed, open and closed, responding to day and night, summer and winter.

GROUND
0   5
m

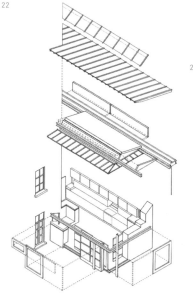

0   5
m

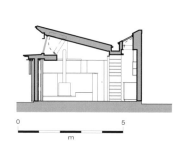

26

27

28

29

MORRISON/GAIT HOUSE
Dirleton, East Lothian; completed 1998

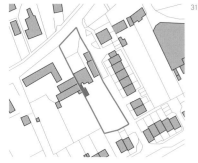

At the Morrison/Gait House in Dirleton, a conservation village outside Edinburgh, a new kitchen and nursery for unexpected triplets, was quarried out of a previous washhouse. (30–36) Semi-demolished stone, expressed steel, flat roof, hidden source of light (this time reflected back from mirrors) and disappearing sliding corner window all re-appear. The kitchen work area itself becomes a banana-shaped console facing the garden. (36) With no room for sliding windows, instead they became counter-balanced horizontally pivoted so that in summer, cooking can almost be in the garden. A further extension for new owners has recently been completed. (30)

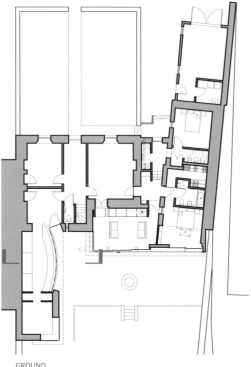

GROUND

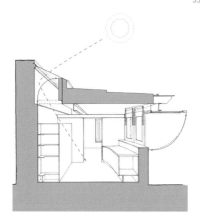

HARRISON HOUSE
Edinburgh; completed 2000

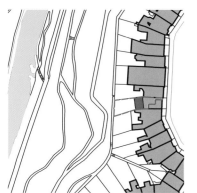

Undoubtedly, the most Soanian-inspired project is the basement apartment for Patrick Harrison, a retired secretary of the RIBA, and his wife, Mary. From a series of sub-divisions, a bizarre flat had been created from the townhouse originally built for Lord Moray. The Harrison apartment (37–45) consisted of flat roofed kitchen extensions, a grand billiard room and was linked to the main street by an umbilical corridor under the original house. (38) The unlikely move was to eschew the billiard room as the living room. Instead it became the principal bedroom. All the previous kitchens and their flat roofs were demolished

and a new kitchen/dining/living space created under a barrel vault. This sits on new thick walls (eroded with shelves, penetrations and mirrors) with circulation on either

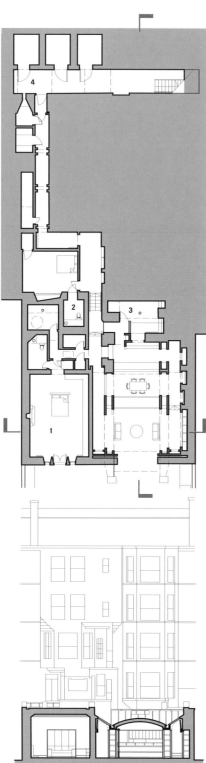

1 FORMER BILLIARD ROOM
2 FORMER STRONG ROOM
3 STUDY
4 ENTRANCE

GROUND

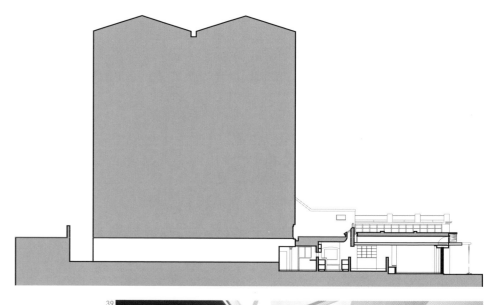

side under roof-lights which bounce light back into the main space. (39–40)

The only available elevation makes a single window to the spectacular vista across the valley of the Water of Leith. In summer the glazed doors disappear into the thickness of the stone walls. At night insulated plywood-finished shutters slide from the same location. Both roof-lights are complimented with giant pivoting shutters operated manually by ship's winches. These give extra insulation at night, and prevent privacy infringements from the apartments above, but again, more importantly, radically change the section. As Mary Harrison put it to a visiting journalist from *The Architects' Journal*, "at night it's like living in a cigar box". (41)

LAMBERT HOUSE

Wooler, Northumberland; completed 2001

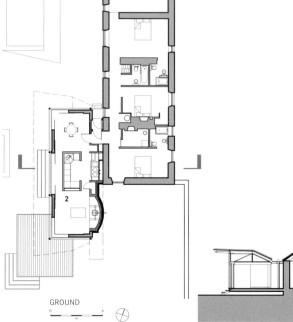

1 FORMER SMITHY
2 NEW EXTENSION

GROUND

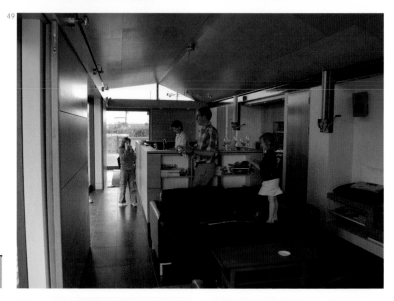

The Lambert House, a holiday home partially inhabiting a former smithy in northern Northumbria, became the site of a large extension. (46–52) The cottage itself was reorganised to contain all the bedrooms and bathrooms. Placed parallel and offset was a single room of dining, kitchen and living area, the kitchen console in the centre dividing the space. Again, windows slide away in summer so that living takes place in or adjacent to the garden. Insulated panels and hinged ceiling panels close down the entire space in winter or when unoccupied. (47, 48) The architecture of steel frame, Douglas fir cladding and aluminium roof floating above the ground contrast with the solidity of the stone and slate cottage and its small windows. It was a battle with local planners to see the logic of this idea, with them preferring the default position of an 'in keeping' extension.

Now however, the original building has all the cellular rooms, the extension has open living; a logical architecture of contrasts each benefitting from the juxtaposition with the other.

Michael Lambert writes:

The Old Smithy at Fowberry in North Northumberland has long family associations; my father visited as a boy and finally purchased it from an elderly great aunt in the early 1960s. Some of my earliest memories are of this place with its majestic beeches and towering pines. Against this backdrop of emotional clutter, change was never going to be an entirely comfortable concept.

Meeting Richard was only partly serendipitous—he has the misfortune to live nearby in Edinburgh and was too polite to refuse my supper invitation with its hidden agenda. Richard's mews house and Maggie's Cancer Centre were, for me, daily reminders of his distinctive style and ingenuity and must have had some subliminal influence. My approach to Richard came at a time when his practice was moving away from smaller domestic projects. He would have been forgiven had he taken a less enthusiastic response to my proposal, though perhaps unsurprisingly Richard relished the idea of his first foray into England, albeit its most northern marches. I think secretly he more keenly anticipated the 'flying visits', by micro-light.

Planners are not so easily persuaded when it comes to something different—perhaps especially in rural Northumberland. Local opposition mounted, Parish Councils petitioned, local newspapers talked of a 'carbuncle' on the countryside and there were times when it was quite a relief to drive back home to Edinburgh. Richard, however, was undeterred. Eventually, after lengthy negotiations, the first Murphy creation in England was under starter's orders.

The exacting tolerances that a Murphy building demands were clearly not something either familiar or necessarily welcome to the local artisans. Walls that slide open and disappear into other walls, a roof that pivots on a piano hinge and requires an array of pulleys and marine winches to open, a shadow gap here, a mirror there were all mysteries that were greeted with bemusement, incredulity and scepticism in even measure. So to pretend that the process of construction was either quick or painless would be to distort reality, but every project like this has its agonies and ecstasies, as we all know.

Well, what of the end result? In summer, it's a light and airy space that opens up to frame the garden and provide a real sense of the outside inside, recalling *der glassraum* in Simon Mawer's recent novel. In winter, the beech panelling reflects dancing shadows from the open stove and you feel safely cocooned from the harsh elements of the Northumbrian winter. A pavilion, if you like, but Barcelona not Brighton.

The experience of being part of this creative process was hugely satisfying. Richard's work is uncompromising. Visionary, yet firmly rooted in the practical detail that makes best use of every 'nook and cranny'. Nearly ten years on and the extension and, thankfully the locals, have gently mellowed. The cedar cladding now has taken on that wonderful silvery hue. The glass room sits in quiet harmony with the old stone smithy and we are greatly content with our little piece of the Murphy legend.

Knox House, Circus Lane, Edinburgh

Building in an Edinburgh Mews

"ARCHITECTURAL STRING QUARTETS"

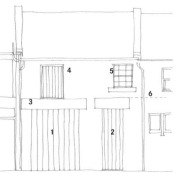

1820

1960

1995

In the space of 12 years the practice has completed six mews houses within the Edinburgh New Town and at the time of writing, the seventh is under construction. By chance three are in one lane, Royal/Regent Terrace Mews on Calton Hill and another three are located in Circus Lane in Stockbridge. Four are new constructions, three are conversions.

Mews lanes are virtually the only places within the New Town where building a new house is still possible, although, from experience, never without controversy. In contrast to the composed elevations of the grand streets of the New Town, mews lanes were developed in a pragmatic way, often sites were left undeveloped and over time they have become a welcome relatively anarchic contrast to the formalities of the New Town. Mews were an integral part of

the design of the New Town; they were accommodation for horses, carriages and stable boys but were otherwise rarely inhabited. Normally a mews was placed at the end of a town house back garden and one of their peculiarities is that the more expensive ashlar facade was placed facing the rear of the parental house since this was the only elevation viewed from the house. (1, 2) The elevation to the mews lane itself was confined to poor quality rubble stone; in other words today, they appear to be built "the wrong way round". The southern half of Circus Lane follows this pattern although the northern half and the Calton Hill lane are unusual, having their mews placed remotely from their parental houses. Typically the plot width would be about five metres and the elevation usually consisted of a wide door for

carriages with an enormous lintel, these being probably some of the single biggest stones found in the New Town. (3) In the centre of its span the lintel was relieved by a hayloft door placed above it. To one side of the main opening was a door and above it a small window. The ground floor would have an unusually high ceiling for accommodating carriages and consequently the low first floor was mostly reserved for hay storage with a small cabin and fireplace as stable boy's accommodation. They were rarely designed as houses, but most of the elevations have now been altered by either widening the stable opening to suit the turning circle of today's cars or, where converted into houses, by pretending that they are ersatz Georgian cottages. Mews lanes are typically only six metres wide. When

converted to residential use the absence of privacy across the narrow lane can become a major problem. The first six projects share similar concerns and are in effect variations on themes. Firstly, since an integral garage was until recently a necessary prerequisite to obtaining planning permission the section reverses the previous ordering; (ie) the first floor is universally lowered to allow significant space to be given to living areas now placed above. Expressing this reversal of ordering on the mews lane facade is a common preoccupation of most of the projects. (7, 12, 20, 21, 36)

Internally, each mews design is challenged to contain as much accommodation as possible; the Calton Hill Mews are only 40 square metre footprints including the garage. In all the designs the main open plan split section spaces created an illusion of space in itself, increased further by mirrors located in the gable walls beneath the roof-lights. Mirrors are frequently found on the front facades to create local illusions of layering. Further enjoyment was found in using fixed furniture; typically, at Colburn House 1, a desk was placed over the head-height of the first stair, a wardrobe over the second and the bonnet of the car slides in under the kitchen washing machine! (8) In Colburn House 2, the desk was transferred to the top of a vertical bookcase 'tower' around which all circulation revolves. (11)

NEW TOWN STREET

MEWS LANE

NEW TOWN STREET

COLBURN HOUSE 1
completed 1995

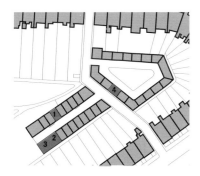

1 COLBURN HOUSE 1
2 COLBURN HOUSE 2
3 FINEGAN HOUSE 1
4 COOKE HOUSE

FIRST

GROUND

The first project, Colburn House 1, was a conversion, although the original carriage door and pedestrian doors had been combined sometime in the 1960s with a new giant concrete beam. (4–9) Much architectural energy was expended in enjoying contrasting the new order with the original openings (in the manner of the then recently completed Fruitmarket Gallery). (4, 7) Here, the idea was to slip a new house in behind the existing facade. The new floor is expressed as a steel channel (which doubles up as a garage door gear runner, an idea lifted from a Victorian conversion two doors down the lane) and a lead panel appears in three different openings. (5) In reality it is three separate lead pieces dressed into shadow gaps or mirrors to maintain the illusion. When the new mews houses were constructed it seemed natural to continue this game of duality in the ordering of their facades.

Internal shutters close all facades at night. At the Colburn House 1 and in the Gordon Houses, two wooden shutters, aligned behind the external lead panel slide in opposite directions to close off the whole facade. Across the lane at Regent Terrace Mews, Colburn House 2, a complex system of sliding and hinging panels closes individual openings. (17–19) (See also page 295)

Preserving privacy led to a process of sophistication of the facades. The Gordon Houses (20–27) were similar to Colburn House 1 but with smaller openings, but at Colburn House 2 (10–19) the decision was made to abandon a horizontal sight line (light is admitted through two glass block panels) so that from the interior, only the cobbled road and the sky are visible. Internal sliding or pivoting shutters give further night-time privacy in almost all the projects. In the Knox House etched glass and vertical timber louvers are used. Indeed, the debt to Japanese design was acknowledged in the planning submission—so much so that the local press dubbed the design "the Japanese style house", a joke taken up by the client with his Japanese 'No Parking' sign!

The admission of light is a significant issue in mews conversions. The plan is relatively deep (exceptionally so in the Gordon Houses) and bounded each side by party walls. (21) The original mews had little need for light and in all the designs top light is used. At Colburn House 1 a ridge roof-light catches light all day. On the other side of the road, Colburn House 2 halves this to have only a south-facing light with a pivoting shutter occupying the opposite space on the north soffit. Richard Murphy observed living in Colburn House 1 that it is possible to have too much light. So deep was the plan in the Gordon Houses that the roof-light was divided into two with a roof terrace placed in between. (24) In the Knox house the south-facing roof-light is the intervening element between the 'traditional' slated pitch to the lane and the necessarily flat roof to the rear which covers the trapezoid geometry of this particular site.

9

COLBURN HOUSE 2
completed 2002

Having established the first floor as *piano nobile*, all successive projects went on to enjoy the same split section. At Colburn House 1 the kitchen was placed at the lower level, the bedroom above as a raised platform to the living area; at Colburn House 2 (where no openings were possible in the ground floor rear wall) the arrangement was reversed although a sightline from the bed diagonally across the section to the front elevation clerestory was deliberately created. (10–19)

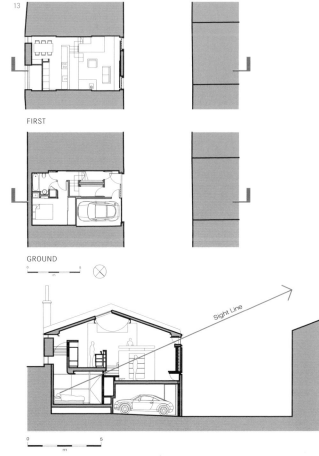

FIRST

GROUND

Sight Line

GORDON HOUSES
completed 2001

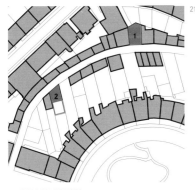

1 GORDON HOUSES
2 KNOX HOUSE

The Gordon Houses are truly Tardis-like. (20–27) From the street they appear to have similar facades to Colburn House 1 although slightly narrower. (20) They also play identical games. However, behind such a facade is a garage, four bedrooms a generous living, dining and kitchen at two levels, two bathrooms and two roof terraces. The deep plan was fully exploited but so too was the section with an additional lower floor accommodating more bedrooms clustered around light wells. (27)

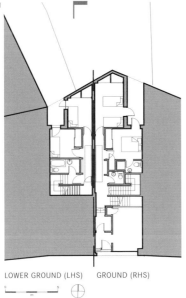

LOWER GROUND (LHS)   GROUND (RHS)

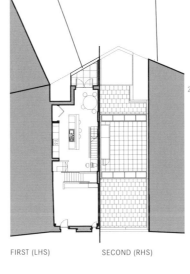

FIRST (LHS)   SECOND (RHS)

Only the Knox House (30–36) was built on undeveloped land and there the clients were able to negotiate for enough land for a private garden so that the opportunity of a major rear elevation was exploited. (34) The garden was located at a half level so that the upstairs living space and bedrooms below could have equal access. The plan form of this house was peculiar. A trapezoid plan resulted from the land subdivisions remaining parallel as the lane curved parallel to its parent Royal Circus. Externally, this was resolved by a trapezoid flat lead roof; internally, the plan pivots around a spiral stair which resolves the geometry and visits four different levels which was a particular client request.

Two further mews properties have been completed on Calton Hill, both predominantly interior projects behind existing facades. Immediate neighbours (Finegan House) of Richard Murphy commissioned him to demolish the interior of their flat (which consisted of only the upper level but had double the footprint). (28) Two minimal bedrooms and bathrooms were created but most of the apartment became a single space with a characteristically expressed lateral steel structure, south-facing roof-light and raised steel desk-study. In Calton Terrace Lane, an unusual mews with equal entries from two sides, one at upper level, the other at the lower level, the Cooke House has been redesigned as an upside-down house. (29) The upper level has been turned into one space, again expressing the volume of the roof and using south-facing roof-lights.

1   LIVING
2   KITCHEN
3   DINING
4   ROOF TERRACE
5   BEDROOM
6   GARAGE
7   CIRCUS LANE

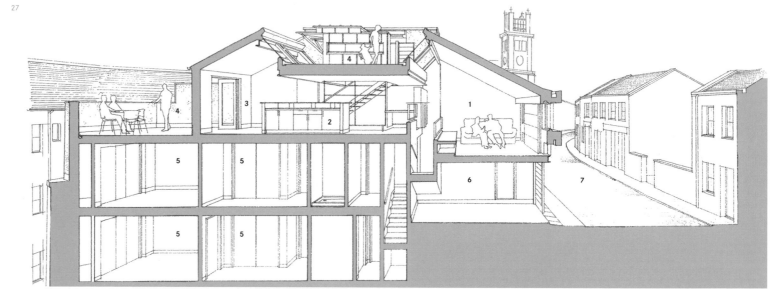

FINEGAN HOUSE 1
completed 2010

COOKE HOUSE
projected completion 2012

KNOX HOUSE
completed 2005

30

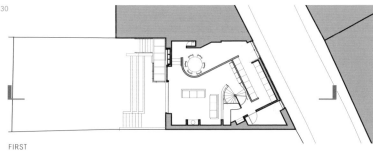

FIRST

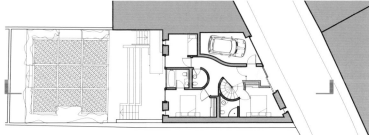

GROUND

32

31

33

These little mews houses have been much published, two have received RIBA Awards, the Colburn House 1 at Royal Terrace Mews even being shortlisted for the Stirling Prize. The filmmaker Murray Grigor describes them as the practice's "string quartets"; developments of architectural ideas in miniature themes and variations, an analogy which is both appropriate and very charming!

Brian and Lesley Knox write:

We began to consider a home in Edinburgh in 1995, because Lesley had grown up there and was making much of her career in Scotland; and later our daughter Ella was to opt for an Edinburgh school. We are both enthusiasts for architecture; Brian writes about that of Central Europe, and together we had built a house in Suffolk. We began the hunt for a site in September 1998, and that year's Open Doors Day introduced us to the work of Richard Murphy at 17 Royal Terrace Mews.

In February 1999 we gave him our brief: ground floor with three bedrooms and garage, multi-purpose space above. After 18 months' search we focused on the unoccupied "mews" site formerly attached to 26 Royal Circus, in September 2000 we took an option to buy it, and we completed the purchase in October 2001. By then the design had progressed far enough to include a spiral staircase, curving walls both for the ground floor circulation and the living space upstairs, and a grand Murphy skylight spanning the lot. Lesley insisted on a fireplace; Richard said "ah, you want what my tutor called a terminal space".

In November 2000 we submitted our first planning application; in spite of the City Planners' support, in the face of over 70 letters of protest ("cheap and ugly and out of place") and the tergiversations of Historic Scotland ("no objection in principle" in 1988, now "opposed to the principle of development") it was turned down in May 2001. The facades gained more stone and we recruited over 50 Edinburgh notables in support, and a second application was submitted in October, to be turned down in December. In April our undaunted lawyers submitted a meticulous written appeal to the Scottish Executive; in June the Inspector called, and in July 2002 he said the Conservation Area would be "enhanced by the innovative design"; appeal allowed.

We continued to refine the plans, as one does, and to confront the cost, which promised to double our initial budget of £200,000. An ingenious basement utility room had to go. Work began on site in January 2004. There were delays with the groundwork; New Year 2005 came and went; to get the taps we wanted we bought them retail in London and shipped them north with the specially tailored double bed. Most of our furniture arrived in April; walls were painted in bold colours: dozens of pictures were hung. In August Richard called and said "it looks like you've been living here for ages".

We participated in Edinburgh Open House that September, to much praise and much wonder what all the fuss had been about. In 2007 Richard was given a RIBA Award for the design, and Brian was elected an Honorary FRIAS, apparently for determination as a client rather than as a historian of architecture. And the *Time Out 2010 Guide to Edinburgh* began a walk of new building in the New Town in Circus Lane with a colour photograph of 10A.

The Architect's House

PRACTISING WHAT YOU PREACH

"And I bet you don't live in a house you designed?" These words, spoken by Prince Charles to Richard Murphy at a reception at Holyrood House are symptomatic of many towards the perceived hypocrisy of architects who "impose their visions" on others and then retreat to the comforts of a Georgian or Victorian villa. On that occasion, Prince Charles was rebuffed, as at that time Richard was renting the first of the two Colburn Houses (see pages 39–40) on Calton Hill. He then went on to transfer his tenancy to the second house on the other side of the street and eventually to purchase it. This highly unusual experience of 'road testing' two of his own designs before purchase also whetted an appetite to build a completely new house unrestricted by the sectional limitations of mews houses. And so, they also became test beds for ideas.

In reality, it is true that not many UK architects do live in houses they have designed, even if they do have the aspiration. Most usually do not get the chance to find a plot or have the means to buy it. An inspirational exception is the London architect, Ted Cullinan's ingenious mews house in Camden which was not only designed by the architect but was in large part constructed by him too. (1)

And similarly, on a trip to Australia in 1996 Glen Murcutt invited Richard Murphy to his holiday house at Kempsey in New South Wales. (3) Murcutt, a Pritzker prize winner, has become internationally celebrated for his single houses, each superbly responsive to their locale and now seen as emblematic of Australia (see page 50). So it was with some amusement that he told Richard, rather sheepishly, that he found the prospect of designing a house for himself too daunting and had solved the problem when noticing a house that he had designed for a client ten years previous, advertised for sale, and purchasing it for his own use!

An enduring inspiration has perhaps been England's most famous architect's own house: the Sir John Soane Museum in Lincoln's Inn

Fields, London. (2) Not only is it full of endless architectural tricks, it was an evolving 45 year long testing ground for the architect's ideas.

Richard Murphy's first attempt was for a site in Bakehouse Close behind the Canongate in the Edinburgh Old Town and the second is in Hart Street in the New Town. At an advanced design stage the purchase of the Old Town plot collapsed, but the second is, at the time of writing, under construction. Both have similar agendas addressing winter/summer variations, complex sections, squeezing many rooms onto highly restricted sites, but above all responding carefully to two very different and in many ways diametrically opposite respective contexts.

MURPHY HOUSE
Bakehouse Close, Edinburgh; unbuilt

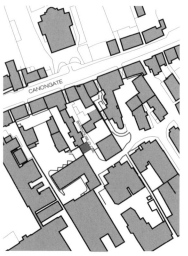

The Bakehouse Close site was a tiny section of leftover space resulting from the reopening in 1994 of this part of a formerly derelict brewery. (5–11) The west elevation was the boundary wall of the then still functioning remnant of that brewery and the north, a gable-end of restored Mediaeval buildings. Internally, the plan spiralled through a series of 'third' levels starting with a garage and then progressing upwards with a second bedroom, an entrance hall (accessed in typically Old Town fashion with an external staircase), a study and then the main space of the living area, and then a kitchen/dining level and finally a master bedroom. Internally there were a number of connections between spaces which could be opened up or closed off.

Externally there were various features of the design which made reference to the pre-eighteenth century buildings of the Royal Mile itself, and in particular, the reconstructed "Mediaeval" architecture. (4)

Already mentioned was the exposed external staircase to the front door; cantilevering gable roofs and other elements at an

upper level; timber screens and modelled timber rooms at upper levels; deliberately reduced windows at the lower level, with a contrasting large amount of glazing at the top.

The main south elevation had a number of sliding elements which enjoyed the ambiguities of levels inside and the theme of "open and closed" on this elevation was to continue right to the roof where an ambitious idea of the two roof pitches opening with hydraulic jacks was to have been attempted. (9–11) Internally, in the winter the ceiling could also have pivoted to a horizontal soffit to cut off the roof-light, preserve energy and change the section.

SECOND

FIRST

GROUND

0   m   5

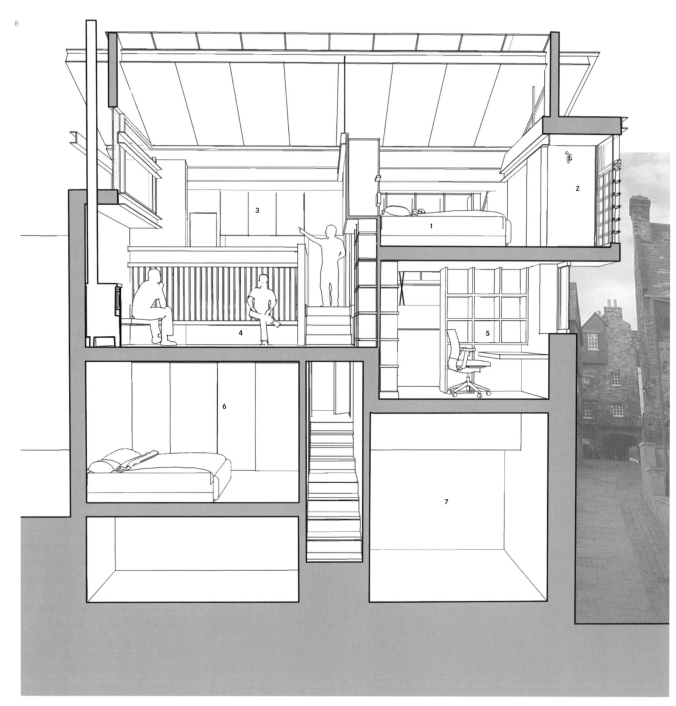

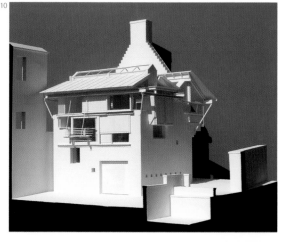

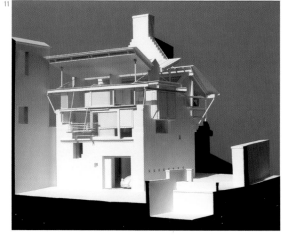

1 BEDROOM
2 SHOWER ROOM
3 KITCHEN (TO REAR)
4 LIVING
5 STUDY
6 SECOND BEDROOM
7 GARAGE

MURPHY HOUSE

Hart Street, Edinburgh; projected completion 2013

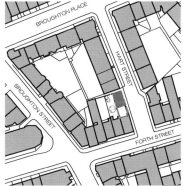

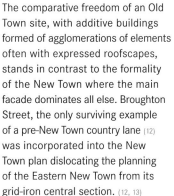

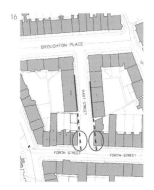

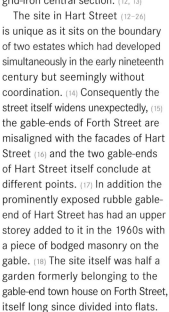

The comparative freedom of an Old Town site, with additive buildings formed of agglomerations of elements often with expressed roofscapes, stands in contrast to the formality of the New Town where the main facade dominates all else. Broughton Street, the only surviving example of a pre-New Town country lane (12) was incorporated into the New Town plan dislocating the planning of the Eastern New Town from its grid-iron central section. (12, 13)

The site in Hart Street (12–26) is unique as it sits on the boundary of two estates which had developed simultaneously in the early nineteenth century but seemingly without coordination. (14) Consequently the street itself widens unexpectedly, (15) the gable-ends of Forth Street are misaligned with the facades of Hart Street (16) and the two gable-ends of Hart Street itself conclude at different points. (17) In addition the prominently exposed rubble gable-end of Hart Street has had an upper storey added to it in the 1960s with a piece of bodged masonry on the gable. (18) The site itself was half a garden formerly belonging to the gable-end town house on Forth Street, itself long since divided into flats.

A right of light angle to the basement flat (24) heavily influenced the final design but the wedge shape of the house could also be read as a deliberate 'bookend' to the Hart Street houses, rising as high as possible to obscure the gable-end; an attempt to resolve a piece of ad hoc urban planning that should never have happened in this otherwise normally highly composed urban milieu.

The resulting south-facing 45 degree roof also lent itself to an interesting energy strategy. The roof design is mostly glazed but incorporates solar water heating panels and photovoltaic cells. Underneath it are a series of heavily insulated shutters which can close in winter or at night and open in the summer and daytime. (23–24) When heat is generated through the greenhouse effect it is to be ducted from the roof apex to the basement and through a rock store. In such a way energy can be stored for evening use and the temperature differential between the top and bottom of the house formed through the stack effect, counteracted. And in summer excess heat is naturally ventilated out at the top of the roof, encouraged by its shape.

The facades of the existing Hart Street houses step up the hill and consist of indented ashlar at ground level, smooth ashlar at the upper level and a prominent cornice completing the facade (ignoring the recently added top storey). Each of these three elements is incorporated into the new facade which has been designed to appear as two fragments at either end of the new house with a steel, timber and glass composition in between (see pages 40–41). The whole site is developed with a garage with a roof terrace placed above completing the plan.

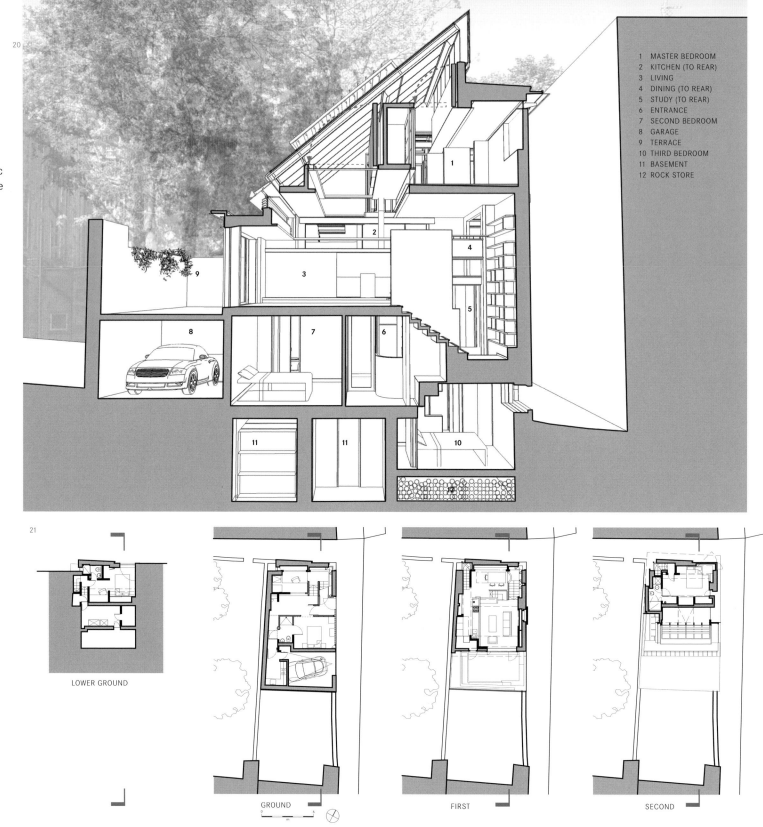

20

1   MASTER BEDROOM
2   KITCHEN (TO REAR)
3   LIVING
4   DINING (TO REAR)
5   STUDY (TO REAR)
6   ENTRANCE
7   SECOND BEDROOM
8   GARAGE
9   TERRACE
10 THIRD BEDROOM
11 BASEMENT
12 ROCK STORE

21

LOWER GROUND

GROUND

FIRST

SECOND

The ashlar is developed in the northeast corner with tiny windows for perpends which translate into window slots integrated into a bookcase internally on the main staircase.

Internally, similar to the Bakehouse Close design, the rooms were organised on one third and two third levels. [20] Entrance at ground floor leads up to a third storey, to a study, and also down to a bedroom partially built into the ground and a storage cellar. Up two thirds of a level from the study is the main living room and then up a third level to a dining area and kitchen. And finally a whole storey above a master bedroom occupies the very top of the wedge. Again, like Bakehouse Close, the staircases are non-repetitive on plan with two of them occupying the illusion of a "thick inhabited wall" (albeit more appropriate to the Old Town than the New Town), an idea which manifests itself around the entire perimeter of the house including the roof terrace.

Asked about the inspiration behind the design Richard Murphy replied that it is a "quarter Soane, a quarter Scarpa, a quarter eco-house and, referring to all the proposed moving parts, a quarter Wallace and Gromit".

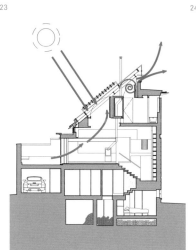

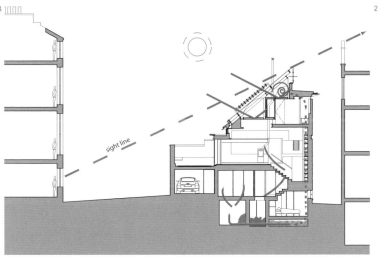

Stoneman House, Co Galway, Ireland

Houses in Landscape

LONG HOUSES, WALLED GARDENS, TOWERS

Architecture Without Architects was the great exhibition and then book by Bernard Rudofsky published in 1964. It exhibited from all over the world the natural beauty of houses, villages and cities built from local materials, with an innate understanding of local microclimate and seemingly without the hand of any overall designer. (1)

The beauty of "vernacular" architecture and the way in which it contributes to a landscape was understood with the Arts and Crafts houses and illustrated in *Das Englische Haus* but particularly in the work of Norman Shaw, Lutyens, Voysey and in Scotland, the two built examples of Mackintosh, which show sophisticated vernacular inspired ideas of working with local materials and landscape. (2)

Almost at the same time, Frank Lloyd Wright showed with his Prairie houses, and later Usonian houses, an idea about how the settler was planting his roots in the American Midwest. (3)

The great accumulations of exaggeratedly horizontal cantilevering roofs, internal spaces leading inseparably to landscape perspectives stretching to the horizon, the kerb stones on which the whole composition sat; all were symbols of an idea of claiming and colonising what was understood to be a virgin landscape. Much more recently, but unlike Wright, in another 'new' country Glen Murcutt in Australia has produced what seems to be an endless series of variations on the long house idea where the section, structure and enclosing envelope are carefully crafted to respond to variations of local microclimate and fauna across that enormous country. (4) But more importantly his houses float above the landscape which remains unchanged, "touching the ground lightly" in the Aboriginal phrase.

If a pattern can be discerned amongst what some might see as a disparate group of designs it is the reworking of a few concepts: the long house, the walled garden and, in particular, the tower house, all present already in the Scottish landscape. (5, 6) Internally, contemporary life is accepted as taking place in one large family-dominated space with the kitchen assuming prime position as the 'cockpit' of family life. A living room often becomes a secondary space

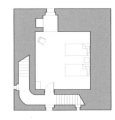

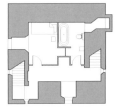

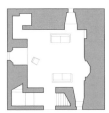

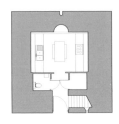

acting as a retreat from the first. An interest in closing and opening facades between winter and summer started with the house extensions and has often been further developed.

In the mid-1970s, well before the legendary property bonanza of the 'Celtic tiger' years in the 1990s, the rapid suburbanisation of rural Ireland with pre-planned bungalows bought from a catalogue called *Bungalow Bliss* (sic) was already destroying the very landscape that was at the heart of a well marketed national identity. (7, 8)

STONEMAN/CLARKE HOUSES

Co Galway, Ireland; completed 1997/2005

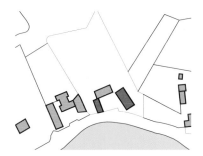

Working briefly as a student in Galway in 1977 Richard Murphy saw this phenomenon at first hand, so it was a providential coincidence that the practice's first commission for a complete new house was in the rural west of Ireland 20 years later. By then the destruction had grown apace so the Stoneman/Clarke house, and its later smaller companion alongside, is an essay in what might have been. (9–17) The simple thatched cottage of the west of Ireland cannot be reproduced, but lessons can be learnt from how it relates to its immediate landscape. Approached down narrow walled lanes it appears as roof first with the roof dominating the composition.

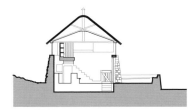

1997 HOUSE

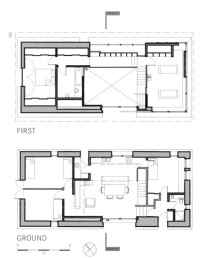

FIRST

GROUND

Frequently constructed in a hollow against the wind it rarely is an isolated building but normally forms space along with out-house buildings. Today's bungalows do exactly the reverse. They seek out the highest point on the land, clear the site so that they become isolated objects, and because the trussed rafter is universally employed to form a cheap roof, the walls dominate. And finally, by law, the lane must be widened to a two way road destroying the scale of the immediate approach.

Like the traditional cottage, the Stoneman house has a single section rectangular plan with a double-height space in the centre. Externally, it adopted a construction technique pioneered by Ted Cullinan at the Fountains Abbey Visitor Centre of an internal blockwork structure and a rain screen of dry stone walling, a craft still very much in evidence locally and used as a way of joining the house to its immediate landscape. (16) The roof takes on the form of an agricultural building completed with mill-finished aluminium with stained cedar boarding and fenestration in between (including two disappearing corner windows).

A smaller guest house lying alongside was completed ten years later, which together with a re-inhabited cottage now forms a little entrance courtyard. (12, 13) The guest house employs a stepped section so that all the main rooms see the view of the sea.

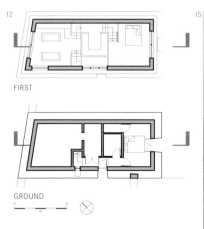

FIRST

GROUND

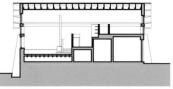

2005 HOUSE

MACKINNON / BRIONGOS HOUSE

Strathaven Airfield; projected completion 2012

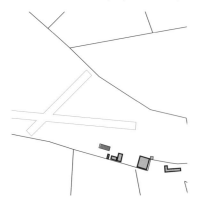

The Mackinnon/Briongos house is a similar roof-dominated house located at Strathaven Airfield in Lanarkshire. (18–23) To a degree there is a superficial resemblance but whereas the Stoneman/Clarke House grounded itself in the undulating sea of dry stone walls of the west of Ireland this house floats above its landscape of uninterrupted upland pasture. The owner of the airfield, also chief instructor, wished to live 'over the shop' but at the same time to preserve his privacy; all the main accommodation is on the first floor, the ground floor being reserved for spare bedrooms, entrance, garage, etc.. A cantilevering structure expresses this idea and the cladding of mill-finished aluminium throughout resonates with the airfield hangars and nearby agricultural buildings.

1 GARAGE
2 BEDROOM
3 WOODCHIP STORE
4 LIVING
5 KITCHEN/DINING
6 TERRACE
7 STUDY
8 SNUG

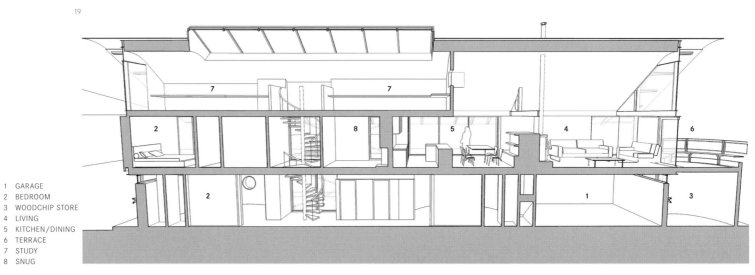

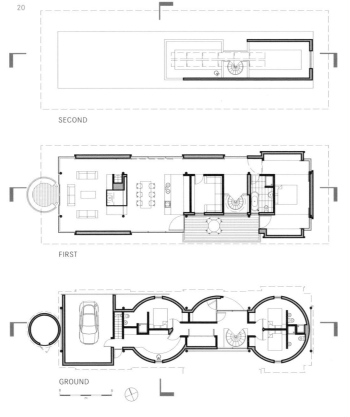

SECOND

FIRST

GROUND

22

23

VAN HULTEN HOUSE

Joure, The Netherlands; completed 1998

24

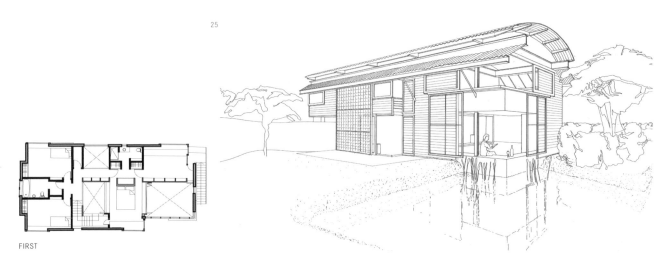

25

FIRST

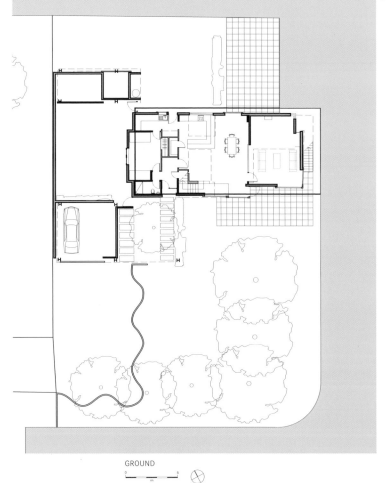

26

GROUND

29

In The Netherlands an unusual opportunity came about to build on the edge of a suburban housing development in the Friesland town of Joure. The Van Hulten House is surrounded on three sides by water. (24–29) The house is an object in the landscape in the manner of traditional combined Dutch farms and farmhouse—great single section buildings. And in the somewhat dislocated environment on the edge of a housing estate it was elected to emulate these forms with a simple building of an extruded section: a barrel vaulted space with two side sections. Clad in cedar and designed to be prefabricated, as is the norm in the Dutch building industry, the house was arranged on the site to give maximum private garden and organised internally with a children's zone near the entrance and a parents' zone towards the lake. At the centre, as a meeting place between parents and children, is placed a double-height family kitchen/dining room able to open directly to the garden. This is a noisy place packed with the daily life of the family and in contrast is the quieter living room linked by sliding screens and fronting both the lake and garden. Above this was placed a mezzanine study.

STEWART HOUSE

Udny, Aberdeenshire; completed 2000

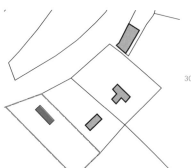

GROUND

SUMMER

WINTER

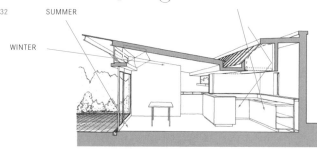

Perhaps mindful of the disaster which has befallen the Irish landscape, in 1994 the RIAS, in conjunction with West Lothian Council, ran a "house for the countryside" competition. (30) The practice's project showed a long house idea and in 2001 this was developed into the practice's first house commission in the UK, in the Aberdeenshire hamlet of Milldale near Udny. A south-facing site completed a small row of houses and looked out at gently rolling open fields. The Stewart House was the first of a series of "long house" designs; mostly single-storey, they are all arranged with habitable rooms in a line facing south, circulation and service rooms on the north side. (31–39) The section, complete with sliding window shutters and pivoting ceiling panels, was developed directly from the Palmer house extension (see pages 30–31) so that south light was directed to the north edge of the plan through a long roof-light. The angle of the roof admitted low winter sun but shaded in the summer. The kitchen remains the 'cockpit' of family activity at the heart of the circulation and the natural fall of the site was exploited to give a higher ceiling to the living space.

MACLEAN HOUSE
Barnton, Edinburgh; unbuilt

This design has been employed in variations almost all, unfortunately, unbuilt for Barnton Avenue (40–42) (complete with granny flat) and Ravelston (43–44) in Edinburgh, Strathtummel (45–46) and Loch Tay (47–49) in Perthshire and in Aberdour in Fife. (56–57) Constructed is a large home placing two long houses 'back to back' as a pavilion between re-inhabited sides of a former steading at Broomhill West Lothian and is another manifestation of the sectional idea. (50–52) A proposal to 'bend' the idea into two sides of what will become a walled garden house in North Berwick is due for completion in 2013. (58–60) The exterior of this house will appear to be an extension of the existing villa on the site in the form of an almost blank garden wall. This latter design is an example of what some call the practice's "stealth projects"; projects which attempt to disguise their presence to the outside world, a tactic required increasingly in conservation areas where planning officials lack the imagination to conceive of anything else. A proposal to build a similar design in Guildford was sadly abandoned after an unpleasant campaign by neighbours; a victory for nimby-ism, now known as "localism". (53–55)

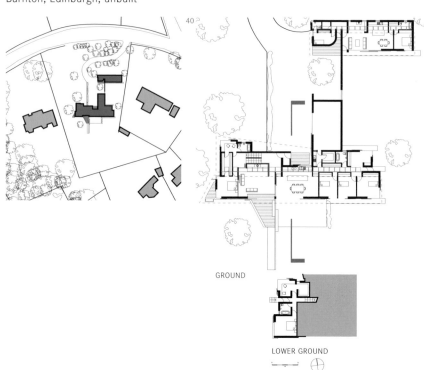

GROUND

LOWER GROUND

MARSHALL HOUSE
Ravelston, Edinburgh; unbuilt

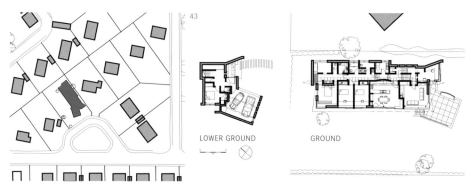

LOWER GROUND

GROUND

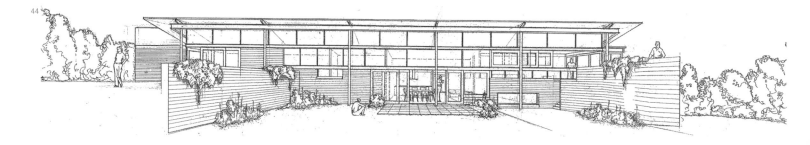

LACKIE HOUSE
Strathtummel, Perthshire; unbuilt

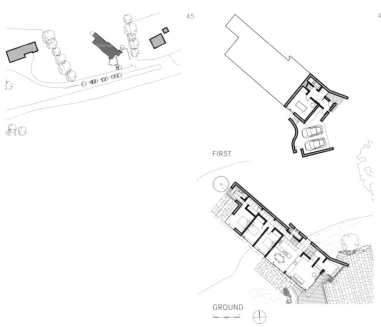

45

FIRST

GROUND

46

BOWDEN HOUSE
Loch Tay, Perthshire; unbuilt

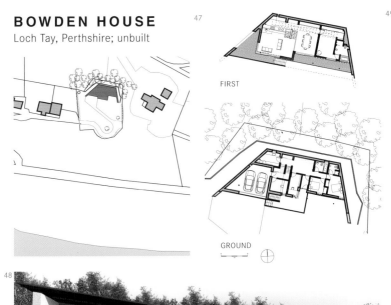

47

FIRST

GROUND

48

49

McCORMACK HOUSE

Broomhill, West Lothian; completed 2001

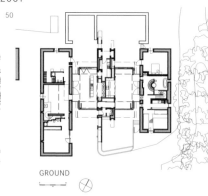

GROUND

FIRST

FORGAN HOUSE

Guildford, Surrey; unbuilt

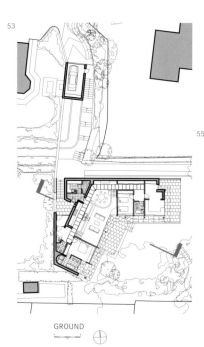

GROUND

HARRIS HOUSE

Aberdour, Fife; unbuilt

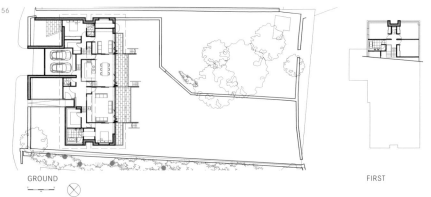

GROUND ⊗

FIRST

CORBETT HOUSE

North Berwick; projected completion 2013

GROUND ⊕

THOMSON HOUSE, EDINBURGH
Completed 2004

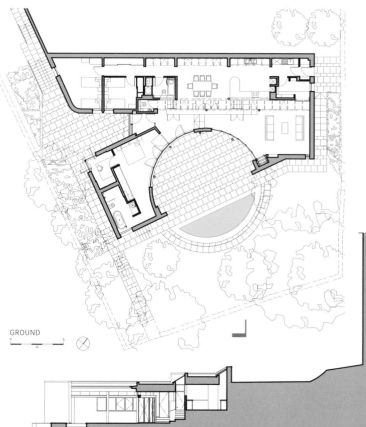

GROUND

A built example of a house that broke all local planning rules is the Thomson House in Colinton, a conservation area on the outskirts of Edinburgh. (61–68) The clients wished to downsize from their substantial Edwardian villa and the new house was placed on the former tennis court at the foot of the steeply sloping backgarden. It was designed to be semi-underground, to be invisible from the main house by having roofs planted in cotoneaster and appear to be a continuation of their garden. The plan focuses on a pool and small garden with the main living spaces being continual but defined by three minor changes of level. Although substantially overshadowed by existing trees lighting levels inside are remarkably high due to two major roof-lights which also mark the changes of level in the plan.

Neil Thomson writes:

Marion and I had a slight advantage over most of Richard's clients in that I had the pleasure of working with him as part of the winning design team on DCA, his first 'big' commission. I knew what I was taking on.

Marion and I had a problem in so far as we had lived for 28 years in a lovely Edwardian house and wished to retire in the same district of Edinburgh and build a modern 'butt and ben'. We spent three years looking for a suitable site to no avail. Marion knew I wanted to commission Richard and induced me to invite him to lunch to at least discuss the prospect. What a fruitful liquid lunch it turned out to be. He immediately spotted that our tennis lawn, several levels down our large garden, could house such a dwelling. I was immediately sceptical and as a surveyor thought only of the difficulties of the site and the cost of overcoming them. Marion being a midwife saw only the 'birth' of a brilliant solution.

We had a year's wrangling with the planners and the local conservation society but by making our building virtually invisible, with an envelope of garden wall stone and a green roof of cotoneaster we eventually won them over. Strangely the house now appears on the amenity association's list of notable houses in Colinton. We found a contractor brave enough to undertake the task and 37 weeks later we had our dream home (any resemblance between the contract period and the length of a pregnancy is purely co-incidental as Marion had no influence in this decision).

Right from Richard's first sketches the building felt right for us, and in practice it has proved to be the case. Richard's clever use of roof-lights and open planning has given us a home that is bathed in light regardless of the weather and a joy to wake-up to each morning. I resolutely stayed out of acting as project manager as over the years I have seen too many building professionals get too close to their own creations and make a hash of them (Richard beware). I was however ideally placed as a client with a bird's-eye view from the old house of the daily building progress.

Marion cleverly made a pact with the workmen that she would bake them cakes every Friday if they performed well on site. Strangely we seemed to have more men on site on the 37 Fridays she baked but it did ensure the design team attended regularly as well. The workmen gave her flowers and a hamper of food at Xmas (who said building tradesmen were hard-nuts?).

The level of detailed drawings provided by RMA was impressive and given the complex nature of the build proved essential. Marion was so taken with Craig Amy, the project architect, that she threatened to adopt him.

The building design won several awards and appeared in at least five house design magazines. Marion and I envisaged this project as a ten year episode in our lives but having lived here for almost eight years we are already revising this upwards before we move into our final 'sheltered housing'.

We have watched with admiration Richard's successes since he started up in practice 21 years ago and as very satisfied clients we can thoroughly recommend his practice to any potential developers in the private or public sectors.

YOUNGER HOUSE

Earlston, Borders Region; projected completion 2013

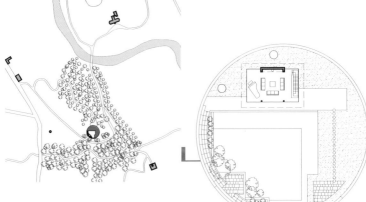

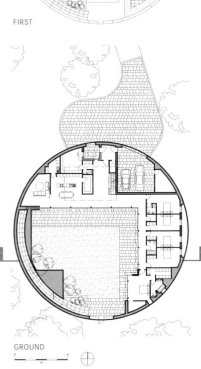

FIRST

Another stealth project is the intriguing possibility of constructing a substantial house at Knock Knowe near Earlston in the Borders Region. (69–70) Restoration from aforestation of a significant detached section of the historic landscape of Carolside House is proposed on condition that permission is given for a new house within it. This apparent contradiction has been solved by creating a circular broch-sized structure (the broch being a uniquely Scottish prehistoric tower dwelling), with a blind stone exterior not recognisable as a house *per se*, but containing within it an L-shaped plan and walled garden. In contrast, a first floor Miesian living room pavilion, with panoramic views of the entire landscape, will be the only recognisable inhabited element seen from the outside. The approach disguised within woodland will add to the buildings mysterious ambiguity.

GROUND

COWAN HOUSE

Inverness, unbuilt

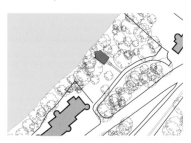

Tower houses pepper the Scottish landscape. Their plans of massive thick walls formed of tiny chambers, stairs and window places, in turn enclosing a single main space per floor, inspired the American architect Louis Kahn. (5, 6) Visiting Borthwick Castle outside Edinburgh he was instantly struck by the power of the idea which resonated with his own evolving ideas of served and servant spaces. The practice has proposed several unrealised variations of the tower with a proposal on the steeply sloping banks of the Ness River representing the closest to being built. (71–72)

Our client spotted the possibility of a house for herself in a wood south of Inverness next to a housing development. A gigantic (and potentially dangerous) Douglas fir sat on the site which we proposed to fell. A three-storey tower was conceived with a tiny footprint (7 x 5 m), which would have sat on the site of the felled tree and cantilever out at the second floor level where all the living spaces would have thus been in the branches of the trees. Access was to be by bridge at first floor level. A ridge roof-light would ensure plenty of daylight in the event of the tree canopy obstructing light. In winter, the section of the roof room would have been lowered so that the ridge light disappeared, replaced by a insulated ceiling.

It was calculated that the entire house construction including both internal and external cladding could have been fabricated from the single felled Douglas fir arguing, successfully, that we were not so much losing a tree, merely rearranging it. The developers, having failed to get planning permission themselves for the plot, then held out for a unreasonable sales price so the project was abandoned.

71

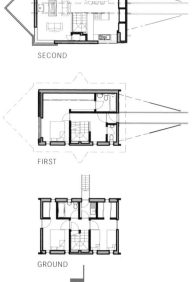

SECOND

FIRST

GROUND

72

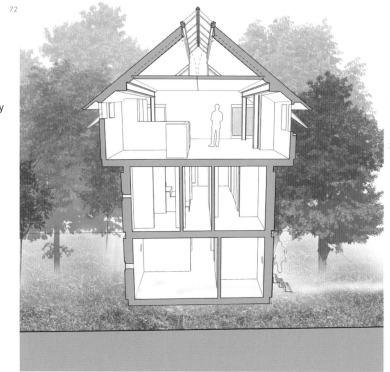

FINEGAN HOUSE 2

Argyll, unbuilt

Although the external characteristics of the Cowan house had the proportions of a traditional tower, the plan had none of their characteristics. However, another unrealised proposal placed a tower on the Island of Seil on the shore of the Argyll coast. (73–76) Here non-repetitive staircase circulation, cupboards, etc., would have formed the thick external walls with a single significant main space at the top crowned with an external terrace. A spectacular view down the Sound of Jura would be captured by a single horizontally pivoting window. (76) The planners thought the idea 'non traditional' (sic) and preferred a slated bungalow, like so many whose mediocrity is gradually dumbing down the Highland landscape. Again the project was abandoned.

73

THIRD

SECOND

FIRST

GROUND

74

ANDERSON HOUSE
Edinburgh, unbuilt

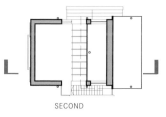

SECOND

FIRST

A tower project situated in an Edinburgh suburban garden was suggested for a rear garden which slopes steeply upwards on the flanks of the city's famous extinct volcano, Arthur's Seat in Willowbrae, a locale comprised of pre-war bungalows. (77–80) In contrast to these, a three-storey aluminium tower was originally proposed with entrance in the middle storey from the adjacent road. (77) The house was designed upside-down, living spaces occupying a cantilevering top floor and external space being a south-facing roof terrace above this while all the habitable rooms look north to an amazing panorama of the Firth of Forth. Cantilevering stairs to either side connected the levels. The project was refused at Planning Committee and a more compact design submitted for approval. (78) Regretfully, this too has been refused, as not "in keeping" with the local bungalows (sic).

GROUND

LOWER GROUND

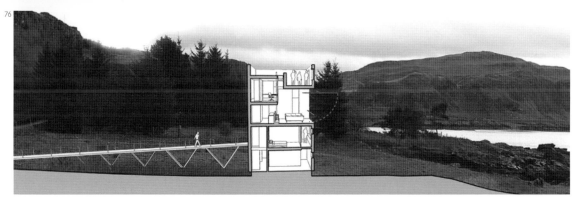

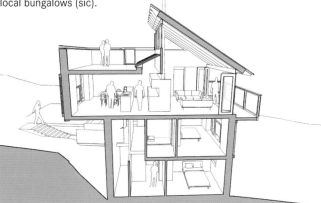

Old Fishmarket Close, Edinburgh

Living in the City

REPAIRING THE STREET

112 CANONGATE

Edinburgh; completed 1999

The concept of the European city made of 'everyday' buildings which form the streets interspersed with 'monument' buildings is well known. Nolli's sixteenth century map of Rome went further and showed inside public space of the monument buildings (predominantly churches) having the same status as outside public space and British nineteenth century maps followed this lead. (1)

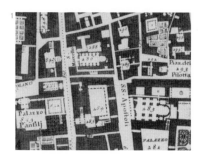

In many ways Edinburgh's New Town is the most perfect UK example, since apart from public buildings (again mostly churches) there are no 'buildings', rather all is composed streets and squares. (2) Most of the everyday buildings, the *poché* of the city plan, were housing but gradually in our city centres over the last hundred years these have been eclipsed by office or retail buildings.

In addition, the principle of joining up buildings with party walls to form streets with recognisable fronts and backs has been diluted with much

post-war public housing taking on the form of free-standing blocks. Dumbiedykes on the edge of the Old Town is a classic example. (3)

Such architectural experimentations with high-rise living and "streets in the sky" are now recognised as not only socially ill-advised, but also essentially anti-urban. Scotland has its own tradition of tenement building distinct from the terraced housing in England, resulting, some would argue, from the concept of the "flying freehold" in the Scottish legal system. Amongst UK cities, Edinburgh generally is an exception in that it has not experienced the same massive haemorrhaging of residential population from its city centre that say, some of the North of England cities experienced; nor has it suffered the so-called slum clearances of Glasgow and elsewhere. The late twentieth century has seen a return to city living, with houses reconverted, empty infill sites developed, and in particular the complete regeneration of the Old Town, which had seriously depopulated from its peak of 80,000 in the late eighteenth century to less than 4,000 in 1981. These seven built projects, two public and five private are primarily from that era and are representative of a deliberately non-inventive pattern of building; more they set out to reinforce patterns of inhabitation already in existence.

Three projects in the Edinburgh Old Town have contributed to its revival, and each makes direct references to the distinct plan and architecture of the historic structures, built to a very high-density, and yet comply with contemporary lighting and privacy standards. A small project for a housing association comprises nine flats and a shop and sits on the site of the former archway to the Holyrood Brewery on the south side of the Canongate in the Edinburgh Old Town. (4–9)

It was a small part of the major revitalisation of a derelict brewery

site master planned by John Hope Architects. The design made reference to buildings of the Old Town which have to a large extent disappeared and been replaced with Georgian and Victorian successors (ironically, the Old Town is now predominantly newer than the New). In particular, colonnades at ground floor level, external staircases, windows frequently arranged as horizontal galleries, and a free-style quality to their general composition were all re-interpreted. The upper storeys of Mediaeval constructions were often cantilevered, (4) frequently made of timber with a roof-top profile of 'roofed rooms', like small independent buildings embedded into the roofscape. The geometry of the plot forms an acute angle between front and side elevations allowing the orthogonal cantilevers to progressively jut out onto the street. The opportunities were taken for stunning views of Salisbury Crags to the south and a chance to make a contemporary addition to the heterogeneous development of the Royal Mile. The top flat with views in all directions as well as generous roof glazing is particularly spectacular. (8)

FOURTH

THIRD

GROUND

7

8

9

OLD FISHMARKET CLOSE
Edinburgh; completed 2004

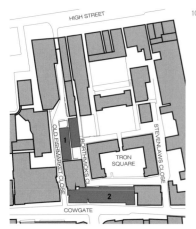

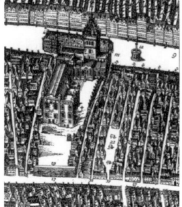

1 OLD FISHMARKET CLOSE
2 COWGATE HOUSING

1647

1780

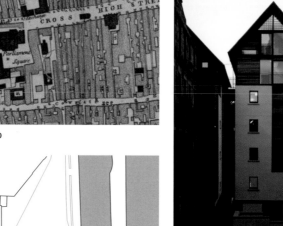

Further up the Royal Mile, just off the much denser High Street (Edinburgh and Canongate were once separate boroughs), the practice won a competition to develop a former three-storey car park on the steeply sloping Old Fishmarket Close. (11–17) The 1867 Improvement Act had amputated many of the 'bones' of the famous kipper-bone plan due to their insanitary state, lack of sunlight (the Edinburgh Old Town had been an astonishingly dense and insanitary place). The project was a simple reworking of the Old Town linear pattern into two parallel but offset blocks and the restitution of a long vanished close between the two; in other words to put back in a contemporary way what had been removed in the nineteenth century. The considerable slope allowed offices and a restaurant to be slipped in under the flats and the top most flats express their maisonette interior with double-height living spaces forming lantern-like windows in the four gable-ends. (14) The form of the building was directly inspired from the famous Gordon of Rothiemays aerial view of the Old Town 1646–1647. (10)

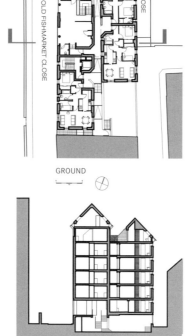

GROUND

COWGATE
Edinburgh; completed 2006

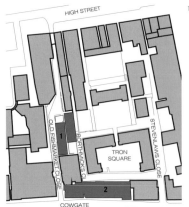

1   OLD FISHMARKET CLOSE
2   COWGATE HOUSING

Old Fishmarket Close housing was part of a wider regeneration project which led to a commission for housing association flats in the valley of the Cowgate and offices on the lower two floors. (18–23) The site is complex, a long narrow strip between a busy and ancient thoroughfare and the nineteenth century three-sided Tron Square social housing, which has demanding daylight and privacy requirements. Guthrie Street opposite leads up to Chambers Street and the topography of this two level part of the Old Town means that there are also views from the upper level of the city from bridges across the Cowgate and through vennels from the High Street to the top of a potential new building. (20–22) The resulting design on a restricted budget built three mono-pitched towers to the street with roof terraces between and with many individual flats having their own terraces. Deck access for the majority of the flats is positioned confronting Guthrie street. (21) The flats above the offices are accessed from hanging staircases to the rear. (23) They were originally to have been bridges to the adjacent square but the idea was vetoed by residents there. (19)

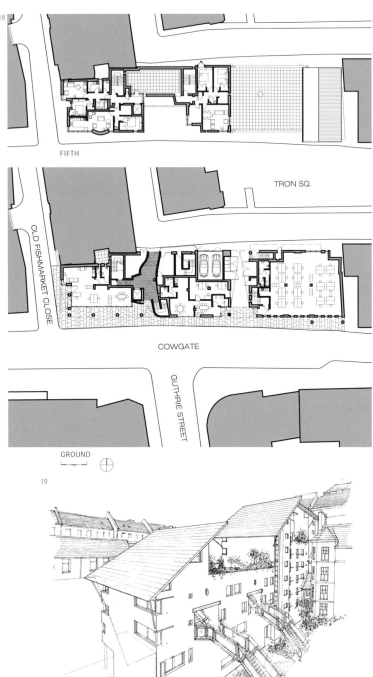

FIFTH

GROUND

DEAN BANK LANE
Edinburgh; completed 2005

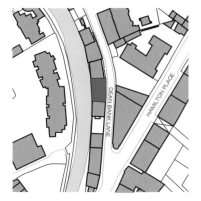

On the fringes of the New Town are two projects which typologically appear to be conservative but internally have unexpected twists. Edinburgh is unusual in having no major river at its centre; instead the Water of Leith winds around the northern suburbs and with the exception of its setting as it passes through New Town gardens it has always been treated as an industrial backwater. At Dean Bank Lane the developer client was persuaded not to refurbish the industrial building on the site to produce at most six flats but to contemplate complete demolition and replacement with a larger project of 11 flats. (24–31) The proposition was that the block should rise a storey to complete a row of tenements to the north before the smaller scale of two-storey houses began to the south. It also went down two storeys to just above the flood level of the river making it total a six-storey development when seen from the riverbank walkway opposite, but a three-storey building in the relatively modestly scaled Dean Bank Lane. The top floor penthouse is set back from the lane to achieve this.

The site is also prominent from the nearby bridge at Stockbridge and the gable-end is divided into two masses separated by an indented terrace to the flat on the penultimate floor.

Architecturally, the idea was of planes of zinc wrapping the sides of the building and folding over to form the roofs with a celebration of the riverside elevation onto which emerges the circulation system at the upper floors.

Medium sized developments such as this, to be efficient in plan, cannot afford two fire escape staircases and over the years building regulations for single staircase blocks of flats, particularly those regarding fire and smoke have progressively tightened. The requirement for there to be naturally ventilated lobbies to all flats entrances if more than eight flats in a block had interesting architectural consequences for both this project and at Belford Road (overleaf).

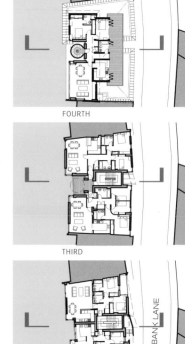

FOURTH

THIRD

GROUND

DEAN BANK LANE

LOWER GROUND

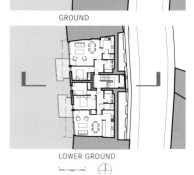

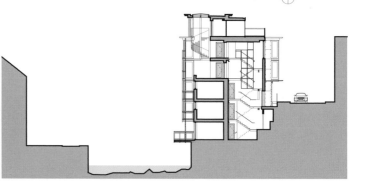

BELFORD ROAD

Edinburgh; completed 2003

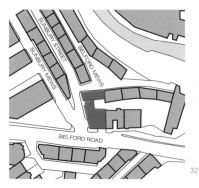

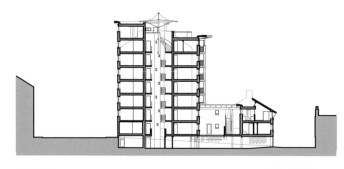

At Belford Road on a very prominent corner of this late Victorian outpost of the New Town is a dense project which on Belford Road itself completes a row of tenements, steps up to turn a corner into Sunbury Street and then to the rear is completed by three upside down maisonettes sitting on top of a semi-buried parking floor which meet the mews scale of the adjacent Belford Mews Lane. (32–36) While the architecture of the block is distinct from its neighbours its urban manners are impeccable. At Belford Road the square plan requires the three available elevations all to be fenestrated with habitable rooms. A centrally placed staircase would have required a pointless corridor stretching to the exterior on each floor. Instead was invented a central tube of outside air at the heart of the plan and around it are balcony accesses to three flats protected from most of the rain by a Teflon canopy floating over the top. So as a type it appears to be "tenement stair" but is, in reality, "deck access". Similarly at Dean Bank Lane, the stair was divided into two; a stair going down to four flats (only the lowest floor flats are single aspect, the floor above benefit from light wells to the lane) but the height of the upper flats still demanded ventilated lobbies so the top three floors are accessed externally, with the penthouse given an appropriate flourish with a suspended spiral staircase as its entrance. From such mundane and sometime perplexing restrictions flow architectural solutions which perhaps are probably more interesting than had a repetitive tenement style stair been still permitted.

32
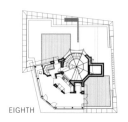
EIGHTH

FIRST

BELFORD MEWS

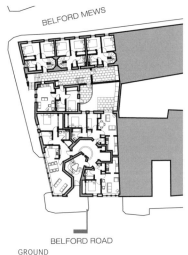
BELFORD ROAD
GROUND

33

35

34

36

Andrew Burrell writes:

Buredi was the imaginative name (or at least the best that we could think of at the time) for the joint venture company formed in the late 1990s between The Burrell Company and the EDI Group. Although both companies had previously worked together it was Richard, by default, who acted as a catalyst to the formation of the venture.

Richard Murphy Architects had won a limited competition run by EDI to design a residential scheme to replace a series of light industrial units behind Dublin Street, in Edinburgh's New Town. EDI had limited residential experience and turned to Burrell who had a track record in delivering bespoke urban regeneration. Thus Buredi was born.

The Company eventually built three projects to Murphy designs, and would have built others had it been successful in acquiring the requisite land. The three that made it were all on difficult sites, all within the historic core of Edinburgh city, and all offered potential that Murphy could exploit whilst sometimes attracting the claustrophobic stranglehold of Edinburgh's NIMBY set.

Dublin Colonies, insisted Richard, was the wrong title as the design was based on the historic pattern of development in the New Town's back lanes of that area. However, always with an eye on the marketing potential, we chose to compare Murphy's low-rise, high-density layout of apartments approached by external stairs, with Edinburgh's iconic dwellings for workers of the nineteenth century.

Number 56 was the much safer title we adopted for the second Murphy scheme, this time on a corner site in Edinburgh's West End at 56 Belford Road. It was a brilliant plan which exploited the use of a naturally vented central stair on this constrained site, allowing a greater density than would otherwise have been possible. The dominant feature was to be the towering corner reflecting the building's important position on the street, and intended to detract from the nearby mediocrity which had recently been built. However, it was to finish as a somewhat stunted corner as one storey was chopped off in discussion with the Planners, another at the behest of the local conservation body, and a third by the Planning Committee that didn't know about the previous slice but whose members knew there was an election imminent.

The Tron, a personal favourite, was the product of another limited competition, and was created on an infill site previously occupied by a Council car park. The design expertly snuggles into the Old Town's pattern of closes and steep slopes where once the rig system of thin elongated land holding dominated. Light is the nutrient which buildings on such sites strive for and Murphy created a mixed-use scheme with the ground floor commercial rising through various apartment sizes and shapes and culminating in double-height end-gable apartments with views across the surrounding roof tops to Arthur's Seat.

Whilst all sites have potential, they also come with their difficulties. But it's the rewarding aspect of the design process that registers in the memory with these developments. Each building designed for Buredi was a considered response to the site, commercially viable, and the architect/client engagement a rewarding experience. Even fun.

Andrew Burrell is a Director of Buredi Ltd. and client for housing at Old Fishmarket Close (pages 74–75), Dublin Street (pages 87–89) and Belford Road.

WHITEHAVEN
Cumbria; projected completion 2014

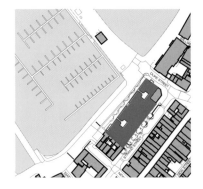

It is still a slight mystery as to why the practice found itself entering a RIBA open contest at Whitehaven on the Cumbrian coast, preferring limited to open competitions. (38–43) The site was almost an urban block on the harbour front and the brief was for 40 flats, each to have a harbour view and 4,000 square metres of flexible office space with underground parking. Astonishingly, the competition attracted 139 entries from all over the world and even more astonishingly, after being shortlisted, the practice won. Unlike most competitors, who proposed variations on a deck access residential block along the front with an office block on the back, the design arranges the flats as three residential towers on top of two floors of offices, with the aim of creating corner windows to exploit the panoramic views. (43) Pairs of upside-down maisonettes at first floor are accessed by external stairs which discharge directly onto the quayside and are implanted into the office design and animate this elevation and also bring down its scale. The maisonettes along the quayside continue the corner window motif and are used to frame a cupola on a fragment of a former swimming baths so as to integrate this element into the site.

The slight change of level is exploited to form a lowered terrace which is partially populated by a cafe within the surviving fragment of the swimming baths. The site sits between the town and the sea and so the two main elevations responded accordingly; a seaside series of towers seen from across the harbour, necessarily at a larger scale, but on the landward side a street elevation of three storeys with upper levels stepped back. The site's depth at 31 metres required light wells to illuminate the offices but these also found a function as two controlled-access courtyards from which in turn two stair/lift cores each were accessed. The central courtyard is internal and roof-lit and forms the location for the main office staircase. In this way, the two functions of the site were integrated rather than the twentieth century tendency of isolation from each other.

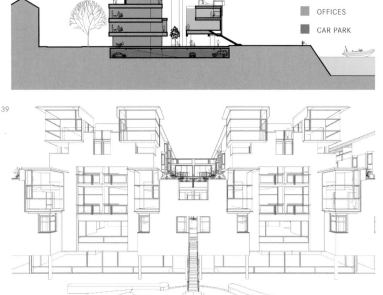

	TWO-BED FLATS
	MAISONETTES
	OFFICES
	CAR PARK

FIFTH

FOURTH

THIRD

SECOND

FIRST

GROUND

42

43

Moore Street, Glasgow

Making Housing Sociable

COURTYARDS AND STAIRCASES

Different countries and cities have produced their own typologies of housing. In Scotland there is the tenement with publicly lit internal stairs and communal back green. In Newcastle are found terraces of Tyneside flats; in London the terraced town house sometimes within a square containing a shared garden and perhaps a mews lane. In Berlin there is the dense tartan grid of the Berlin block; in Paris the courtyard apartment block; in Prague the balcony accessed gated street; in Amsterdam the communal porch to three flats, etc.. Interestingly, between the wars "red" Vienna produced the Wienerhof which is effectively a Scottish tenement turned inside out. These arrangements can produce varying degrees of sociability depending generally on how much semi-private space is available outside the entrances to individual apartments. The tenement scores lowest in this respect; a tenement stair being an internal means of access and nothing more.

However, Edinburgh is the home to another typology, unique to the city. The "colony" house, so-called as they were built originally for colonies of artisans on the edge of the middle class New Town. (3–5)

Superficially they appear to be two-storey terraced houses with attic dormers. However, they are in fact flats with the ground and first floors accessed from opposite sides of the block with gardens on each side and a central road between each terrace. Consequently, the front of the ground floor flat is the rear of the first floor flat and *vice versa*. Highly distinctive are the external staircases protruding at right angles to the block, shared by two front doors and articulating the gardens on that side of the block. The ground floor is a single storey but most of the upper flats have developed their attics so they are in fact maisonettes. The colony house, however, did not invent the external staircase; many of the Old Town's tenements were accessed, certainly at their lower levels, by stairs which spill out directly onto the streets. One of the most beautiful surviving examples, although heavily restored, is at Whitehorse Close (1) where the flats also enjoy a courtyard setting. A revival of this idea was the Mediaeval inspired student housing inspired by Patrick Geddes at Ramsay Gardens. (2)

For 15 years Richard Murphy lived in an upper colony house in the city's Abbeyhill district. Opposite was a standard Edinburgh tenement and he observed that it was only on his side of the street that all the neighbours knew each other. In the summer residents sit outside their front doors, and converse across the gardens. Even the simple act of climbing the staircase becomes a little piece of theatre, an opportunity to stop and say hello to neighbours whilst on the other side of the street; residents live anonymous lives! (5)

3

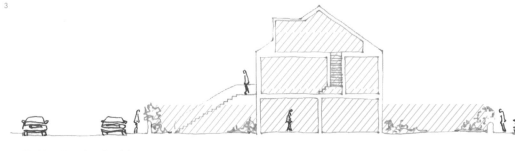

DUBLIN STREET COLONIES

Edinburgh; completed 1999

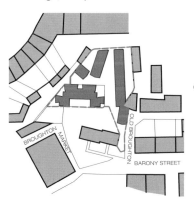

As part of their ill-fated bid to become UK City of Architecture 1999 Edinburgh City Council's own development company EDI launched a limited competition for a New Town back-land site in 1994 behind Dublin Street. (6–14) Semi-derelict industrial buildings incapable of conversion existed on the site but after examination of historic maps it became apparent that these were in fact the remnants of the pre-New Town village of Broughton. (6) Scheduled for complete demolition in the 1820s, it had instead been encircled by New Town tenements. (8) The practice's successful entry decided not only to preserve the spirit of the village by constructing apartment blocks approximately on the footprint of the existing buildings but also to celebrate the Mediaeval idea of the external staircase which had hitherto been found only in the Old Town. Three blocks of three-storey flats and a small block of six houses were constructed with a sequence of informal spaces between them. Residents have since described being there as like living in a secret village; exactly the intention!

1747

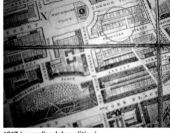

1817 (unrealised demolition)

1851

GROUND

13

14

GRAHAM SQUARE

Glasgow; completed 2000

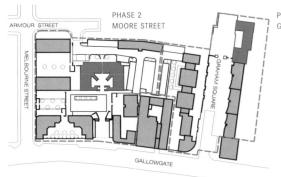

The idea of an external stair was repeated in Glasgow where Molendinar Park Housing Association asked the practice to convert the derelict Market Hotel, a former meat traders' lodging that had been part of the now demolished market. This was part of a larger project with Page/Park and JM Architects and became known as Graham Square. (15–20, 23) Both the hotel and the attached market archway were grade B listed. The central section of the hotel was unsafe so it was proposed to demolish this and replace it with a new section set back from the street so as to create a courtyard with external stairs beneath a glass canopy held behind a preserved remnant of the former front wall. The two side wings were then to be converted. Later these side wings were also deemed to be unsafe and they were demolished and rebuilt during the course of the building contract. The hotel entrance was preserved as a gateway in the courtyard wall, and here is found the entry-phone which gives access, making the courtyard itself private to the residents.

The combination of controlled communal courtyard and external staircases has been such a huge social success (the courtyard has been planted and maintained entirely by residents) that when the same housing association launched a limited competition for a larger adjacent site the controlled communal courtyard became the chief idea of the practice's entry.

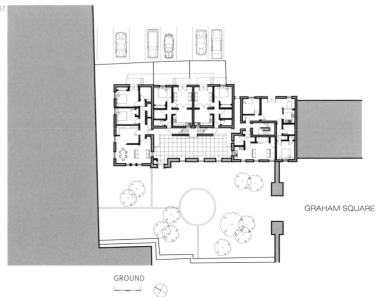

GRAHAM SQUARE

GROUND

MOORE STREET

Glasgow; completed 2008

Moore Street had also been part of the meat market and another archway existed on the site. (22–32) The practice's competition entry proposed this as the main access to a central courtyard from which four other controlled courtyards would be accessed. (22) The idea was victorious although it was later diluted through a consultation process. (23) The three other architects (the Graham Square team plus Elder and Cannon) all produced variations on the theme and the whole site was wrapped in a dark blue brick wall inset with ceramic tiles, the idea being a distant memory of the enclosing copper boundary wall of the Scandinavian embassies in Berlin. The practice's own project for 22 flats sat axially on the archway and, unlike the three Glaswegian practices, who opted for the familiarity of the repetitive tenement staircase, once again all circulation was made external. A symmetrical U-shaped block forms the court with two main staircases climbing into the two corners. Two other suspended staircases at the front give access to two upside down maisonettes, and also help to passively supervise the central courtyard. Great effort was made to celebrate with terraces, seats and plant pot holders, the territory outside each apartment's front door and again the project has been a huge social success. (29, 30, 33) An interesting consequence of these access arrangements is that each floor's plan is non-repetitive, with the top six flats celebrating their position with distinctive lantern living rooms.

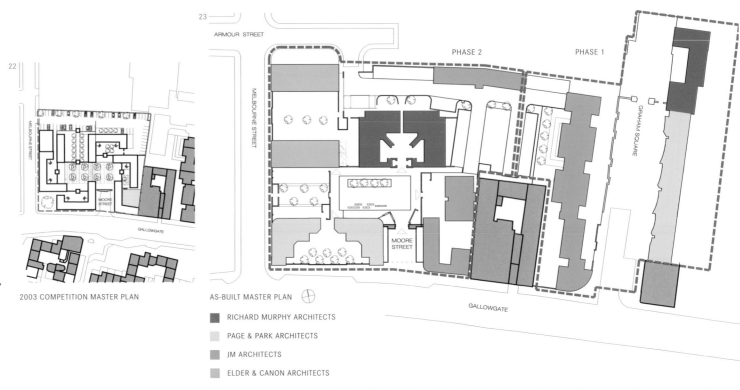

2003 COMPETITION MASTER PLAN

AS-BUILT MASTER PLAN

◼ RICHARD MURPHY ARCHITECTS

◻ PAGE & PARK ARCHITECTS

◼ JM ARCHITECTS

◼ ELDER & CANON ARCHITECTS

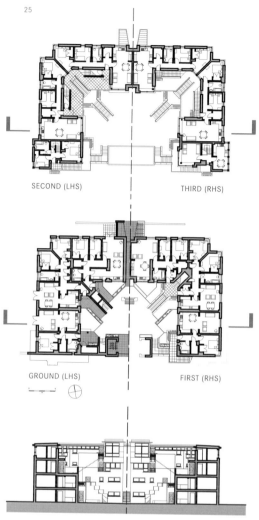

25

SECOND (LHS)   THIRD (RHS)

GROUND (LHS)   FIRST (RHS)

26

27

Rob Joiner writes:

Molendinar Park Housing Association's housing at Moore Street sits alongside our earlier Graham Square development and completes the redevelopment of the old Glasgow Meat Market site. Despite the success of Graham Square and the many awards it won (or, perhaps, because of this) it took nearly seven years to obtain funding from Glasgow City Council for Moore Street. Although this was frustrating it did give us plenty of time to assess how Graham Square had performed in relation to our expectations.

Richard Murphy's courtyard development at 50 Graham Square was definitely one of the successful features and we were pleased that his master plan for Moore Street developed this model further. While each of the four architectural practices involved, interpreting the courtyard concept in their own way, produced beautiful and interesting housing, Richard Murphy created a strikingly innovative form of medium-density residential development.

The flats at 20 Moore Street share some features with 50 Graham Square—the common entrance through the courtyard and the external stairs, for example—but develop the concept further with space to sit out around the entrance to each flat and more dramatic staircases which alter the experience of accessing an upper floor flat. The external stair seems less demanding than the traditional tenement stair and, whether entering or leaving, a bit more interesting than usual—even in the rain!

Creating buildings and spaces which give pleasure is, of course, one of the purposes of architecture and one for which Richard Murphy is rightly recognised. However, this building does more than that. The shape of the building and the positioning of the stairs and flat entrances ensure that each flat is approached openly and visibly. There is no anonymity, as in traditional flatted developments, as every front door can be seen from at least half the other flats even when residents are not sitting outside their front doors. This makes it a very unwelcoming place for those who are up to no good. The form which has been developed here is an interesting one—it is neither a traditional urban nor suburban building—and it is an approach which I believe can be developed further and used for different client groups and in a variety of locations. I hope Richard will find the time, and the clients, to enable him to further explore this concept.

John Ruskin wrote, "When we build, let us think that we build forever. Let it not be for present delight, nor for present use alone; let it be such work as our descendants will thank us for." As funding for affordable housing reduces even further and our government reverts to encouraging standardised, uninspiring housing Richard Murphy's work for us is like a beacon against the approaching darkness.

Rob Joiner is Director of Molendinar Park Housing Association.

MAXWELL DRIVE AND ST ANDREWS CRESCENT
Glasgow; unbuilt

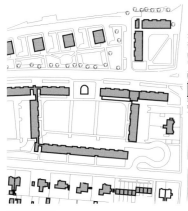

EXISTING SITE

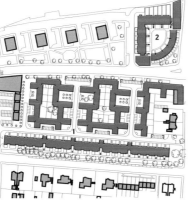

PROPOSED MASTER PLAN

1   MAXWELL DRIVE
2   ST ANDREWS CRESCENT

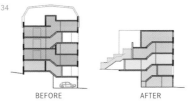

BEFORE   AFTER

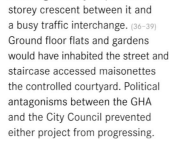

BEFORE   AFTER

Moore Street has been much visited by other housing associations and it led to an invitation by the Glasgow Housing Association (GHA) to make proposals for a large area of 1970s deck access housing in the Pollockshields area of the city. (33–39) The existing six-storey flats have a bizarre section; down the centre the floor plates had been slipped by half a level so that every flat is a split level whilst at the same time being denied the usual benefit of varied ceiling heights. This has produced the most extraordinary series of convoluted plans accessed from two horizontal decks. The design proposed removing all the deck accesses and the lifts and converting the structure of the block to externally accessed flats, allowing the top flats to benefit from the split section. Colony-style stairs accessed the first floor with private gardens between them for the ground floor flats. A terrace of town houses was proposed for Maxwell Drive in the centre of the site with streets made of linked Moore Street-style three sided courtyards. (33–35) Nearby on a smaller site on St Andrews Crescent the practice proposed the same idea for an existing L-shaped block, but then completed a courtyard with an Edinburgh Colony-inspired three-storey crescent between it and a busy traffic interchange. (36–39) Ground floor flats and gardens would have inhabited the street and staircase accessed maisonettes the controlled courtyard. Political antagonisms between the GHA and the City Council prevented either project from progressing.

WESTPORT

Co. Mayo, Ireland; completed 2005

site 'takes possession' of the view. One side consists of the interlocking flats already described, with their end conditions celebrated with external terraces and the other becoming a convex crescent of town houses. These also enjoyed a complex section allowing the living rooms to also enjoy higher ceilings. A similar section was also used in terraced town houses at both Cramond and Harlow (see pages 108–111 and 112–115).

Manipulating the section within an apartment block is not often attempted. At Westport in the Irish Republic the practice was invited by the Irish practice, Taylor Architects, to collaborate with them on the design for a site on the edge of this planned town. (40-51) A section was invented where two flats on top of each other enjoyed one-and-a-half-storey height living spaces; the upper flat accessed by an external staircase and having two floors of other accommodation. (42) The site is egg-timer shaped and sits above the town alongside a disused railway cutting with a distant view of the famous local pilgrimage mountain of Croagh Patrick, a kind of Irish Mount Fuji. The view was at the end of the site so two convex crescents of housing on either side were created, and the mountain was visible through the 'gun-sight' created at the narrowest point between them. In this way, everyone entering the

42

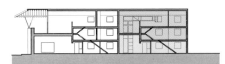

SECOND

FIRST

GROUND

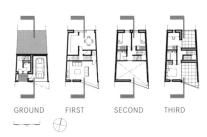

GROUND   FIRST   SECOND   THIRD

43

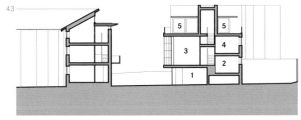

1 GARAGE
2 KITCHEN/DINING ROOM
3 LIVING ROOM
4 BEDROOM
5 TERRACE

44

TIMMER MARKET

Aberdeen; completed 2011

The success of the two Molendinar Park Housing developments in Glasgow has convinced the practice to pursue the courtyard and external stair idea as a typology. In Aberdeen the combination was used again this time winning a competition for social housing and accommodation for the Salvation Army at Timmer Market. (52–56) The site sits adjacent to a very hostile busy inner city ring road but had the opportunity of turning its back on this to create a south-facing courtyard solely for pedestrian access. The Salvation Army were on the lower floors with the housing above. A lowered courtyard gave entry for the Army with flats accessed from an upper court level by spiral stairs. When the Salvation Army withdrew, a nursery school was substituted and again external stairs were proposed this time very much based on the Moore Street Glasgow model. (55) But what can be built on a housing association budget in Glasgow apparently cannot be built in Aberdeen so the final built version (now with an NHS drug rehabilitation centre on the ground floor) sadly adopted more conventional internal tenement staircases but the controlled courtyard access remains. (56)

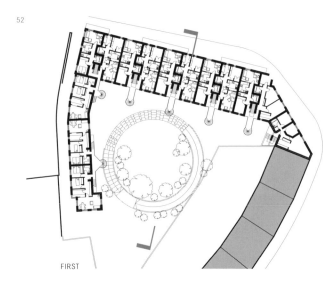

FIRST

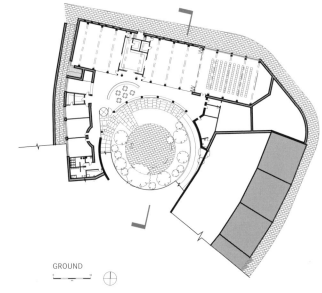

GROUND

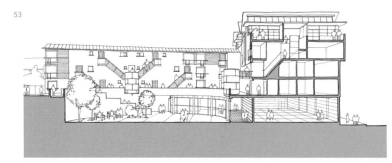

Q10 FORMER ROYAL INFIRMARY

Edinburgh; projected completion 2013

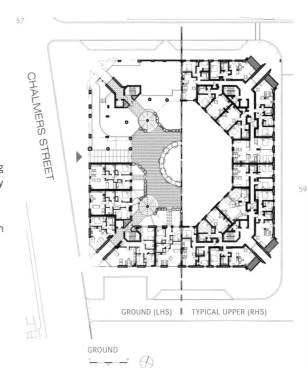

GROUND (LHS) | TYPICAL UPPER (RHS)

GROUND

Another courtyard is the very dense social housing at the former Royal Infirmary site in Edinburgh. The project, Q10, as originally designed, had its numbers considerably increased when the residential accommodation in Foster & Partners' overall plan for the former Infirmary was increased. (57–60) The resulting density of a scheme creating 174 affordable apartments in a single block broke all local guidelines. The practice proposed a version of a Wienerhof with a single entrance to a courtyard with a lift and stair towers in each corner. The massing was eroded towards the southwest corner to admit as much sunlight as possible, and in compensation for the small amount of communal space in the centre many of the flats have their own generous roof terraces and corner balconies. The exterior of mottled grey terra cotta tiles makes reference to Foster's own (more expensive!) metallic cladding nearby. (60) Corners are celebrated with balconies and an oversailing zinc roof. The common stair areas, although deep in the plan, are still naturally lit with a view to the outside at each floor. The interior of the courtyard is white render and glass with a planting regime that is hoped will completely cover the elevations with greenery. The building will thus have a hard exterior shell but a semi-private green heart. Space has been reserved at the ground floor for management office, a nursery and a cafe.

Newhall, Harlow, Essex

The Architect in Suburbia

MAKING PLACES OUT OF HOUSES

The very term "suburban" is pejorative for many architects. Almost entirely in the hands of volume house builders, UK suburban housing is generally an architect-free zone obsessed with the concept of the detached house, mass-produced, with a range of veneered styles marketed with nostalgia for Elizabethan, Georgian or Victorian eras. (1) Contemporary design rarely features.

As demand has increased and developable land restricted, plots have become smaller and houses have moved closer together, but still stubbornly remain as objects surrounded by space rather than in any urban sense joining together to form spaces. It is sad to reflect that the country which invented the Garden City ideal should have now so diluted and distorted it into the thousands of endless identical cul-de-sacs of little boxes which litter the edges of all our towns and villages. (2)

Perhaps the UK detached suburban dream is some distant memory of the country house. In Denmark by contrast Jørn Utzon identified the Danish equivalent suburban ideal as the farmhouse, or perhaps more accurately the farmyard, i.e. the space formed by farm buildings. His two brilliant housing projects at Fredensborg and Helsingør turned the concept of a house into a courtyard; a square plan containing an L-shape of rooms all facing onto a walled garden. (3–5) Externally the identity of the house was suppressed behind an anonymous brick wall but within the courtyards the perimeter garden wall was lowered to give a framed view of a wider shared landscape beyond.

Heavily influenced by these projects is Peter Aldington's own grouping of three courtyard houses built in the 1960s at Haddenham (6) (of which Richard Murphy is a trustee) and his later grouping of six small houses for retired workers on the Carrington estate in Bledlow, also in Buckinghamshire. (7–8)

Both of Aldington's projects are sometimes referred to as "romantic" perhaps because they are roof-dominated and made of local materials, but this is to miss the point. It is their planning that is radical as they have eschewed the individual front and side garden in favour of the shared courtyard and have suppressed the identity of the individual house in favour of the group. The houses are no longer objects in space; rather together they make spaces. How UK suburbia might have been different if developers had taken notice of these two beautiful (and very marketable) projects.

RIAS HOUSE FOR THE FUTURE COMPETITION
unbuilt

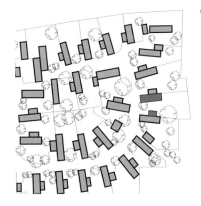

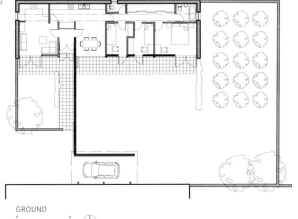

GROUND

In the RIAS "house for the future competition", the practice developed the rural house idea (see page 58, figure 30) but placed it in a suburban context and made single storey long houses set at right angles to the street. (9–12) There was to be no front garden but rather each house would look into private walled gardens with the blank rear wall of the adjacent rear house forming the boundary. The roof profile varied depending on either a south or east-/west-facing orientation. Only one house on a suburban plot was required by the competition but the idea was expanded to show how the houses might agglomerate into "walled lanes" very much in the manner of the walled developments of the Victorian Edinburgh suburbs of Murrayfield and the Grange. (10) The RIAS competition was one of several that have been staged over the years with some such as Future World at Milton Keynes in 1996, and more recently the Highland Housing fair in Inverness in 2009 being assemblages of different individual house designs, a kind of architectural chocolate box. Interesting as it is to have individual new house designs what is surely more relevant and urgent is to find a new way of combining houses to make particular places.

CRAMOND HOUSING
Edinburgh; completed 2011

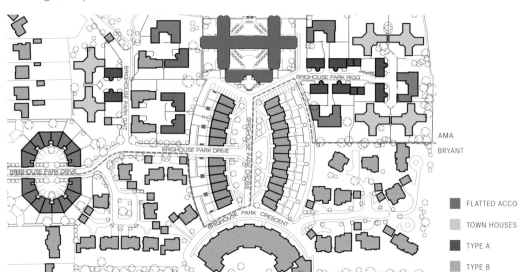

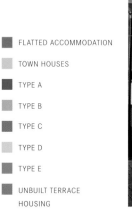

AMA
BRYANT

■ FLATTED ACCOMMODATION

TOWN HOUSES

■ TYPE A

TYPE B

■ TYPE C

TYPE D

■ TYPE E

■ UNBUILT TERRACE
HOUSING

The practice has been commissioned by two developers who were capable of operating outside the mainstream suburban thinking of the mass house builders. At Cramond on the northwestern edge of Edinburgh they were invited to master plan a former educational campus divided between their developers and a mass house-builder. (13–27) The plan necessitated a scrupulously equal division of the site so as to present equal development opportunities to the two parties. A plan was proposed, which, divided by a central access road running east–west, leads in turn to two crescents facing each other and bookended by two blocks of flats running north-south. Around this semi-urban central layout are four areas of detached houses. Each developer received one of each type of flats and townhouses and two quadrants of housing. At the entrance to the site was proposed an as yet unbuilt octagonal space formed by two-storey terraced houses.
The project is necessarily schizophrenic with one side of the site an up-market but otherwise essentially standard suburban layout whilst on the other side of the line the practice was able to develop a range of house types that combined into courtyards. Five house types in all were developed.

None have front gardens and consequently all have unusually large walled rear gardens addressed by all the principle rooms. Two L-shaped house types form the corners of courtyards, one type act in pairs as gatehouses to larger models. Two create their own walled hard paving front court. All five types display a standard semi-circular stair protruding from the house and placed adjacent to the front door. This both marks each house and its entrance and also unifies the whole design across the site. The town houses use a split section which achieves a one and a half height living area on the first floor. (19) Their plots are entirely developed with a kitchen dining area extending out to a terrace over a double garage accessed from shared lanes to the rear. The master bedroom at the top is expressed with its own roof.

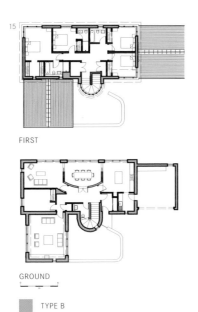

15

FIRST

GROUND

■ TYPE B

16

FIRST

GROUND

■ TYPE A

17

FIRST

GROUND

■ TYPE C

18

The flats (not complete at publication) are arranged in a double cruciform with cores at the centres, creating two major and four minor walled gardens. (26–27) Four of the eight wings are developed as maisonettes at their upper level with roof terraces allowing the bulk of the building to step back at the front. Four flats form two quasi collegiate-like entrance lodges with the upper flats having external staircase access and a roof extended across the gated entrance, where all the entry bells are found.

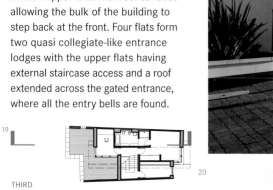

THIRD

SECOND

FIRST

GROUND

▢ TOWN HOUSES

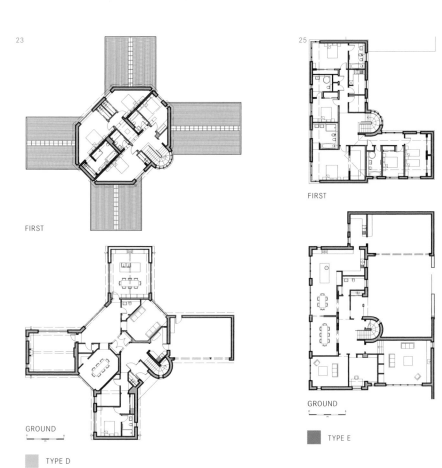

23

FIRST

GROUND

TYPE D

25

FIRST

GROUND

TYPE E

26

SECOND (LHS)

THIRD (RHS)

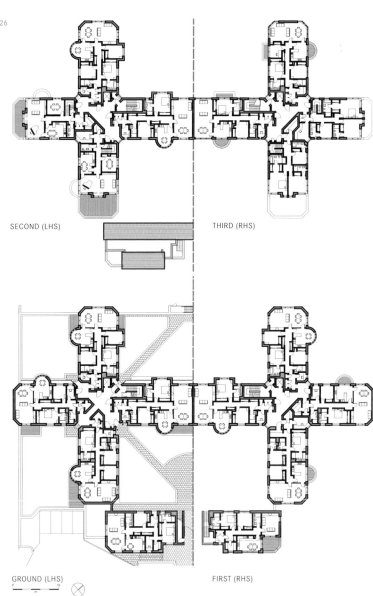

GROUND (LHS)

FIRST (RHS)

FLATTED ACCOMMODATION

24

27

NEWHALL, HARLOW
Essex; completed 2008

FLATTED ACCOMMODATION

TYPE A

TYPE B

TYPE C

TYPE D

28

29

31

For UK suburban planning the Cramond housing was radical even if the language of the architecture itself was more conservative than might have been intended. The house types grew in size (and expense) during the design process, but in a second opportunity for suburban experimentation at Newhall, Harlow in Essex, the house types suggested were more modestly sized. (28–43) Newhall has been developed progressively by the remarkable Moen brothers, and has been a hot-bed of architectural experimentation. The project obliged architects to build within a pre-existing master plan by Roger Evans Associates (now named Studio Real). This envisaged a network of small pedestrian-friendly roads, but resulted in relatively shallow plots so that the courtyard housing model, similar to the Cramond or Aldington models, could not be attempted. Immediately adjacent and preceding the practice's project is a design on which can be counted no less than 12 external materials, including the world's first mono-pitch thatch roof! To counter

such an extraordinary melange, the practice opted to deliberately restrict materials to a palette of slate, brick and stained shiplap boarding, as found in the Essex countryside.

Like Cramond, there was a very high parking requirement (250 per cent) and again townhouses, detached houses and flats were required. The houses use the idea first developed in the RIAS competition of forming long houses perpendicular to the road with a blank elevation bounding a neighbour's garden. Here, however, they are two-storey but dominated by mono-pitch roofs allowing clerestory light into bedrooms and directing the view from the main bedrooms down into the gardens. The terraces of town houses have a simple split section (very similar to the project in Westport in Ireland—see pages 98–101) and their parking needs are accommodated by mews lanes to the rear. A double garage can be accessed from a main house's rear garden, an idea lifted directly from the Edinburgh New Town mews (see page 30). In order to ensure that these garage lanes are inhabited, flats were invented to sit above the garages, accessed by external stairs and with small roof terraces. In this way the large amount of parking effectively disappears and although density over the whole site is very high, all the houses have comparatively larger private gardens than their equivalents elsewhere. A small block of flats and a shop at a road intersection gave another opportunity for external access staircases. (39, 41, 42) The top flats continuing the mono-pitch theme form upside down maisonettes and are particularly spectacular spaces.

34
SECOND
FIRST
GROUND
TYPE A

35
FIRST
GROUND
TYPE B

36
FIRST
GROUND
TYPE C

37
FIRST
GROUND
TYPE D

38

40

39

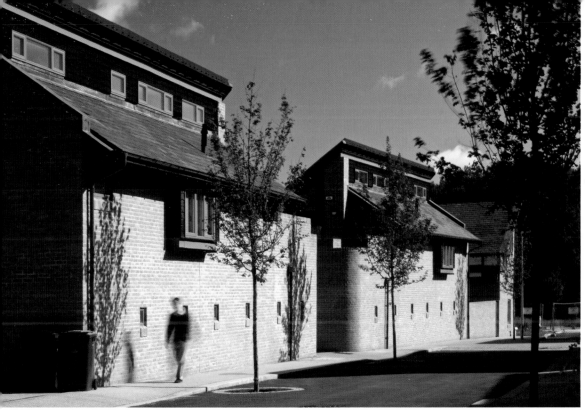

SECOND

THIRD

GROUND

FIRST

FLATTED ACCOMMODATION

DIRLETON

East Lothian; unbuilt

Other similar projects developing the idea of courtyard housing were unsuccessfully developed at Haddington, Balerno and at Dirleton. (45–49) This last example is telling as the developer using the same brief opted instead for the "traditional" approach which has been reproduced here. (44, 46) East Lothian is a fiercely protected and conservative county dominated by stone and pantile roofed architecture, and Dirleton Village itself is a conservation area. The site sits close to the centre of the village. The proposed design showed variations on a T-shaped plan with all the main social spaces looking either southwest or southeast and facing onto enclosed gardens. Two groups of four houses detached but linked with garden walls would have formed courtyards. The house types were identical in size to those constructed and yet private usable garden would have been on average 24 per cent greater than the built alternative. And, unlike the built examples, almost all major rooms open onto these large private gardens and none have northerly aspects. Like Harlow the designs were dominated by their roofs, which would have been pan-tiled so that from across the landscape they would have been the dominant element. It is a continual puzzle as to why UK mass house builders remain so extraordinarily conservative when clearly there are better models on offer for the same price.

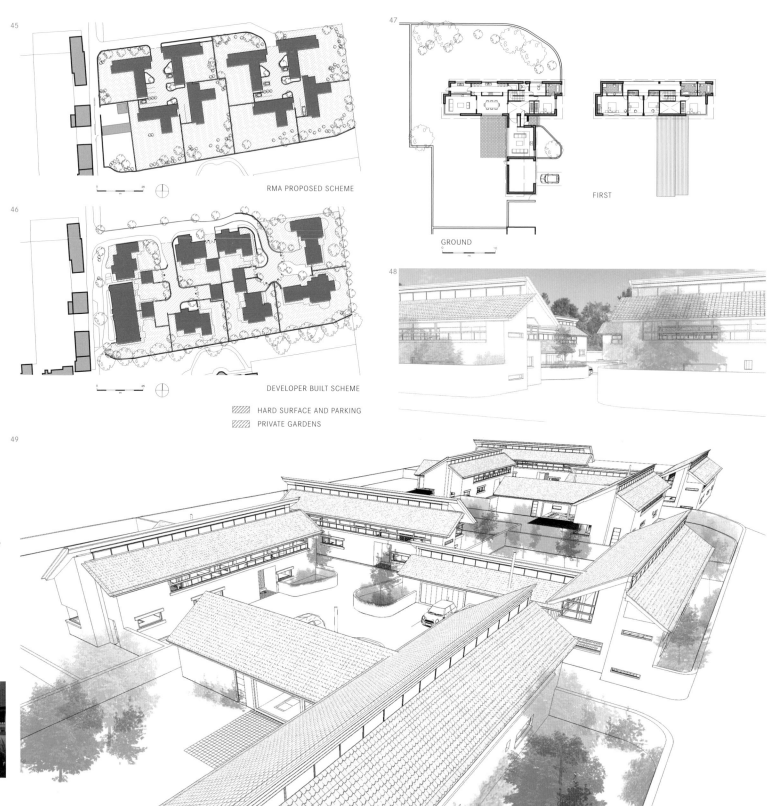

RMA PROPOSED SCHEME

DEVELOPER BUILT SCHEME

//// HARD SURFACE AND PARKING
//// PRIVATE GARDENS

FIRST

GROUND

FAIRMILEHEAD
Edinburgh; unbuilt

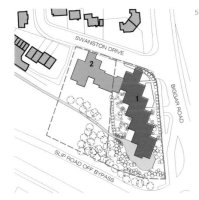

1 PHASE 1
2 PHASE 2

Two further city edge developments were designed to quite an advanced stage but both were abandoned. Both were flatted and both had a communal garden as a major focus of the design. The site at Fairmilehead is at the beginning of the outer edge of Edinburgh on its southern approach, adjacent to the city bypass. (50–53) Busy roads are on two boundaries but with a view of the nearby Pentland Hills. The project was to be developed in two phases; the first being 23 flats on the site of a former pub, the second, if the land could have been purchased, to expand the design by ten flats and houses to make an extensive garden across both sites for the residents. The site falls towards the south where there is a small burn. The project envisaged a deep plan formed of Z-shaped individual flat plans made of two parallel wings; bedrooms in one and living/kitchen in the other. Adjacent flats stepped down by a half level each, following the site topography. All the living areas focussed on the hills with terraces to the west. "Thick walls" of accommodation would have run parallel to the block mostly containing storage, the geometry being expressed in

the barrel vault of the topmost flats' roofs. The burn was to have been dammed so that the building concluded by sitting in a small lake. The second phase continued the idea of parallel barrel vaulted blocks but mostly reduced their height to form into houses and create a south-facing communal garden defined by a crescent of housing and houses. Although planning permission was achieved, the developer never completed on the purchase of the site.

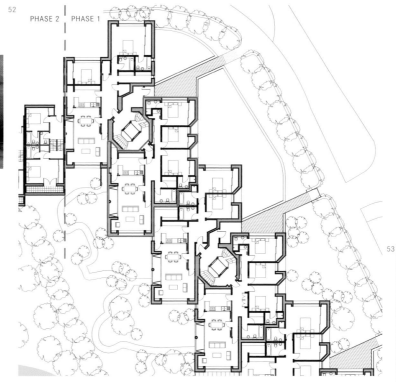

GROUND

FERRY ROAD

Edinburgh; unbuilt

6

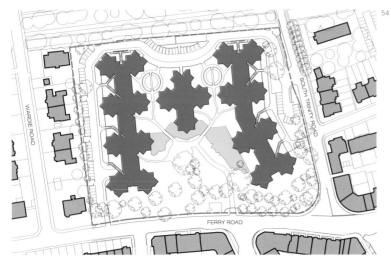

54

GROUND   FOURTH

At Ferry Road, on the opposite side of the city, was a site on the corner of two major roads and contained a strange three-storey office building which had been constructed in the 1970s. (54–56) It had occupied two very large domestic gardens full of mature trees and had been something of a cynical exercise maximising office space whilst avoiding trees which had tree preservation orders, rather than any positive attempt to make a garden or landscape. The design for 256 flats was on paper, a dense development of 20 flats per hectare. It created a U-shaped plan which formed a south-facing private shared garden containing many of the mature trees on the site. The landscape was divided into an upper formal lawn (which marked the roof of semi-buried parking) and a wilder woodland landscape beyond. In between, a lake with access bridges was proposed with the car-park wall exposed as a lake quayside. A perimeter road would have provided access to all addresses. The flat planning was developed using a 45-degree geometry. This provided many opportunities for corner window

living rooms (often in the branches of trees like tree-houses) and 70 per cent of the flats would have had a view of the communal garden. At the top, the geometry was developed into lantern-like rooms reminiscent of the Sea Captains' towers of the nearby Victorian suburb of Trinity. Construction started but was halted in the economic crisis in 2008. The site was sold to another developer who has commissioned an alternative design.

55

1

Reinhabitation

NEW HOMES IN OLD BUILDINGS

ANCOATS
Manchester; as yet unbuilt

The reuse of building stock for new functions from their original purpose is today an everyday phenomenon. Indeed, in Edinburgh the case might be made that perhaps it has become too prevalent. In this book, the Fruitmarket Gallery, Eastgate Theatre, Dundee Contemporary Arts, John Muir Visitor Centre, Poltimore House are all examples of radical transformations of warehouses, a church, a country house, etc., into arts venues. This chapter, however, looks at the more repetitive agenda of placing apartments and hotel rooms within existing multi-windowed structures. A Victorian warehouse complex in Manchester, the disused Royal Infirmary in Edinburgh and the former Donaldson's Deaf School, also in Edinburgh, are the host buildings.

'Loft living', invented in Manhattan, rapidly became chic, but it usually relied for its effect on generous spaces (the original disused New York warehouses had been relatively cheap to purchase) and the preservation of much of the warehouse 'as found' interior. (1) Translated to this side of the Atlantic, flats' plans became much smaller.

In the few Edinburgh examples (mostly in Leith) circulation is often condemned to be depressing internal wandering corridors and there is often no evidence internally that residents are actually in a converted warehouse at all.

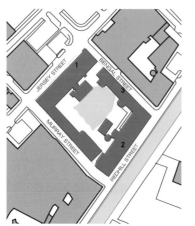

1 NEW MILL
2 OLD MILL
3 HOTEL

At Ancoats, an inner city area of Manchester undergoing re-inhabitation, an ambitious project envisaged the redevelopment of an entire historic mill complex, Murrays' Mills, which itself formed a complete urban block. (2–6) Built between 1798 and 1806 (by Scots!) the building represented the oldest surviving cotton mills in the city. Three sides survive, a fourth having disappeared in a fire. The two main mills, the Old Mill and the New Mill, sat opposite each other. The scheme proposed a mixed-use for the site consisting of 112 apartments and 1,700 square metres of office space within the mill buildings and engine houses; a textile resource centre/fashion centre of excellence within the Murray Street building; and, a 60 bedroom new build 'boutique' hotel on the vacant eastern side of the quad. The proposal would also reinstate the canal basin at the centre of the courtyard, which had originally been connected to the adjacent Rochdale Canal by underground tunnel.

The architectural vision for the re-inhabitation was to create an enclosed central space and to make new architecture which clearly would differentiate between the restored historic buildings and new insertions. Externally, the new elements were to consist of corten steel staircase/lift towers to the old mill and the old mill engine house (echoing the form of the existing staircase); new external staircases to the first floor flats in the new mill; and a glazed lift to one side of the old mill's existing brick staircase.

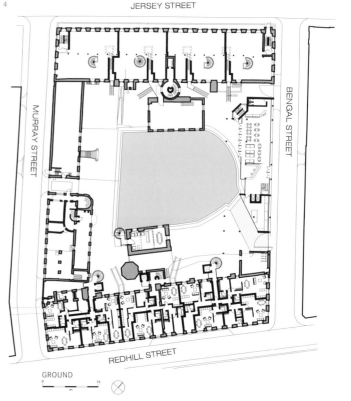

GROUND

FORMER ROYAL INFIRMARY
Edinburgh; unbuilt

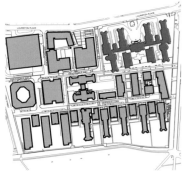

In Edinburgh, two highly visible and important buildings have been subject to two conversion projects, each for apartments and five star hotels.

The former Edinburgh Royal Infirmary is a large city centre site master planned by Foster Associates. (See also social housing Q10 on the same master plan, page 103.) (7–12) They invited the practice to be responsible for the conversion of the only grade A listed building on the site—the original David Bryce 1870 Infirmary itself, incorporating fragments of the previous William Adam building. The six wings of wards were to be converted to bedrooms necessitating elevations, plan and section collaborating, but although there was a convenient rhythm of windows, the plan of the former wards was too narrow to make the usual critically efficient double-loaded corridor and the section was in this instance too high to make sensibly proportioned rooms, but not high enough to insert a new hotel floor. To the rear, all the non-residential accommodation was created, and a new building separated from the old by a line of roof-lights. The Bryce grand entrance led directly to a contemporary foyer. (10)

The fall in the site allowed the creation of two lower floors

1 ENTRANCE
2 FOYER
3 KITCHEN
4 PRIVATE DINING
5 BALLROOM
6 RETAIL
7 RESTAURANT

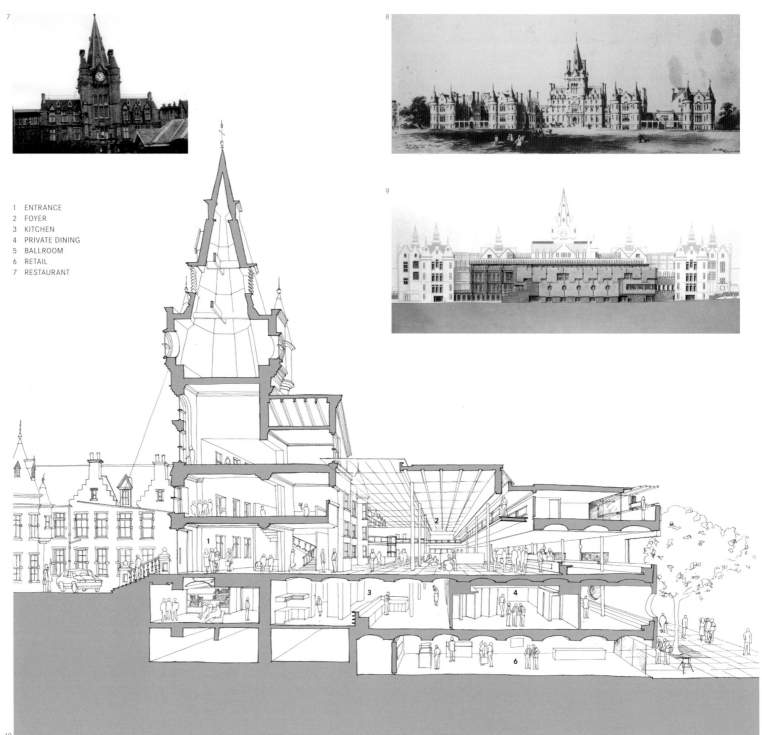

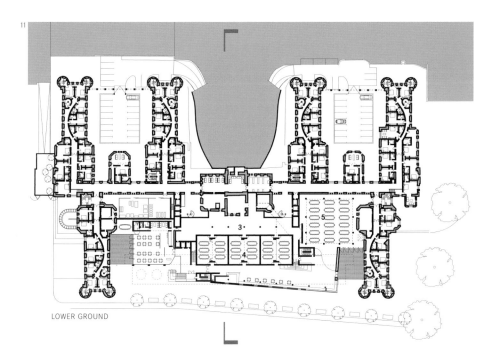

LOWER GROUND

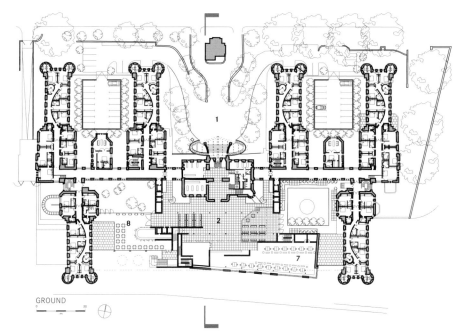

GROUND

including a top-lit function suite, private dining, gym, etc., and the all important location of the kitchen. For a five star hotel, this is the most critical room in the facility with the most strategic location.

Eventually it was concluded that the hotel was not financially feasible and various residential options have been designed including this option, which divides the ward down their length to make pairs of 'long flats'. (12)

DONALDSON'S, AS HOUSING
Edinburgh; unbuilt

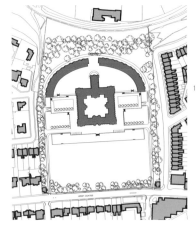

GROUND

FIRST

An almost identical situation was presented with Donaldson's School, but this time the first suggested conversion was for apartments, also with new apartments to the rear and only much later was a five star hotel conversion contemplated. (14–26) Donaldson's School for the deaf is one of the most famous and distinctive buildings in Edinburgh and was designed by Edinburgh's foremost nineteenth century architect, William Playfair in the 1840s. Playfair was quite open that the design was derived entirely from the Elizabethan manor house Burghley House in Northamptonshire, although cost savings reduced it to two storeys (*plus ca change*). (13) The school decided to relocate in 2003 and the successful bidders for the site at this point employed the practice.

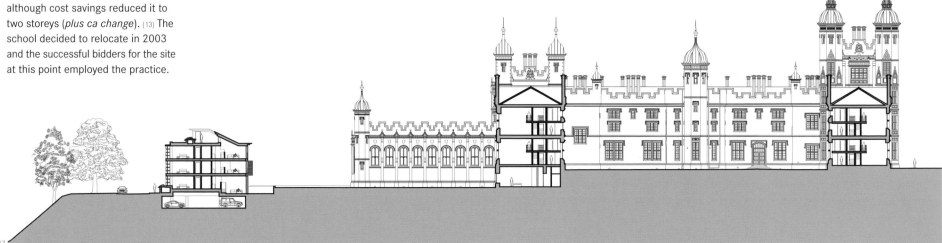

17

The project proposed converting the existing building into approximately 70 flats with the construction of a further 70 on land to the north hidden from view of what is considered to be the important vista of the building. Whilst the exterior of the building and indeed the elevation of the central courtyard is a wonderful Elizabethan fantasy, the interiors of the building are very utilitarian.

On the ground and first floors the classrooms and dormitories of the former school are sufficiently high to allow subdivision vertically into maisonettes. (23) Living room floor levels were raised to allow for views out of the classroom windows (the cill height of Victorian school room windows was always set at a height to prevent children looking out) so that the apartments became interestingly multi-levelled. (14, 21–26) Generally, these are organised in such a way that the new construction is clearly delineated from the original interiors. The proposed flats to the rear were already sunken using the topography of the site so that they would be virtually invisible from the south. (19) However, they form a grand crescent broken in the centre to allow views of the chapel from the north. This grand crescent was united by the device of a moving louvred facade so that the simplicity of the facade would contrast with the complex nature of the Playfair original. The flats themselves are on three storeys with the top storey having access to private roof terraces which give extensive views not only of the Donaldson's magical turreted roofscape, but also out towards the north over the trees and towards the sea.

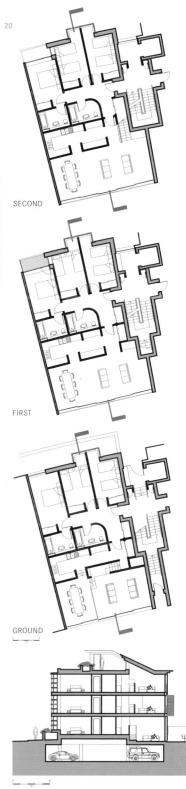

SECOND

FIRST

GROUND

DONALDSON'S, AS HOTEL

Edinburgh; as yet unbuilt

The residential project collapsed with the 2008 property crash but hotel use at the time of writing is still an economic possibility. (28–32) Like the Royal Infirmary, however, the existing building makes for a difficult conversion into rooms; as few as 45 grand bedrooms and suites. The solution is to create a new plinth of formal gardens containing sunken courtyards able to light new rooms beneath. Ted Cullinan's brilliant office-cum-garden for Ready-mix Concrete Headquarters was the inspiration for this idea. (27) In this way, both the historic building resumes a pre-picturesque setting that would have been appropriate to the original inspiration, Burghley House, but also the presence of the new rooms is hidden behind a plinth wall. Two front and rear lakes are to be created to give the building a more spectacular setting. The courtyard is to be roofed over to create an enormous foyer but with glazing organised so that the historic roof silhouette can be seen from within. The project offers the exciting possibility of a 'county house hotel' in the city centre. (31)

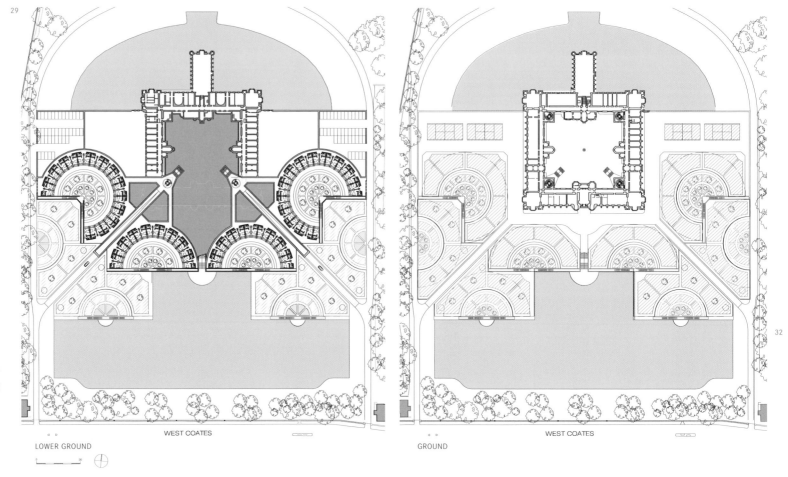

WEST COATES

LOWER GROUND

WEST COATES

GROUND

Queen's University, Belfast

Housing Students

KITCHENS, STAIRCASES, TERRACES

The most traditional way of accommodating students was the monastic Oxbridge model of individual rooms accessed directly off a staircase with staircases themselves distributed around courts or quads. (2–3) Generally, dons and students were interspersed and all took their meals in the College dining hall. That model was exported to America, although Thomas Jefferson developed an alternative at the University of Virginia Lawn. (4) There, students are housed in rooms directly accessed from a colonnaded court ("the lawn") which is occasionally interrupted by professors' pavilions. Significantly, only three sides of the building define the campus. Jefferson left the fourth open facing the 'frontier' of the west where the young republic was expected to spread. In the late nineteenth century, with the construction of Keeble College Oxford, the "hotel" model of rooms off a double-loaded corridor began but it is only fairly recently that the concept of a "student flat" with a degree of communal living and self-catering has been promoted.

Sir Richard MacCormac's pioneering work in various Cambridge and Oxford Colleges came at a time when the traditional Oxbridge stair model was being challenged. Observing that kitchenettes on staircases were the most sociable places, he developed over a number of projects the basic theme of rooms clustering around kitchens often with ingenious non-repetitive staircase journeys from floor to floor or kitchen to kitchen. While in his office, Richard Murphy worked on one in particular, New Court at Fitzwilliam College, Cambridge. (1)

JESUS COLLEGE
Cambridge; unbuilt

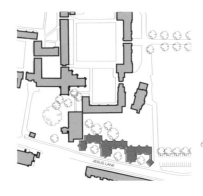

The idea of engendering sociability has been at the heart of proposals for five separate university student housing projects. The kitchen as a social heart, both within a flat and between flats, has been a common theme. In a limited competition for 120 undergraduate rooms at Jesus College, Cambridge (which the practice missed winning on the casting vote of the Master) the proposal was to build another version of the pattern of the College's three-sided courts, looking out to landscape which had grown centripetally over 500 years (see page 190 for a brief explanation of the historic development of the college). (5–13) The stairs were arranged around three miniature three-sided courts with six students sharing a dog leg stair with the kitchen at a half-level. The lowest room sat half a level above the court with the kitchen projecting out as a three-sided elevated pavilion above the entrance to each stair. The section was organised so that the circulation within the stair was observed from the kitchen; all the comings and goings of the six students could have been observed from their social meeting place. (13) The distinctive 45-degree chimneys of the original buildings

were reinterpreted as bathrooms, an idea visited a second time in the, this time successful, competition for the College (see pages 198–203). (5)

FIRST

JESUS LANE

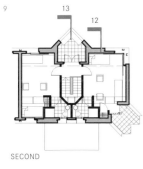

SECOND

FIRST

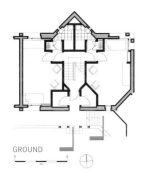

GROUND

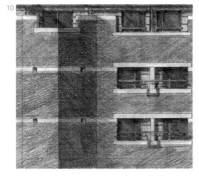

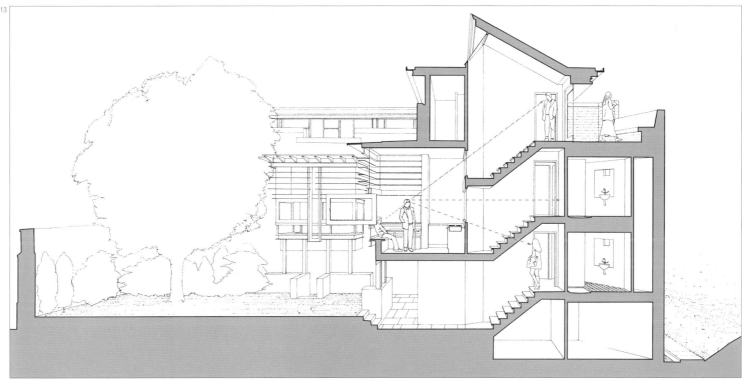

UNIVERSITY OF WARWICK
unbuilt

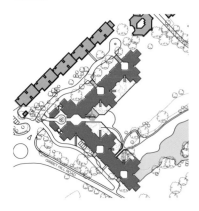

By contrast the campus plan at Warwick University is the complete opposite. (14–19) Where Cambridge is defined by spaces made by buildings, Warwick is made up of isolated buildings surrounded by space, albeit generously landscaped. (14–15)

CAMBRIDGE 1:20 000

WARWICK 1:20 000

Sadly, as elsewhere, existing student accommodation has adopted the corridor hotel model with the unfortunate effect of diluting any sense of sociability or individuality of the flats; one flat opens to another with effectively 24 rooms and three kitchens stretching along a seemingly endless central corridor. The competition brief sought 62 flats of eight students each. All flats needed to have lift access, so a degree of plan repetition was inevitable. To avoid the need for lengthy corridors, the proposition was to make clusters of three flats per floor around a small open court with deck and open spiral staircase access. (17) Four floors of rooms would make a social grouping of 24 students per floor or 96 students per court. Over the entrance to the court it was proposed to place a warden's maisonette. The three kitchens per floor were placed adjacent to the entrance to their flats and within sight of each other and also those at other levels, again to encourage sociability. (18) Using two wardens' houses, the corner was elaborated into an enclosed vehicle drop off court and an outer garden court for the particular use of conferences. Four and two half courts were proposed to form an L-shaped block, which implied a public front and private lawned back (unusual at Warwick where all space is equal). The disposition around the edge of the site would have preserved the majority of the open green space. The block was extended slightly off the designated site boundary so that a sequence of protected linked ponds could themselves have been extended to meet the building. The project was placed second in the competition and a project which proposed more of the same isolated object buildings was selected.

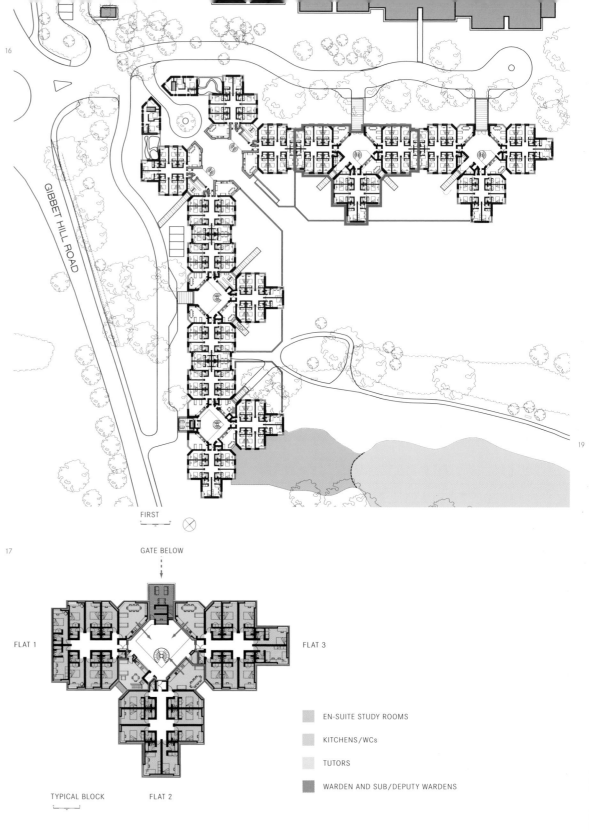

GATE BELOW

FLAT 1

FLAT 3

FLAT 2

FIRST

GIBBET HILL ROAD

TYPICAL BLOCK

EN-SUITE STUDY ROOMS

KITCHENS/WCs

TUTORS

WARDEN AND SUB/DEPUTY WARDENS

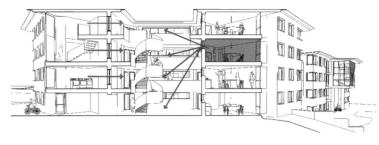
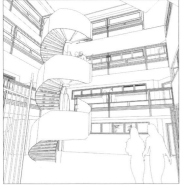

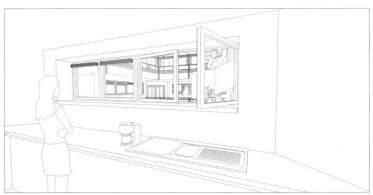

QUEEN'S UNIVERSITY

Belfast; completed 2012 and designed in collaboration with RPP Architects

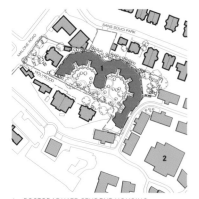

1 POSTGRADUATE STUDENT HOUSING
2 EXISTING UNDERGRADUATE VILLAGE

By coincidence, Queen's University, Belfast (QUB) and the University of Edinburgh have both commissioned projects for 260 bed spaces for postgraduate students. (20–25) But there the similarities ended. QUB requested a variety of flat types from studios to four-person units; at Edinburgh generally six-person flats were required. In Belfast, the site is a 0.85 hectare semi-derelict garden with mature trees; in Edinburgh the site is a 0.19 hectare empty urban corner, bounded by roads on three sides and located on the edge of the Old Town. The Belfast design has two objectives—first, to give the postgraduates a sense of exclusivity; and secondly, to engender sociability within the postgraduate community. Many postgraduate students come from foreign cultures and might stay for as little as a year; encouraging them to meet other students is a key concern. The design encloses three sides of garden, the fourth side to the south is enclosed by a bank of mature trees and a residential side street. An octagonal pavilion in the centre of the garden divides the space into two. A single pend entrance from the undergraduate estate creates the exclusive entrance and beside

this was placed the common room as gatehouse. There is no internal circulation. Instead, all flats have external front doors and at upper level are accessed by open stairs. The section is key to the layout. The lower two levels are deep plan (as fire escape can be directly through bedroom windows). At the upper two levels rooms must be entered from a protected lobby so this was minimised by entering all flats in the centre of the plan, placing living rooms/kitchens to the front with most bedrooms to the, quieter, rear. (23) In this way the flats are clustered around assemblages of stairs and terraces which quarry into the depth of the block and a very wide variety of flat plans results.

FOUR BED FLAT

THREE BED FLAT

TWO BED FLAT

BEDSIT (ONE BED)

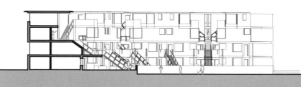

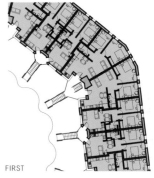

THIRD

SECOND

FIRST

GROUND

UNIVERSITY OF EDINBURGH

projected completion 2013

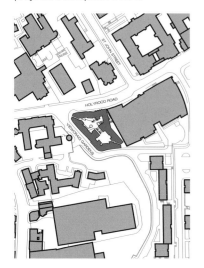

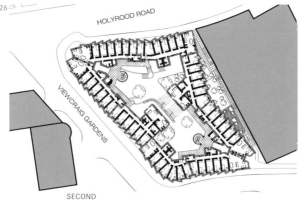

SECOND

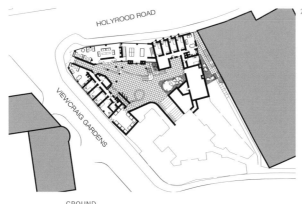

GROUND

The University of Edinburgh's brief was much simpler than that at QUB and needed to conform to height and massing restrictions already laid down by a master plan. (26–29) A perimeter design was proposed which, like Belfast, places all the bedrooms on the exterior facades. Access to the flats is gained exclusively from within a central courtyard. The most prominent urban corner was chosen for the main entrance and like Belfast a common room is placed beside it to act as a social meeting place as well as giving active frontage to Holyrood Road, the principal street. (29) A secondary entrance is placed at the opposite corner, defining an upper and lower court. Once again, a driving motivation of the design is to avoid internal corridors so that the flat plans are largely single sided with internal circulation day-lit from within the court. External circulation is by access decks reached via lifts and two spiral stairs suspended above the entrances. Living rooms to the 45 flats occupy either the corners of the wings or are placed as towers within the courtyard. (28) The

scheme was designed to encourage social interaction within the central court whilst giving every student a private room on the outer edge.

KING'S CROSS
London; unbuilt

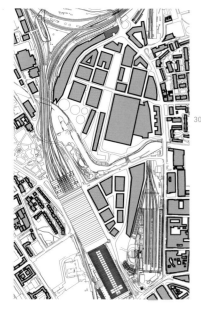

The final project is an unsuccessful entry to an invited limited competition run by Argent Developers as part of their gigantic King's Cross development in London. (30–32) Sitting at the end of row of proposed residential buildings, all approximately 12 storeys high, there was a desire to create a tower to conclude the street. The restricted site backed onto the High Speed Channel rail link. Communal facilities were required at the lowest two levels. The design developed as two buildings, an eight-storey block concluding to the street and a semi-isolated tower which would have curved around the urban corner. Between these two, where lifts were located, were proposed three-storey winter gardens stacked on top of each other with the idea loosely based on the Warwick competition, that this could have made a 'sub unit' of six kitchens, each looking onto the south-facing glazed space which contained local distribution stairs between the three floors. (32)

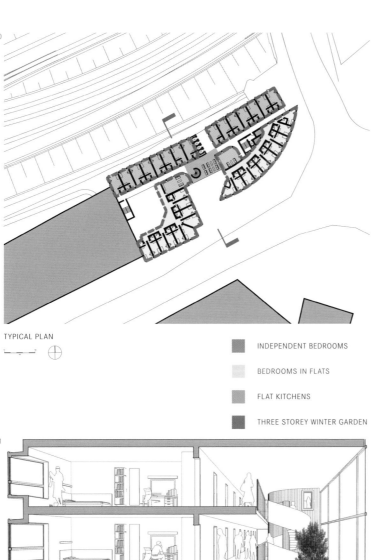

TYPICAL PLAN

█ INDEPENDENT BEDROOMS

░ BEDROOMS IN FLATS

▒ FLAT KITCHENS

█ THREE STOREY WINTER GARDEN

Conan Doyle Medical Centre, Edinburgh

Building for Health

CRUSADING AGAINST THE CORRIDOR

What makes an institution? Quite quickly, the image of an artificially lit double-loaded corridor comes to mind. In buildings for health, be it doctors' surgeries, old people's homes or small or large hospitals, it seems to be the ubiquitous organising device, usually festooned with way-finding signs and sometimes even coloured lines to follow on the floor. (1)

For patients, their relatives and visitors, disorientation leading to anxiety is a frequent phenomenon. Indeed, in larger hospitals these spaces can be expanded to also include permanent work spaces for hospital staff who must labour all day in artificial light and with no connection to the outside world.

No matter how small or large, two issues remain critical: orientation and hierarchy. Wherever possible, all the designs here show circulation placed along an outside wall so that it is day-lit and the exterior, a garden or courtyard becomes a natural orientating device.

In addition, there is an aim to merge purely circulation space with some other informal activity, chiefly waiting areas or simply seats in lay-by spaces so that it can become the place for informal meetings.

On entry to any health building, a patient or relative has to navigate their way usually to one final destination; in the Maggie's Centre there were

only six, whereas in the design for St Andrew's Hospital there were potentially a bewildering 67 final possible destinations! These need to be broken down into recognisable hierarchies ("bunches of spaces" as Aldo Van Eyk called them), and each building takes this issue as a major preoccupation. A number of buildings and projects develop this theme starting with the smallest Maggie's, increasing in size and complexity. (2)

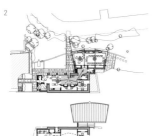

1   MAGGIE'S CENTRE

2   CONAN DOYLE MEDICAL CENTRE

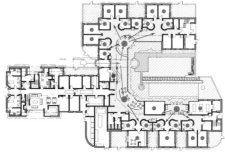

3   OLD SEE HOUSE

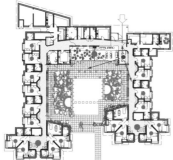

4   STRATHEDEN ELMVIEW

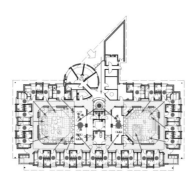

5   STRATHEDEN MUIRVIEW

   ENTRY

   WAITING AREA

   DESTINATION—CONSULTATION/
TREATMENT ROOM

   STAFF SUPERVISION POINTS

→   TRAVEL TO RECEPTION

→   SIGHT LINES

   CIRCULATION

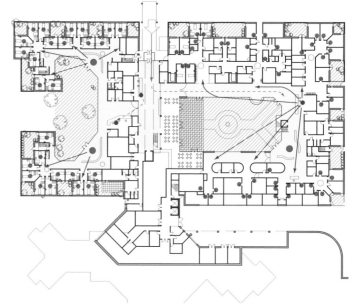

6   ST ANDREWS COMMUNITY HOSPITAL AND HEALTH CENTRE

MAGGIE'S CENTRE

Edinburgh; completed 1996 and extension 2001

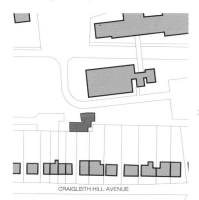

CRAIGLEITH HILL AVENUE

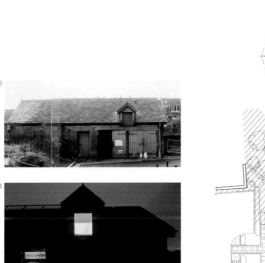

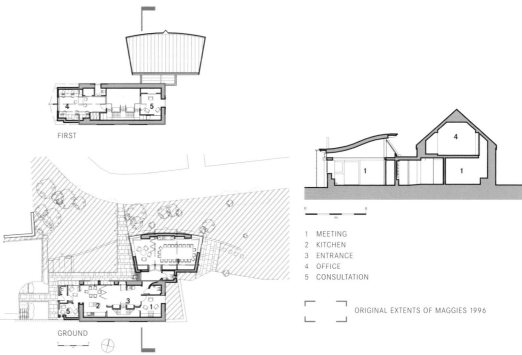

FIRST

GROUND

1 MEETING
2 KITCHEN
3 ENTRANCE
4 OFFICE
5 CONSULTATION

ORIGINAL EXTENTS OF MAGGIES 1996

The first Maggie's Centre was tiny and is housed in a disused stable building at the Western General Hospital in Edinburgh. (3–14) Born of the experience that Maggie Keswick Jencks had on diagnosis with cancer within the NHS, her vision was a place and an organisation that offered individual advice and solace, group therapies and access to information. Above all it was to have the intangible quality of a refuge, a home from home, a place set apart from the clinical processing of the nearby hospital, a meeting place, maybe a return to the idea of medical care with a human face. Although she never lived to see the first building complete, a new one has opened on average every two years and a galaxy of international architectural celebrities have been commissioned by her widower, the architectural critic, Charles Jencks.

The design for the first Maggie's Centre was conceived as a little house with the recognisable elements of kitchen and living space immediately obvious on entry. Completed in 1996, an extension in 2001 doubled the size and extended simultaneously in two directions in order to keep the main double-height space the centre of the larger building.

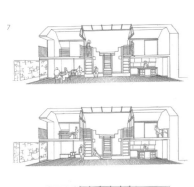

As well as aiming to create an atmosphere of domesticity as much accommodation as possible was needed to be created within the very limited volume available and this to be transformable in its spatial division; the centre is capable of being combined into a series of progressively larger spaces or divided into individual rooms. (7) There are no 'doors', rather rooms are closed using sliding screens or sliding-folding partitions so that when not in use the room is left open to view. (8, 10)

The main move of creating a double-height central space was considered extravagant by some, but it was essential to ensure that all four spaces could be seen immediately on entry. The issue came far more to the fore when the building was doubled in size. To ensure no circulation was introduced, it extends in opposite directions so preserves a domestic scale and the double-height space as the centre of the larger building. All activities in the new area are visible from the original centre space, which still functions as the front door to the centre. Externally, the construction is viewed as a building within a building with a new inner language of steel, lead, glass blocks and timber sliding behind stone, very much in the manner of completed projects at the Fruitmarket Gallery or Colburn Mews Houses. When the extension was commissioned, this existing inner language was extrapolated in both directions to continue the language; consequently the joins between the phases are impossible to identify.

The extension to the west is two-storey with administration on the top floor and an additional consulting room on the lower floor. The extension to the northeast is conceived as an independent but linked building to the original. This is a single volume which can be divided unequally and extends with a rendered retaining wall along its northern boundary to form a terrace on the eastern side and a boundary to the garden on the western side. Again, materials are the same as the other extension with a lead roof, steel framing and douglas fir framed windows. The mono-pitch roof is designed to admit south light into north-facing rooms whilst its sinusoidal form deliberately avoids any conversation with the roof pitch of the existing building. At the practice's instigation the hospital closed a road and in its place the Friends of Maggie's have created a wonderful garden.

CONAN DOYLE MEDICAL CENTRE

Edinburgh; completed 2007

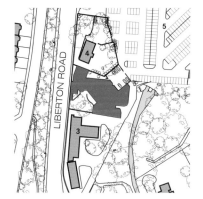

The Conan Doyle Medical Centre project at Nether Liberton, Edinburgh, originally began as a design for two doctors' practices (a larger and a smaller practice) who wished to keep their identities and yet share certain non-public facilities. (15) The design in a semi-wooded site and adjacent to a local river, the Braidburn, is also adjacent to Cameron Toll Shopping Centre and includes the site of Liberton Bank House, a derelict cottage which had become famous as the place where Conan Doyle spent his summer holidays, hence the title for the Centre. Its proposed demolition had already been the subject of a notorious planning battle. The original design placed clinical activities on the ground floor, with combined non-clinical offices, common room, etc., above. (15) The two doctors continued to maintain separate front doors at ground floor and other than a shared education room, kept separate identities. Each waiting area looked out onto a shared walled garden centred on a mature chestnut tree. All surgeries looked onto small pebbled gardens planted with bamboo. An existing scout hut on the site was to have been demolished and rebuilt as part of the master plan and the whole complex,

including the refurbished cottage, now a school, was to have been wrapped in a mostly impenetrable brick wall to suggest the idea of a walled garden, in particular the ambiguity between what is building and what is garden that that device creates.

The cottage next door was converted simultaneously by Nicholas Groves-Raines Architects for the Cockburn Conservation Trust, acting on behalf of Dunedin Special School.

Eventually, the project proceeded on the basis of the one larger practice on half the site with the scout hut remaining on the other half, the hope being that another doctors' surgery might one day occupy the remaining site. (16–24) The plan continued to revolve around an inner "secret garden".

ORIGINAL DESIGN

1 SMALLER GP PRACTICE
2 LARGER GP PRACTICE
3 SCOUT HQ
4 SCHOOL
5 SHOPPING CENTRE CAR PARK
6 DOCTORS CAR PARK

FIRST

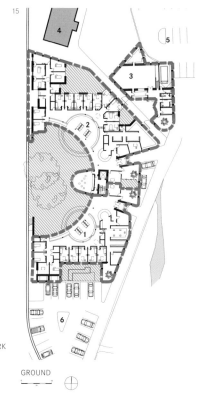

GROUND

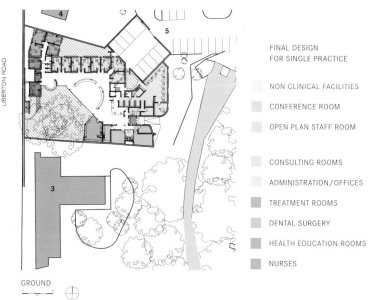

GROUND

FINAL DESIGN
FOR SINGLE PRACTICE

NON-CLINICAL FACILITIES

CONFERENCE ROOM

OPEN PLAN STAFF ROOM

CONSULTING ROOMS

ADMINISTRATION/OFFICES

TREATMENT ROOMS

DENTAL SURGERY

HEALTH EDUCATION ROOMS

NURSES

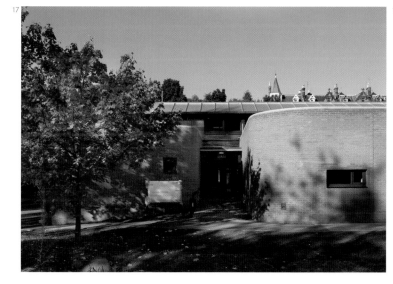

In contrast to the six destinations at the Maggie Centre, this doubled at the Conan Doyle: eight doctors, two dentists and two nurses. Here the main surgeries form an L-shape which holds a semi-circular waiting area looking away from the surgeries towards the walled garden. There is no waiting 'room', but rather circulation is held apart from the waiting area by a half-height wall allowing doctors to summon patients but at the same time to provide some privacy for patients exiting. The reception desk welcomes and supervises the whole space. (21–22) The dentists have their own defined territory and similarly do the nurses who are given their own smaller waiting space. On the first floor are non-clinical facilities which themselves are organised on an L-shape around a staff social area with a terrace overlooking the garden. A minor operations suite is the only section with a corridor.

21

22

23

24

OLD SEE HOUSE
Belfast; projected completion 2013

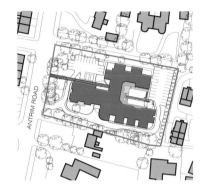

At Old See House, in Belfast, with colleagues RPP Architects, the practice is realising a ground-breaking mental health facility which brings together three functions never before co-located. (25–31) First, is a consulting facility where outpatients have appointments to see psychiatric consultants, in the manner of seeing a GP. Second, is a day centre where patients are encouraged to attend for a whole or half day and to engage in various forms of therapy. Third is an eight bedroom short-stay residential section designed to be an alternative to residence within an acute hospital where patients might go for between one night and two weeks respite. The site is in a mostly residential area and is fortunate in being surrounded by mature trees.

The residential section has its own entrance and presence on the site, akin to a gatehouse. It is designed as much as possible to be an ordinary two-storey house, but with a double-height living area around which all the main spaces gravitate. This came from the experience of designing two houses for six children each at Harmeny School and the issues are similar: engendering a sense of community, ensuring the first floor world of bedrooms is not isolated and making night time supervision of two floors by a single member of staff relatively simple.

And like the Stratheden project (see pages 156–159), each of the bedrooms also becomes a little roofed room.

A service section connects the main building to the residential section but there is deliberately no internal patient access between the two parts of the building.

Like Conan Doyle, the plan focuses on a walled garden; and again like Conan Doyle, consulting facilities form an L-shape of rooms around a waiting area with the day therapy roughly doing the same around a cafe around the opposite corner. Together, they make a U-shape with the entrance in the centre. The total number of destinations is however far greater than Conan Doyle. The consultation suite alone contains 13 psychiatrists' consulting rooms and smaller interview rooms, all needing to look out onto gardens. In the circumstances, it would be easy to resort to the double-loaded corridor, but instead the cellular accommodation has been bent with consulting rooms as 'roofed rooms' on the exterior and interview rooms on the interior on one side of circulation alone. These latter could have easily degenerated into their police station equivalent, so here the furniture of a corner seat is identifiable from the circulation area and the space connected through a clerestory light. (29, 30) Five rooms share a walled, pebbled garden and care is taken with the fenestration to ensure privacy in each room. Office accommodation for outreach staff and administration on the first floor of the main building completes the design.

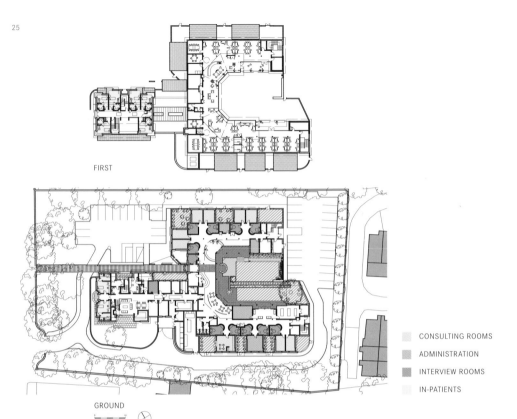

FIRST

GROUND

CONSULTING ROOMS

ADMINISTRATION

INTERVIEW ROOMS

IN-PATIENTS

COMMUNITY HOSPITAL AND HEALTH CENTRE

St Andrews; unbuilt

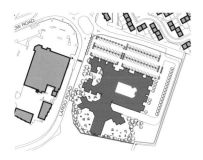

A real test of ideas about circulation and hierarchy came with the unsuccessful competition for a PFI Community Hospital and Health Centre on the edge of St Andrews. (32–35) The hospital comprised a three practice medical centre with a total of 26 consulting rooms and associated accommodation, a minor injuries unit, an x-ray unit, a diagnostic treatment centre, a 40 bed in-patient department and office and administration section. It was a high priority to produce a circulation system that was legible to those entering the building for the first time. The design proposed that most journeys would be day-lit and circulation would almost always be adjacent to a garden. Whilst highly mindful of all the clinical adjacencies that needed to be satisfied, it was felt that the quality of the 'patient journey' was crucial.

There would have been clear hierarchies of space. It was proposed that the internal organisation of the hospital would revolve around a top-lit north–south atrium from which all major departments would be accessed. (35) This would contain the hospital cafe. To the west would have been a two-storey primary care facility organised around its own garden. Reception and waiting areas were derived from the Conan Doyle plan with clustering of consulting rooms, many given pitched roofs, all looking into small walled gardens. (33) This plan came directly from the Old See House design. Administration would be entirely on the first floor. To the east would be a two-storey diagnostic treatment centre, containing all the other outpatient facilities, including day surgery. This could easily be the most bewildering part of the hospital; instead the 'courtyard garden' becomes the key organising element with departments seen around and across it. (34) The different departments, each would have had their own threshold with service rooms in the centre of the plan and clinical rooms adjacent to light and gardens.

To the south the hospital is raised one storey on the natural topography of the site so that inpatient wards would have been placed at ground level which is first floor elsewhere and arranged in a configuration of three wings going out into the landscape. Circulation must be double-loaded here, but would have been top-lit to compensate. This part of the site faces south and is also the quietest boundary condition which would have allowed all the wards to connect directly to south-facing gardens.

A number of roof lanterns were proposed which would have penetrated through first floor level to bring light and ventilation into deep plan spaces. They would also have chimed with the roofscape of St Andrews contributing a new element to the towers and spires of the existing silhouette. The design was judged no more expensive than the others, and without exception the entire staff of the hospital and the three GP practices voted for it, but it was not chosen.

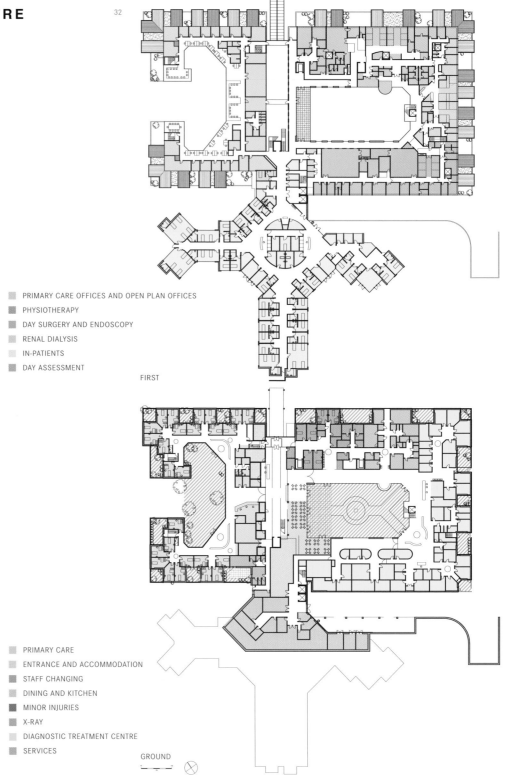

32

35

■ PRIMARY CARE OFFICES AND OPEN PLAN OFFICES
■ PHYSIOTHERAPY
■ DAY SURGERY AND ENDOSCOPY
■ RENAL DIALYSIS
■ IN-PATIENTS
■ DAY ASSESSMENT

FIRST

■ PRIMARY CARE
■ ENTRANCE AND ACCOMMODATION
■ STAFF CHANGING
■ DINING AND KITCHEN
■ MINOR INJURIES
■ X-RAY
■ DIAGNOSTIC TREATMENT CENTRE
■ SERVICES

GROUND

ELMVIEW

Stratheden, Fife; completed 2009

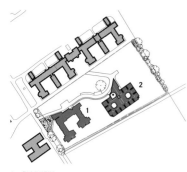

1   ELMVIEW
2   MUIRVIEW

Designing for dementia is fast becoming a health service priority and the practice had the opportunity to design for the relocation of an 18 bed facility from Kirkcaldy to the grounds of the rural mental hospital at Stratheden. The facility is called Elmview. (36–43) This move coincided with the end of multi-bed wards so that three six bed wards were replaced by 18 single rooms each with en-suite.

The existing Kirkcaldy plan was a double-loaded corridor and with the new proliferation of destinations there was pressure to simply extend the concept, particularly for night time supervision. That pressure was resisted and after several developmental consultations an unequal U-shaped plan was agreed. Bedrooms are split into two wings, initially managed as male and female, and the communal facilities and entrance located centrally between them. The whole building focuses on a south-facing semi-secure garden for patients with the southern edge of the garden walled and framing the view south toward hills. (42) The design allows for patients to wander freely around the building and into the garden.

Each bedroom has a bay window elaborated into a window seat with views out into the grounds of Stratheden. (41) Each bedroom is identifiable by individual pitched roofs. For many patients this will be their last home and this was an attempt to give a sense of identity to each room, in the manor of a tiny house. Movement of light stimulates so each room has a secondary source of clerestorey light resulting from the section. (36) The circulation has small alcoves with built-in seating for patients to stop and sit and look out into the garden, so that circulation becomes an active and inhabited space. (43)

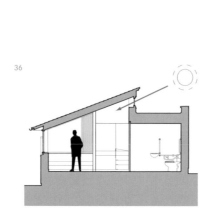

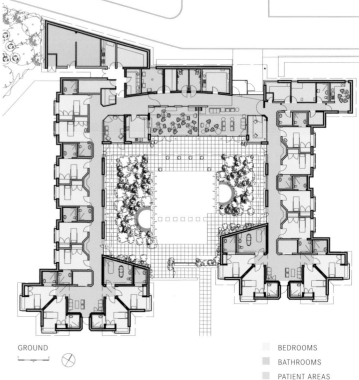

GROUND

                        ◼ BEDROOMS
                        ◼ BATHROOMS
                        ◼ PATIENT AREAS
                        ◼ STAFF/CONSULTING
                        ◼ SERVICES

MUIRVIEW
Stratheden, Fife; completed 2011

The second facility at Stratheden, Muirview, was built alongside the first and adjacent to a single mature elm tree. (44–48) The patient group is different. These are younger patients with either organic or functional mental disabilities. This could range from early dementia through to temporary depression. Accommodation needed to be more secure and initially it was thought the two groups could not be mixed. As the building reached completion that view was relaxed. Two symmetrical closed courtyards were designed with 12 ensuite rooms in each half. The central spine provides services and living/dining spaces on either side. These can be combined so, as patients are now sometimes mixed together, one side has become a large living space and the other a combined dining area. Although the rooms are smaller than Elmview, they maintain the idea of bringing in light from two sources. Circulation also contains lay-by seats which focus on the courtyards. Each of these is alive with the sound of running water from small ponds and their micro-climate is proving to be very successful for patients and plants alike. Quiet rooms on the external corners give patients the alternative opportunity of looking out at the landscape. To the east of the entrance is a rotunda of staff meeting, rest and consulting rooms and nurses' accommodation. (45) Supervision in both centres is crucial and on each occasion this now takes place across courtyards rather than down a corridor as before.

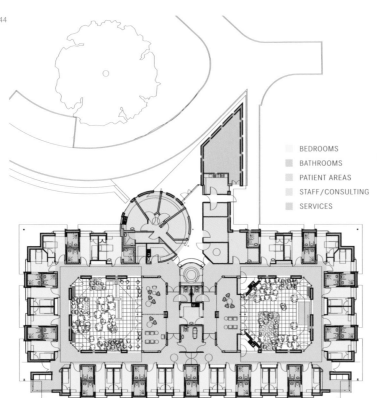

BEDROOMS
BATHROOMS
PATIENT AREAS
STAFF/CONSULTING
SERVICES

GROUND

Dennis O'Keeffe writes:

Thinking of RMA, Shakespeare's words "Poor and content is rich and rich enough..." resonate in my mind. The Breakfast Mission is always so full of vibrancy! You can tell straightway they are not in it for the money! No, no. They are 'in it' hook line and sinker, to relish and to rise to the difficult challenge that is excellence in architecture, and for that they are rich, and rich indeed.

Where do these Sisyphean tendencies come from? Well, from Richard Murphy himself I believe. Richard has remained unflinching in his quest for excellence and it is this that rubs off on his staff and frankly everything that they do. I am delighted to be able to say that I have known Richard for over 15 years and most recently as a client. He is for me certainly the most authentic architect's architect that I know of. Two primary and reciprocal features permeates his work: a deeply felt set of personal convictions, that is entirely focused on producing human-centred architecture and his refusal to compromise on anything that in any way falls short of these convictions. Not for him flagrant iconicism, or submission to some yoke of dull bureaucratic 'guidance': Richard's and RMA's work is always fresh, intelligent and consistently pursuant to a deep concern with the life that goes on inside a building and as determined by its users.

Never more is this so self-evident that in some of his recent healthcare architecture for the NHS here in Scotland. I happen to share Juhani Pallasmaa's observation of the pathology of today's architecture: "that often the most technologically advanced settings such as hospitals can evoke a sense of alienation, detachment and solitude owing to the ocular dominance of our sensory systems in relation to culture and architecture in particular". When Richard worked for us in NHS Fife his practice went beyond such mere externalism, functionalism or worst still, reductionist, deterministic notions of audit check-lists (or as Prasad more eloquently puts it the... "Intrinsic ossification of evidence orientated bureaucracies"). Richard sticks and stays true to his convictions. Never fazed by the challenge at hand, he digs deep into his experience and influences such as the geometry of MacCormac, the patterns of Alexander and (even with NHS budgets) entirely appropriate touches of Scarpa's tectonic and sensuous materialism. Add to this a twist of wit and good humour and *voilà*! another RMA building comes into being most importantly through the social interaction with the end-users. And please, don't get me wrong: this is not to represent some well-trodden linear 'problem-solving' endeavour. The reality of a RMA design journey, witnessed many times, is one of gentle, patient acquisition, intuition, social negotiation, tireless iterations and most of all emergence, all intertwined and inextricably linked to the end-users. For me, as Robert Chia puts it, developing a design with RMA is a becoming ontology beginning with an attempt to acquire a deep understanding of the client's tacit knowledge and then gently, patiently, probing and teasing out needs from wants. Complex, always. Complicated, often. Simple, never.

As NHS Fife's Design Champion, I too share this passion for better design, focussed, as you would expect on healthcare buildings. Imagine then how exciting it was for my NHS colleagues and me to work with RMA in developing our ideas for the Elmview and Muirview units at NHS Fife's Stratheden hospital for persons with dementia and other learning difficulties. How much more rewarding it was for us all, not just to pick up design prizes aplenty, but to hear the wonderful NHS nurses and staff and the patient's carers say this place is the best hospital building I have ever worked in or visited and, as on-going research is demonstrating, a building that allows everyone to provide better patient healthcare outcomes.

Well done Richard, well done RMA: I feel quite honoured in being asked to make this small contribution to Richard's book and for everyone who works in the Breakfast Mission.

Dennis O'Keeffe is Projects Director and Design Champion at NHS Fife.

48

Schools of Thought

BUILDING FOR CHILDREN AND TEACHERS

EDINBURGH ACADEMY NURSERY SCHOOL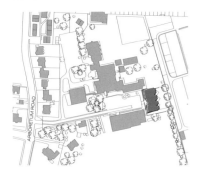

completed 2008

In the 1990s state school building underwent a private finance boom, although the system of selecting designers has led to very patchy results. The government's procurement system has made it virtually impossible for many practices to design schools, particularly smaller practices or those who have not designed in the field before and Richard Murphy Architects is no exception. Instead school commissions have come from either the private sector or from abroad.

A long running association with the Edinburgh Academy has produced a master plan for both their junior school and senior school sites, a new nursery school and new junior school classrooms. (1–7) The nursery school is arranged entirely on the ground floor with the main teaching accommodation in three linked rooms, one of which, for the two to three year old group, is capable of subdivision. Each of these rooms gives onto landscaped play terraces and also has external covered space and internal bay windows spaces. In the centre of the plan are all the necessary services and storage and at the entrance elevation is a large cloakroom arrival point for distributing children to the different classrooms.

Observations from other nursery schools show that the place where children and parents are separated and later reunited and where coats and shoes are taken off invariably hosts the most traumatic moments of the day and requires generosity of space. Storage for the children's shoes and coats was fashioned into a sinusoidal entrance wall which in turn forms an entrance to the nursery at one end and the after school club above at the other. Small child level windows give views out. (3, 4, 7)

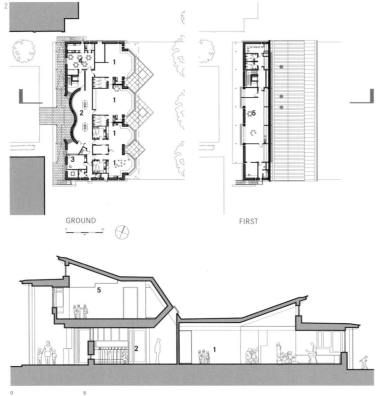

GROUND

FIRST

1 CLASSROOMS
2 CLOAKROOM
3 STAFF
4 DINING
5 AFTER SCHOOL CARE

HARMENY SCHOOL
Balerno; completed 2000

1 ORIGINAL HOUSE: NOW ADMINISTRATION
2 SIX CHILD HOUSE (CONVERSION)
3 MUSIC ROOM
4 KITCHEN
5 CLASSROOMS
6 STAFF ROOM/OBSERVATION
7 SPECIAL CLASSROOMS
8 COOKING CLASSROOM
9 GYM
10 SIX CHILD HOUSE (NEW BUILD)
11 MAIN COURTYARD
12 MINOR COURTYARD
13 SERVICE COURT

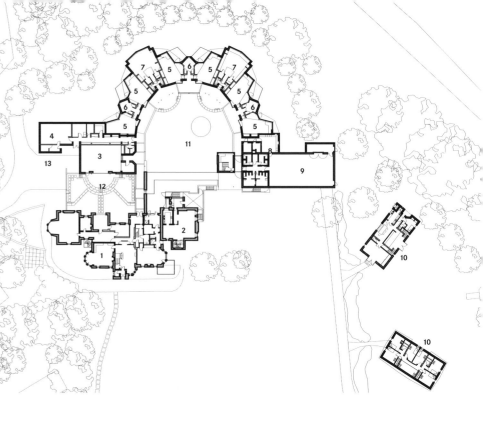

GROUND

Although a private charity, Harmeny School, located just outside Edinburgh, receives most of its funding from Scottish local authorities. (8–17) The residential school serves children between eight and 12 years with severe emotional and behavioural difficulties. The school is based in a listed country house built at the turn of the nineteenth century and set in extensive grounds on the outskirts of Balerno, near Edinburgh. The house was extensively remodelled by Lorimer in 1910, adding a pitched roof storey, a wing and a tower and reversing the entrance from south to the north. (8)

The initial project involved a radical reassessment of the school's brief, emerging as a long term programme of construction to provide two new houses in the grounds for children, a crescent shaped development of classrooms and specialist teaching rooms, including sports hall and music room, substantial alterations to the existing listed country house, together with the preparation of longer term development and woodland strategies for the whole site.

Children are taught in six classes of six each and are potentially easily distracted. Each of the classrooms looks onto mature woodland, but has high cilled windows to an

interior break-out courtyard. (17, 11) The classrooms themselves are an informal shape with a teaching area, wet area and individual study against the window. Observation panels from adjacent staff offices allow children occasionally to be monitored. Each classroom has its own roof and is surrounded with views of trees. The cloistered courtyard between new and old serves as a break-out space for children having an individual crisis and at the same time prevents them escaping into the wider world. Ensuring that the school remains a school and has no connotations of a prison became a major objective.

The crescent is terminated by a gym on one side presenting a 'garden wall' appearance to the formal south front of the house while the other is finished with an assembly/music room, on axis with Lorimer's Tower. Between the two is a second 'quiet courtyard' containing an external auditorium for events staged in the new room.

The two new houses are identical and placed in the old kitchen garden. (13) Each contains six children's rooms in the roof, but they are deliberately architecturally quiet to provide a base of 'normality' for the children's lives. A one-and-a-half-storey living room allows night time supervision of the upstairs from a carer situated below.

13
14
15
16
17

SECONDARY SCHOOL

Mosta, Malta; completed 2011

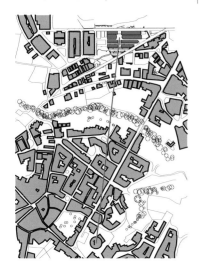

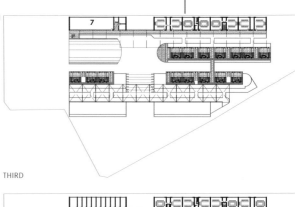

THIRD

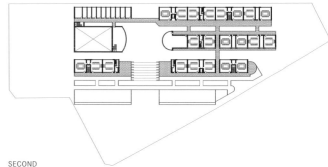

SECOND

In Malta a competition was held by the 'Foundation for Tomorrow's Schools' for a new boy's secondary school on the edge of the town of Mosta in the centre of the island. (18–24) Local architects, JB Architects, invited Richard Murphy Architects to take the design lead and the competition was won in April 2006. (22) Only about half of the main island remains undeveloped and the remaining landscape is distinguished by small fields separated by terraces of dry stone walls. (18) The site slopes towards the town and the competition design envisaged a landscaped inspired form with terraced streets of classrooms organised along the contours of the site, with a complex section, the streets roofed with Teflon. (19) The roofs of the classrooms are greened with pergolas. Thick walls of storage sit between each class. A heavyweight construction helps moderate classroom temperature but also these 'thick walls' contain air ducts from proposed water storage tanks beneath the lowest classrooms. Water

storage is a major issue in Malta and the idea here was to allow cooled air to help reduce temperatures.

After the competition, the design underwent the usual development process benefiting from dialogue with the client (although being a new school no leading staff had yet to be identified) and the plan progressed to having a centralised piazza at its heart which included an external raked auditorium, the backdrop to which was a framed view of Mosta's most famous building, its domed church. (24)

1 THE DOMED CHURCH
2 SPORTS PITCH
3 CENTRAL SQUARE
4 ENTRANCE
5 ASSEMBLY HALL
6 LIBRARY
7 STAFF AND ADMINISTRATION
8 CHAPEL

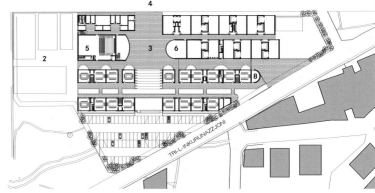

FIRST

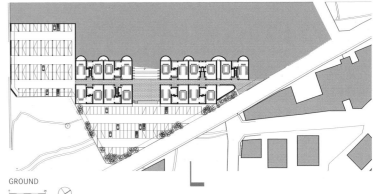

GROUND

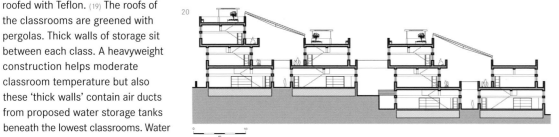

22

23

WELLS CATHEDRAL SCHOOL

Somerset; unbuilt

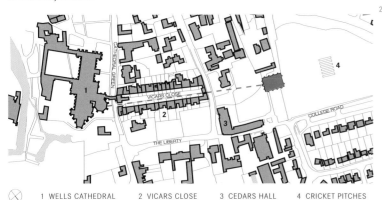

1 WELLS CATHEDRAL   2 VICARS CLOSE   3 CEDARS HALL   4 CRICKET PITCHES

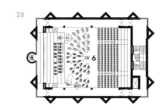

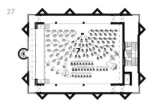

SECOND

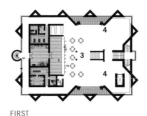

FIRST

GROUND

1 MAIN ENTRANCE/BOX OFFICE
2 PRACTICE AND TEACHING ROOMS
3 BAR/CAFE
4 BREAK OUT SPACE AND SEATING
5 MAIN AUDITORIUM AS CHAMBER
  PERFORMANCE AND AUDIENCE
6 MAIN AUDITORIUM AS 70 PIECE
  ORCHESTRA AND AUDIENCE
7 MAIN AUDITORIUM AS 120 PIECE
  ORCHESTRA REHEARSAL STUDIO

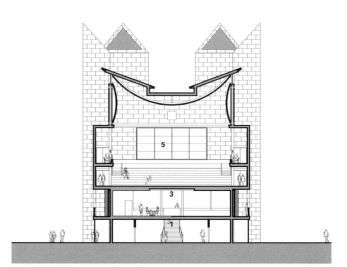

Another invited limited competition by a private school was held by Wells Cathedral School (25–31) in Somerset. The school was founded in 909 AD and is one of only four in England to receive special government assistance for music teaching. For such a comparatively small town, the school of about 750 pupils is very large, but inhabits a variety of scattered accommodation. The Cathedral itself has acted as the main performance and assembly space, but as the acoustic is musically very limiting, the school resolved to construct its own purpose designed, multi-functional music auditorium for chamber music with a small audience of 350, or a reduced audience to make room for a 70 strong orchestra, or finally to be used for a 120 strong orchestra rehearsal. (25–27) In addition, there was to be a foyer, sectional rehearsal spaces and teaching accommodation and the hall should have a public presence as well as being a school facility. The site chosen was in front of the main administration building, Cedars Hall, but to one side of the view from the Hall to the school's cricket pitches. (30)

The competition proposal made a vertical building: teaching accommodation, green rooms, etc. on the ground floor, the first floor reserved entirely for foyer with the auditorium at second floor level with third floor balconies. Retractable seating allows for the three main configurations. A heavy construction was proposed with natural ventilation chimneys; the result was a verticality of form located within the Gothic tradition of the Cathedral and chapter house and yet recognisably of our own time.

The overall size and presence of the building deliberately emphasised the intention that not only was this a new construction, it would also have been the most important and public building that the school would have constructed within its thousand year history. It would also have taken its place as one of the most recognisable and significant public buildings within the town.

The practice was unsuccessful on this occasion and a more self-effacing design was preferred.

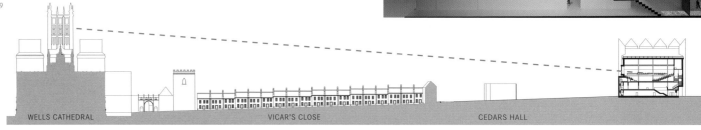

WELLS CATHEDRAL   VICAR'S CLOSE   CEDARS HALL

Higher Education

UNIVERSITIES, ANCIENT AND MODERN

KIRKINTILLOCH ADULT LEARNING CENTRE
Completed 2003 and extension 2009

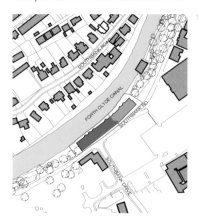

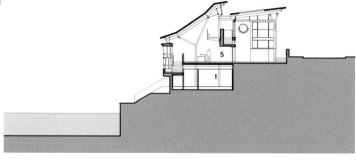

1 OPEN PLAN RESOURCE AREA
2 CLASSROOMS
3 OFFICE
4 CAFE
5 ENTRANCE/RECEPTION

The practice has designed extensively for higher education institutions across the spectrum. In doing so, two tendencies have been observed. First, at the detailed level is the change in modes of teaching, resulting from computer and laptop ownership. It seems that it is the "new universities" who are challenging the traditional ways of teaching, in particular with the invention of the "computer library", a 24-hour open access facility, parts of which can also be used for whiteboard style group teaching, but simultaneously through computers. Small lecture theatres are being amalgamated into facilities for mass lectures and libraries are transforming themselves into "learning resource centres".

The second tendency is to observe the ad hoc way in which universities grow. Rarely conforming to a master plan, buildings are often constructed to meet a particular need at a particular time, often at some speed. The consequential spaces that result between buildings are rarely actively considered but are an unfortunate by-product of this process.

Two opportunities have arisen, both illustrated here, for the practice to counter this trend. One built example at The University of East London's Stratford Campus and one unrealised at Edinburgh Napier University's Merchiston Campus.

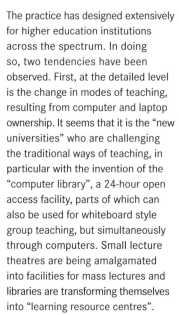

A building with no surrounding campus, Kirkintilloch Adult Learning Centre was constructed in two phases and later became an outpost for Cumbernauld College. (1–8) The aim of the project was to provide an open learning environment which draws in potential students from all sectors of society and also provides a new home for the classes already located within Kirkintilloch by Strathkelvin Further Education Centre.

The building houses a computer orientated open learning resource centre, as well as more traditional teaching rooms. The site forms part of the narrow strip of ground between the Forth-Clyde Canal and Southbank Road in the centre of the town. The canal bank itself slopes steeply into the water and was previously covered in scrub vegetation. The building is laid out as a linear plan with a two-storey block to the south side housing classrooms and offices. Against this sits a cranked pitched roof, freestanding and supported on steel trees, which houses the open learning facilities. All circulation takes place within this two-storey space.

The entrance was located at one end of this linear plan, facing towards the town centre with a

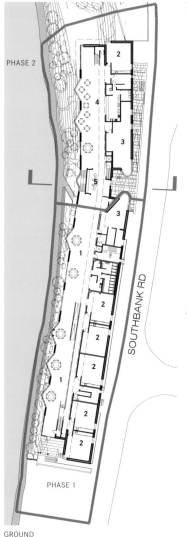

GROUND

view that a future extension might locate it in the centre of a larger building, a speculation at the time which was fulfilled by a decision to expand the building in 2007. (5)

Entering the main space, students can instantly grasp the layout of the building. The open learning space looks over the canal with a series of triangular bays forming workspaces almost amongst the trees retained on the canal bank. (2, 3) Circulation is from open galleries on each floor, the aim being that all activities take place in the open learning area except individual classrooms. (6, 7) The cranked roof and the classroom roof are separated by a continuous roof-light which allows sunlight into the main space.

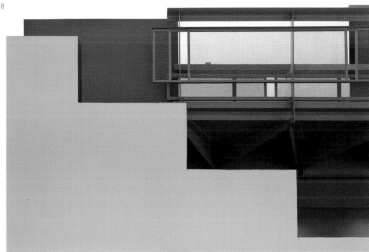

EDINBURGH NAPIER UNIVERSITY COMPUTING CENTRE

Edinburgh; completed 2001

A complete example of the new techniques of teaching and learning was presented by the chance to design a 500 terminal computer 'library' for Edinburgh Napier University. (9–16) Situated in the middle of a 1960s complex in their Merchiston campus, it replaced engineering laboratories which were demolished. The space created had no elevations and is entirely top-lit, care being taken to avoid light falling onto computer screens. The brief was very simple and could easily have been interpreted as calling for a gigantic column free shed, with no subdivisions or defined circulation. But for the users this could have been a daunting prospect. Instead the practice elected to immediately subdivide the space into a matrix of 5 x 4 bays defined laterally by five parallel barrel vaults and longitudinally

by a stepped hillside of four terraces. A tartan grid of circulation weaves its way, under valley gutters in one direction and vaults of light in the other. The roof is supported on clusters of four columns at circulation intersections and the entire composition is surrounded by light from hidden perimeter roof-lights where there are also ramped access routes. Obviously, the parallel arrangement of vaults and tartan grid has a superficial resemblance to Kahn's Kimbell Gallery in Texas. (10, 11) But, there the vertical Texas sun is admitted in the centre of the vault and reflected back onto the vault soffit. In Scotland light is far more horizontal and the vaults themselves are lit from the sides by sunlight reflected upwards. (10, 12) Placed centrally within the matrix is the main support desk, providing both a commanding overall view of the facility and also of the main entrances. At the top of the 'hillside', where the vaults form the most intimate spaces, are the five bays which can be converted into class-style teaching. Further bays down the hill are also capable of this function as required.

9

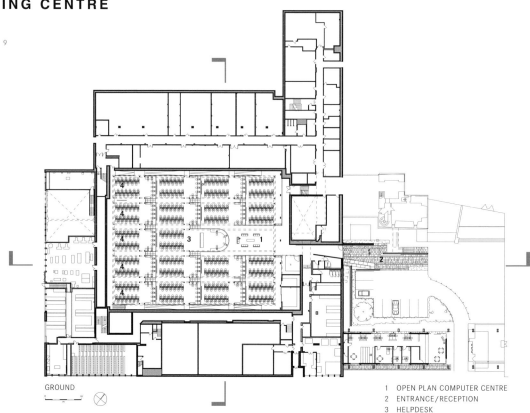

GROUND

1 OPEN PLAN COMPUTER CENTRE
2 ENTRANCE/RECEPTION
3 HELPDESK
4 TEACHING BAYS

10

11

12

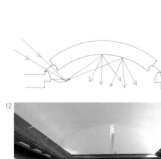

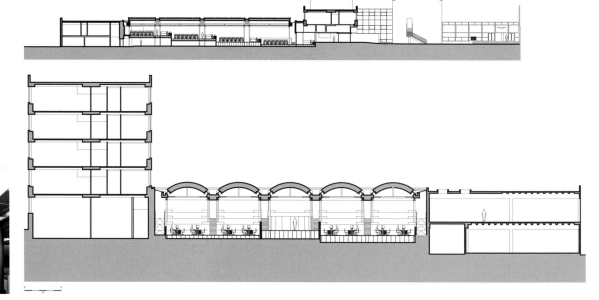

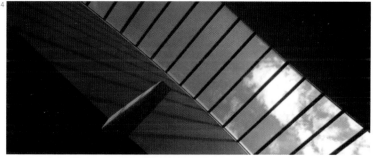

EDINBURGH NAPIER UNIVERSITY, MERCHISTON CAMPUS MASTER PLAN

Edinburgh; unbuilt

After the completion of what became known as the Jack Kilby Centre, further work for Edinburgh Napier led to an exciting possibility of reorganising the University's entire Merchiston Campus. (17–19) The campus is surrounded by Morningside middle class housing and had already been well developed up to its boundaries. Amongst the students it is also the most popular of the University's four campuses, so the study initially looked at ways of increasing accommodation there.

In the centre of the campus sits the tower house of Sir John Napier, the discoverer of logarithms. (17) Astonishingly, in the 1960s this was skewered by the main internal circulation which then developed around the campus as a typical wandering labyrinth of mostly artificially lit corridors.

The practice took this opportunity to introduce the ancient idea of the cloistered court in which would sit

the tower, now de-skewered and landscaped with a reflecting pool. At a stroke, the campus would have had a recognisable heart, but more importantly, the entrances to all the major destinations would have been located within the cloister. The geography of the entire campus could thus be grasped on entry. The existing single-storey chaotically planned library was to be relocated to a new atrium design in the current service courtyard and new teaching accommodation constructed where it had previously stood. And significantly, much of the overall current experience of long, winding corridors would have been removed. A second later study maintained the cloister concept, but looked at making a music auditorium as a base for the Scottish Chamber Orchestra alongside a relocated music facility instead of a new library. A decision to concentrate the future of the University at its Sighthill Campus effectively put an end to both ideas.

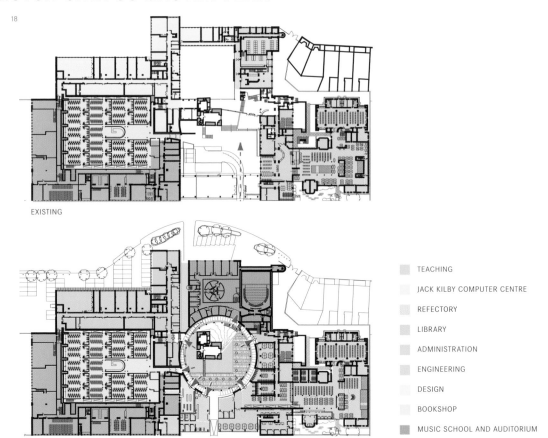

EXISTING

PROPOSED

TEACHING

JACK KILBY COMPUTER CENTRE

REFECTORY

LIBRARY

ADMINISTRATION

ENGINEERING

DESIGN

BOOKSHOP

MUSIC SCHOOL AND AUDITORIUM

UNIVERSITY OF EAST LONDON MASTER PLAN
Stratford; completed 2009

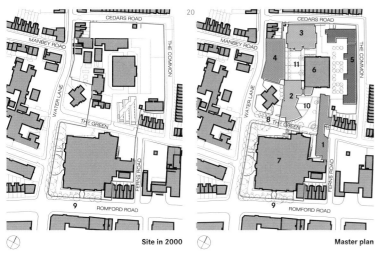

Site in 2000

Master plan

1   CLINICAL EDUCATION CENTRE
    (PODIATRY AND PHYSIOTHERAPY)
2   COMPUTING AND CONFERENCE CENTRE
3   CASS SCHOOL OF EDUCATION
4   PROPOSED NEW LIBRARY
5   PROPOSED STUDENT HOUSING
6   ARTHUR EDWARDS BUILDING
7   UNIVERSITY HOUSE
8   NEW CAMPUS ENTRANCE
9   ORIGINAL CAMPUS ENTRANCE
10 NEW CAMPUS GREEN
11 SECOND COURTYARD

1900

The master planning of the Stratford Campus of the University of East London (UEL) came about almost by accident. (20–26) The University had three campuses—their flagship new campus at Docklands, designed by Ted Cullinan and two inherited technical colleges at Stratford and Barking. The latter was eventually sold and the practice began work at Stratford, initially to solve the problem of inserting a dismantle-able lecture theatre into a Grade 2 listed hall. The commission grew to master planning the whole campus, refurbishing existing buildings, constructing three major new buildings and planning a fourth. The campus already consisted principally of two buildings. The larger one was a Grade 2 listed former Edwardian Workers' Education Institute, (21) which itself had had the function of library, (22) museum, (23) exhibition hall (24) and educational institute, (25) each with their own front door but with a chaotic internal circulation system. This is now called University House. The second, the Arthur Edwards Building, is a sadly all too typical 1970s concrete slab six-storey tower. (26) Various other insubstantial, isolated

buildings festooned the campus and a public road bisected it.

At UEL, security was a serious concern, so a closed campus with limited entrances chimed with the vision of a modern interpretation of Oxbridge courts. But Universities want buildings which house teaching and research facilities; they rarely think of making external spaces or a legible campus geography; why should they? At Docklands, the Cullinan master plan has not been followed through and a series of disconnected object buildings have been built since to its detriment, some good, some less so, but none contributing to any coherent campus spaces. But at Stratford, the practice had the unusual chance of working constantly on a campus for almost a decade, master planning and then building three buildings as well as a number of smaller projects and responding to the University's changing requirements during that period. The result is not just buildings, but a campus with a green heart, an oasis in this dislocated section of East London. In that period, it has been transformed in the students' eyes from the least favoured campus to the most popular.

The University were persuaded to close the public road and eventually make a new entrance into the centre of the campus and consequently reverse the circulation system in University House. This was confirmed by the first major building, the Podiatry and Physiotherapy Departments stretching along the eastern side of the campus (Ferns Road) completing a gap in the street and starting the process of making a central College Green. Various ideas were put forward to demolish the Arthur Edwards building or to disguise it by converting it into a library. Eventually, the second building, a computer library, teaching accommodation and 400 seat lecture theatre make the other two sides of the court with the computer library deliberately stacked up against the Arthur Edwards Building to disguise its dominance. A second court accessed by a pend was planned. Here the new Education Faculty was placed and the location established for a fourth building, the proposed new library, to form its fourth side. Further courtyards of student housing were planned on the remaining two sides of the Arthur Edwards building.

UEL CLINICAL EDUCATION CENTRE

Stratford, completed 2006

The Clinical Education Centre at UEL is now home to the Department of Podiatry, the London Foot Hospital, formerly in Fitzroy Square, and a relocated Department of Physiotherapy. (28–33) In the Podiatry section, issues of patient privacy were paramount. Patients elsewhere typically sit either facing other patients (as at Fitzroy Square) (27) or walk past them on their way to the podiatrist's chair.

of city connecting an isolated group of houses on Ferns Road with other University buildings further down the street, as well as form one side of the new proposed open College Green. A public entrance for podiatry patients is located external to the campus in the two-storey section which is deliberately scaled to meet the adjacent terraced houses. (31)

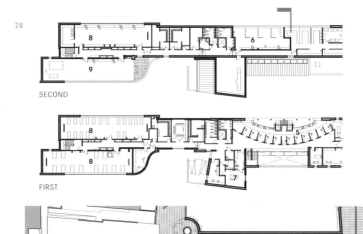

SECOND

FIRST

GROUND

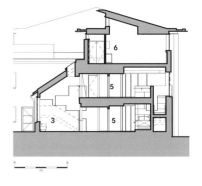

1 PUBLIC ENTRANCE
2 UNIVERSITY ENTRANCE
3 WAITING AREA
4 ADMINISTRATION/RECEPTION
5 PODIATRY TREATMENT
6 GAIT ANALYSIS, ETC.
7 MINOR OPERATIONS SUITE
8 PHYSIOTHERAPY
9 SPORTS SCIENCE LABORATORY

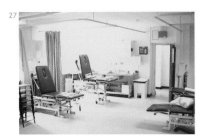

The solution was a two-storey space with 24 cubicles arranged in a gentle curve. Patients access the space from a two storey waiting area via individual doors to their respective cubicles, in the manner of opera boxes in a opera house, and every patient has a view of the green. (29) In this way patients never see other patients being treated and at the same time four academic staff can easily each supervise a group of six students in their charge. The building goes over the former road "The Green" connecting to five physiotherapy laboratories and on the roof is a sports science laboratory which has the benefit of a roof terrace. Finally, on the top floor of the podiatry section are found all the semi-public facilities such as biomechanics and gait analysis.

The building not only attempts to perform its functions well, but also tries to repair an abandoned piece

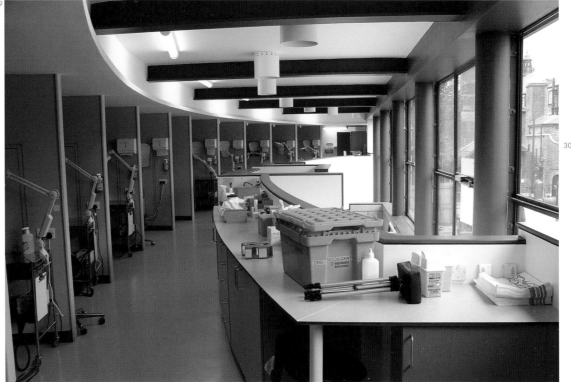

31

32

33

UEL COMPUTER AND CONFERENCE CENTRE

Stratford, completed 2009

The second commission from UEL, a Computer and Conference Centre, accommodated 400 computer terminals and like Edinburgh Napier before it, is organised into approximate groups of 30 for both teaching and open access. (34–40) Computers are organised in a two-storey galleried space which allows students to look out onto the new College Green. Three staircases between the levels divide the computers into the teaching bays and colour-coded light using light reflectors is admitted over each stair. The building was completed with a 400 seat lecture theatre, seminar rooms and a University entrance foyer. The lecture theatre, unusually, is expressed externally so it can be recognised as a destination and sits as a hinge between the entrance road and the courtyard. (35–36) Beneath it is the University entrance foyer and security point and this doubles as a gathering space for the 400 seat lecture theatre above. A staircase gives independent auditorium access and the foyer is also freely connected to the computer facility. The L-shape plan forms the final two sides of the adjacent central College Green at the heart of the reorganised campus. The building also deliberately acts as a visual block to the formerly dominant Arthur Edwards building and forms a gateway to a second University quadrangle.

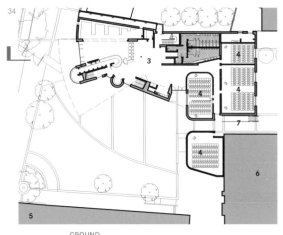

GROUND

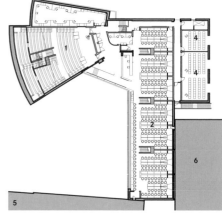

FIRST

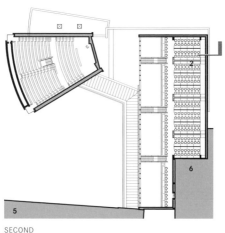

SECOND

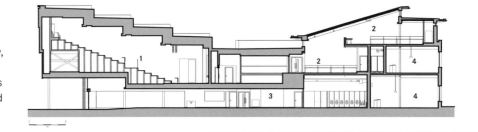

1 400 SEAT LECTURE THEATRE
2 COMPUTER LIBRARY
3 FOYER
4 GENERAL TEACHING ROOMS
5 CLINICAL EDUCATION
6 ARTHUR EDWARDS BUILDING
7 PEND TO SECOND COURT

37

38

39

40

UEL CASS SCHOOL OF EDUCATION

Stratford, completed 2009

The final major commission from the University was the Cass School of Education. (41-46) The building was placed at the northern side of the proposed second quadrangle. The other sides are the existing Arthur Edwards building, the completed Computer and Conference Centre and a future new library. The Cass School of Education is one of the fastest growing and successful schools within the University. The building is organised around a central atrium space with three levels of teaching accommodation on the north side and four levels of office accommodation to the south. (46) The teaching spaces require higher ceiling heights than the administration so the floor levels differ on either side of the atrium with the intervening staircases developed as a journey alternating between each side. These are accessed by open walkways (there are no corridors) that overlook the atrium and all rooms feature extensive glazing to the atrium elevations so that all the activities of the building can be seen from the atrium and walkways. (44) In the words of the Vice Chancellor, when a student walks in "everything appears to be available". Within the atrium is placed a drum-shaped tower of student consultation rooms that is cantilevered from the upper floors over a circular reception area on the ground floor. (45) Additionally, a lowered floor area within the atrium provides a breakout space for the main music practice room, this was extracted from the brief and turned into a miniature public performance space. The atrium is designed to be a busy interactive place with cafe, information point, and exhibition area.

1 ATRIUM FOYER
2 RECEPTION
3 ADMINISTRATION
4 MUSIC ROOM
5 EXHIBITION/MUSIC ROOM FOYER
6 TEACHING
7 MUSIC PRACTICE
8 STAFF OFFICES
9 STAFF COMMON ROOM AND HEAD OF SCHOOL
10 INTERVIEW ROOMS
11 CONFERENCE

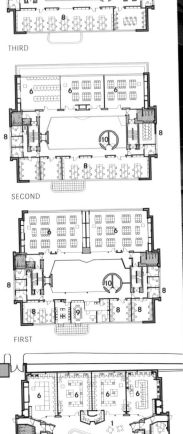

THIRD

SECOND

FIRST

GROUND

UEL LIBRARY

Stratford, unbuilt

The fourth project for UEL was designed to be the architectural climax of the practice's work on the campus. The design of a library has long been an ambition and the master plan placed it on the west side of the second court. (49, 50) Inspired by Asplund's great library in Stockholm, (47) but also by Aalto's smaller examples of 'cascade' libraries such as Viipuri, Otaniemi or the University of Jyväskylä, (48) a hillside of books was proposed with a zigzag plan which would have provided long shelf runs and study spaces at different levels with stacks and group study rooms within the hillside facing Water Lane.

The library hillside was to have been exposed to the new courtyard through a glazed facade whilst the Water Lane facade was mostly masonry against the noise of the street. An urban window was proposed which interrupted both the facade and the hillside addressing the axis down Manbey Street and would have given a glimpse from outside into the campus interior. Sadly, the very visionary Vice Chancellor, who was the practice's great supporter, moved to another university at a crucial moment and this commission was lost to a local architect.

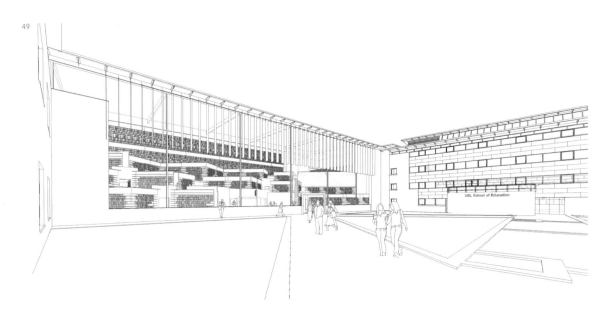

49

47

48

50

Professor Michael Thorne writes:

I first encountered Richard Murphy Architects (RMA) when I was Vice Principal at Napier University. We were looking for extremely creative consultants who could turn a disused engineering workshop which occupied multiple buildings on multiple levels into a huge open-plan student computing facility which would be the envy of the university sector and do it on a small budget. No small order! As well as a number of, at the time, more well-known architectural practices, we invited RMA to become interested because of their stunning success with the low budget development of the Dundee Contemporary Arts Centre. During the formal selection process we deliberately provoked the presenting teams of architects to see if they could respond to our needs as clients with different schemes from those that they had inevitably brought along to show their thinking. RMA were unique in that the more we said we didn't like a particular scheme the more they relished coming up with new ideas to address our thinking. It was clear that rather than an architectural practice looking for a good home for a building they had designed for themselves, RMA were determined to give us what we wanted—and within the budget (which by the way several firms of architects said was "impossible"). Completed more than a decade ago, the Jack Kilby Centre (as it became known) still attracts visitors from universities looking to provide computing facilities to students in an innovative way.

When I moved to the University of East London as Vice Chancellor and embarked on a massive redevelopment of its entire estate across three sites, RMA were successful in their bid to help us on one of them. Their breakaway design for the Podiatric Medicine Centre had clinical areas in which patients could be treated surgically yet still have views out of windows (and so avoid that imprisoned feeling which hospital treatment rooms so often invoke) was followed by another large-scale student computing facility and a wonderful new building for the School of Education. This latter, again on a very tightly constrained budget, used the good old-fashioned idea of a quadrangle but also incorporated the newer thinking of open classrooms and flexible spaces which could be shrunk or enlarged as numbers in different education specialities changed. For staff and students another triumphant success within the modest means available to the public sector.

Professor Michael Thorne BSc (Hons) PhD FIMA FBCS FRSA has been Vice Chancellor at Anglia Ruskin University since 2007. Prior to this, he was Pro-Vice Chancellor at the University of Sunderland 1993–1997, Vice Principal at Edinburgh Napier University from 1998, before becoming Vice Chancellor of the University of East London in 2001.

POSTGRADUATE STUDY CENTRE, FACULTY OF DIVINITY

St Andrews; unbuilt

1 ST MARY'S COLLEGE QUAD

1854

Two projects for ancient universities, neither realised, necessarily began as careful exercises in reading their respective sites. St Andrews University (53–58) occupies a number of sites within the original town defined by its three parallel streets (54) and intervening 'riggs' or parallel alleyways. The Faculty of Divinity wished to create a facility for postgraduate student individual study rooms, student social spaces, some collective facilities of seminar rooms, a small CD library and computer facility and four additional staff teaching rooms. The current accommodation for the students was in various ad hoc corners of their existing buildings, often overcrowded with two or three persons to one room.

The starting point for the design was the observation that a postgraduate's study of Divinity can often be an individual, indeed solitary affair. Providing single student studios but at the same time engendering sociability became the objective of the design.

The 'rigg' system of long backland development separated by narrow alleyways or closes, overlaid St Mary's College on South Street, interrupted only by the quadrangle of the college itself.

The width of the site for the proposed facility takes up two riggs, each of which have closes which are currently closed to the street. Three independent buildings were proposed, each with pitched roofs and arranged in a way that they would form a natural continuation of the rigg system whilst also forming a small courtyard space between them and between the existing buildings. (58) In such a way the building would have been able to satisfy both the informal grain of the rigg of the town and also make a formal statement about a University faculty organised around a small courtyard fronting the quadrangle.

Internally the students' study rooms were to be arranged on first and second floors around the double-height communal spaces; ten students in each of the three buildings. At ground floor, vaulted spaces were to contain the remainder of the accommodation and would have been a link to Mediaeval vaulted spaces found elsewhere in the town. The project collapsed due to lack of funding.

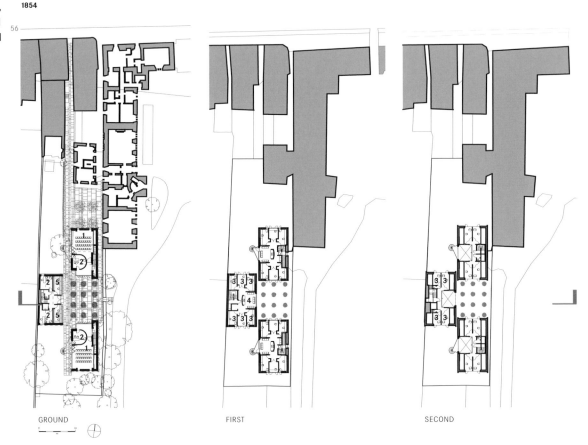

GROUND

FIRST

SECOND

1 SEMINAR ROOM
2 STAFF STUDY
3 STUDENT STUDY
4 STUDENT SOCIAL SPACE
5 CD/COMPUTER LIBRARY

JESUS COLLEGE AUDITORIUM AND HOTEL
Cambridge; as yet unbuilt

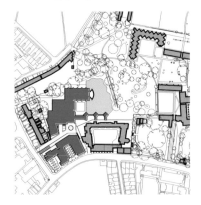

In Cambridge, Jesus College invited the practice to compete for the second time, ten years after being finalists in a 1998 competition for student accommodation (see pages 134–135). (59–69) This competition victory against two London studios and the Spanish architect, Rafael Moneo was for a larger and much more complex brief at the opposite end of the College, partially on the site of a former garage. The project brief consisted of, in the first phase, a music auditorium for an audience of 250, foyer, practice rooms and a 70 bed boutique hotel, the latter to be an independent facility on Jesus Lane. The music auditorium was to be linked to the hotel for conference purposes and although primarily a College facility, it should be accessible to the public without them having full access to the College. Incorporating three existing squash courts, a second phase proposed a sports gym capable of conversion to a studio theatre, (with similar dual access arrangements). Thirdly was to be a small research institute which could also have conference access and connection to the hotel. Clarity of circulation for the various user groups and connections between different combinations of facilities

was seen as a major challenge and represented an unusually complex brief.

Jesus College has a highly distinctive development and is generously endowed with space and landscape. Over its 500 year development from the small cloistered court of the former nunnery a pattern can be discerned of successive three-sided courts looking out to distant landscape and organised approximately centripetally from the original cloister, First Court. (63) Making this idea possible is the unusual college access called "the Chimney", a walled pedestrian route placed between the Master's and Fellows' gardens. (60) The proposed student housing project had followed this pattern ten years previously.

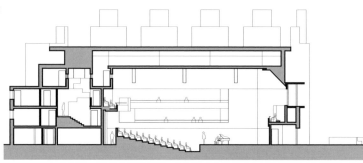
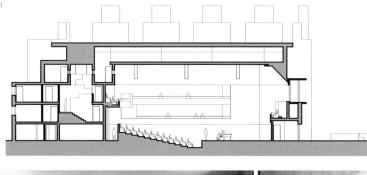

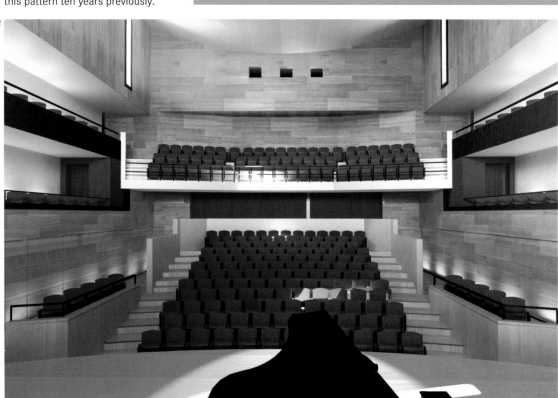

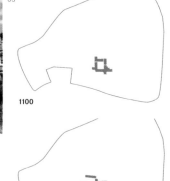

1100

1690

1870

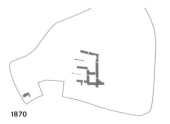

1928

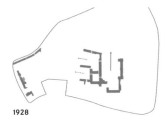

1965

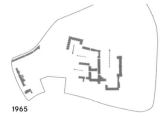

1996–2001

1   AUDITORIUM
2   FOYER
3   SPORTS HALL/STUDIO THEATRE
4   NEW COURTYARD
5   NEW LAKE
6   PRACTICE ROOMS
7   WESLEY HOUSE
8   HOTEL RESTAURANT
9   HOTEL BAR
10 HOTEL FOYER
11 GYM AND SQUASH
12 CHANGING
13 BACK STAGE
14 HOTEL COURTYARD ENTRANCE
15 HOTEL CAR DROP OFF
16 CENTRAL DOMED COURTYARD
17 GALLERY
18 RESEARCH INSTITUTE
    (NOW 'LITTLE TRINITY')

- - - - -   COLLEGE
            BOUNDARY

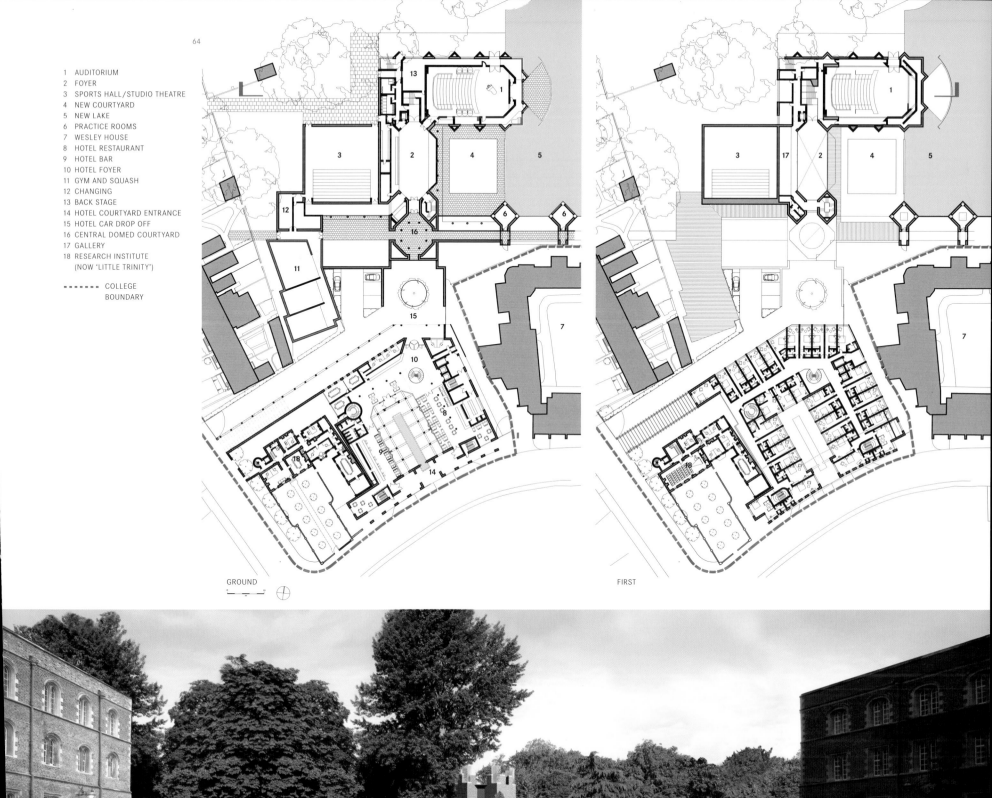

GROUND

FIRST

The site for the new development was detached from the existing College and was obscured from it by substantial trees. Even though detached it was thought appropriate to conceive of it as a three-sided court design again even though in this instance it would have looked back into the direction of the original College rather than outward from it.

It was proposed that the auditorium and foyer would form an L-plan with the third side formed by a loggia and the three music practice rooms which were extracted from the brief to form independent garden pavilions. The foyer opened to the new court and addressed the distant landscape. Beyond the foyer, a dramatic 'cascade' staircase lit with a hidden source of light sat on the entrance axis and gave access to the upper galleries of the auditorium. (68) An upper window behind the stage gives gallery audience members a view of the College from across the tree tops. (69) The foyer was to be a room in its own right and has an upper exhibition gallery with seminar rooms on the top floor. Behind it was the sports centre/studio theatre designed as a simple box, its bulk shielded from the College by the presence of the auditorium and foyer, but linked to the foyer so that it could be used for theatrical purposes. Back stage areas are also interconnected.

Externally the auditorium was marked by brick chimneys topped with etched glass lanterns. These would help ventilate the building and obviate the requirement for artificially chilled air and act as giant lanterns by night. It was proposed to set the whole composition in a small lake and to fell a small number of trees so that the auditorium would appear as an object building when initially first seen from First Court. (65) A small circular colonnaded courtyard roofed with a domed pergola represented the crossing points of routes to and between auditorium, sports centre, new exterior entrance and hotel, and would, in effect, act as a secondary entrance to the College as a whole. The route from the College to this circular court passed along a hedge adjacent to Wesley House, a building which dominates this part of the College but is not in college ownership. In this way, its presence would have been completely obscured.

The hotel was to have 87 rooms, arranged around its own entrance courtyard addressing Jesus Lane. Bar and restaurant would form the two long sides to the court at the ground floor on the journey to the main entrance, joined in the foyer, but a secondary entrance vehicle drop off was to be placed at the rear and this entrance would also link direct to the College when the new auditorium was used for conference purposes. The college is currently seeking a donor for the project.

ANGLIA RUSKIN UNIVERSITY
Cambridge; projected Phase 1 completion 2013

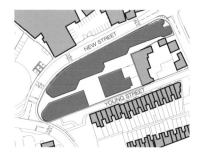

The practice has unexpectedly found itself building elsewhere in Cambridge, this time for Anglia Ruskin University. (70-75) The University has purchased a site to expand from its now completed East Road Campus nearby. The site contains a disused Victorian primary school, known as the Ragged School, derelict buildings, and with the exception of a nursery school and two private residences, the University owns the entire block.

It is the intention of the University to develop in three phases. The first phase will house the relocated Faculty of Nursing Studies. Later phases are to include administration, academic buildings and a 200 seat lecture theatre. The rehabilitation of the Ragged School for a Music Therapy School is also included. The campus has been developed to contain significant green space within it and not to overwhelm the diminutive scale of the terraced houses on Young Street. The presence of the large law court building adjacent prompted the raising of the heights of buildings at the west end of the site and to make the campus main entrance there as a pend between phases one and two. (71)

In the nursing faculty the teaching accommodation is on two floors accessed from a double-height foyer. The top floor is reserved for academic offices with a meeting room rising at the east end above that. The second phase will contain at an upper level a large lecture theatre whose profile and presence is signalled in copper cladding. A third phase will continue the architecture of the first to the end of New Street where there will be an external faculty entrance.

The environmental performance of the nursing building is critical to understanding its design. The lower two floors will be entirely naturally ventilated with air admitted via floor

1   EXISTING NURSERY
2   CAMPUS ENTRANCE
3   NURSES FOYER
4   SKILL LABS
5   CAMPUS WORKSHOP
6   TEACHING ACCOMMODATION
7   FORMER RAGGED SCHOOL
    —NOW MUSIC THERAPY DEPARTMENT
8   ADMINISTRATION
9   COURTHOUSE

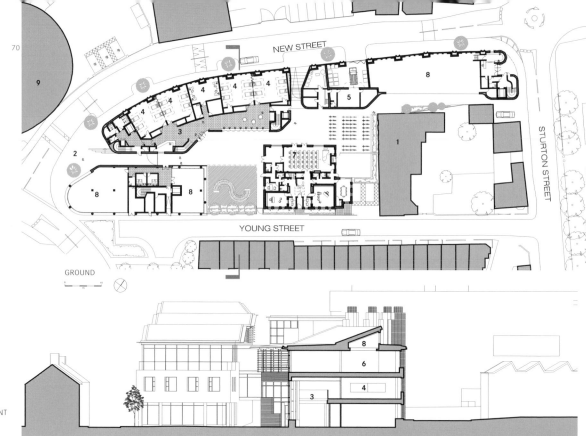

GROUND

vents to the ground floor rooms and ceiling vents to the first floor rooms. External acoustic conditions obliged the fenestration on New Street to be sealed and so extract is via externally expressed brick chimneys. (73) These have been designed to form a major architectural feature to this elevation and, of course, there are obvious references to the famous elevation on Trinity Lane in the centre of the city. (72)

They will eventually form the entire southern elevation of New Street. The north and south elevations deliberately contrast, the former being essentially a masonry wall punctured with windows whereas the south will be predominantly glazed and protected with louvres from overheating. (74) The main access staircase on the southwest elevation will be expressed in the glazing which steps up to the meeting room at the very top.

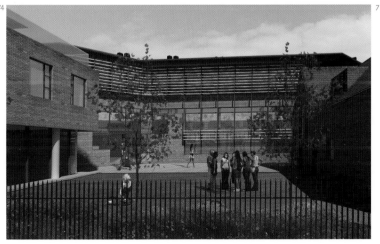

Artrium/Office, Justice Mill Lane, Aberdeen

The Commercial World

WORKING, EATING, PLAYING

OFFICE FOYER
Bath Street, Glasgow; completed 1998

Around the art of office design, a mystique has grown up that has led to a subculture of architects, agents and others convincing themselves that designing for this fiercely competitive market involves such a massive learning curve that architects who have never designed an office before can rarely be trusted to design one! The practice found itself in this dilemma for 15 years until the vicious circle was finally broken by a competition win for a development of offices, hotel and housing at Justice Mill Lane, Aberdeen.

The tragedy of offices is that the concept of "lettable" office space has become so formulaic that all sense of place or hierarchy has disappeared. (1) Indeed, it is always noticeable in magazine reviews of office buildings that much attention is given to the facade, the entrance, maybe an atrium, even the toilets, but rarely the actual office itself! As Richard Murphy put it: "I have rarely seen a speculative office design where I would want my own office to be."

Prior to Justice Mill Lane in Aberdeen, the practice's only constructed building in the field was a new foyer on the front of the former 1970s Glasgow Health Board Offices in Bath Street in the centre of Glasgow. (2–6) Also the result of a design competition and won against established office designers, it features a cranked steel roof profile that provides the building's distinctive angled soffit planes.

These are visible through the large structural glazed facade that steps to form a covered external entrance area. By night, their interior illumination gives a highly visible focus to the whole development within Glasgow's central business area and distracts attention from the banality of the surrounding office block. During the day, a hidden source of light on the rear wall from a roof-light running laterally between new and existing animates the space.

BATH STREET

GROUND

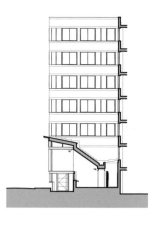

OFFICE

Edinburgh Park; unbuilt

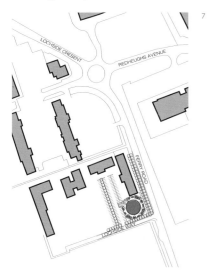

ROOF TERRACE

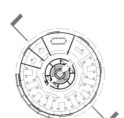

TYPICAL

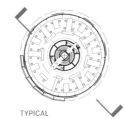

TYPICAL

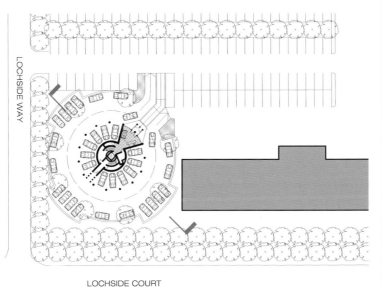

LOCHSIDE WAY

LOCHSIDE COURT

GROUND

Two unsuccessful competition entries attempted to break into this market and challenge the norms of office planning. The first was for a speculative office in Edinburgh's business park in 1999. (7–9) To make a landmark in this undistinguished office landscape, the obvious solution of a three-storey rectangular block was discarded in favour of a six-storey circular tower proposal. Round buildings have been taboo of course, until that is Foster's Swiss Re broke that particular 'rule'. The design proposed a single central core of lift, WCs and two spiralling interlocking staircases that would have given the office spaces 360 degrees panoramas and a very high gross/net ratio of 85 per cent. The usual roof-top plant room was to be piled up to make a lantern tower liberating most of the roof to be used as a communal garden with hot tub, sauna and picnic facilities. Parking in a semi-excavated ground floor would have continued the circular theme. The glazed facade was to be protected by a screen of louvres. These were to be movable, covering only 25 per cent of the facade, but would have continually circumnavigated the building once a day tracking the sun and shading the offices when needed, leaving an uninterrupted view at all other times. (9)

SCOTTISH NATURAL HERITAGE HQ

Inverness; unbuilt

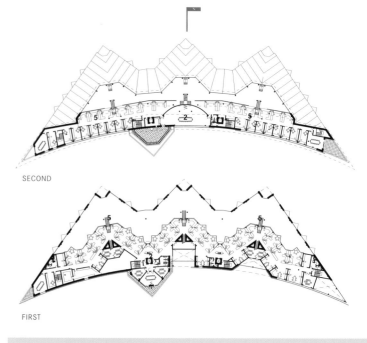

SECOND

FIRST

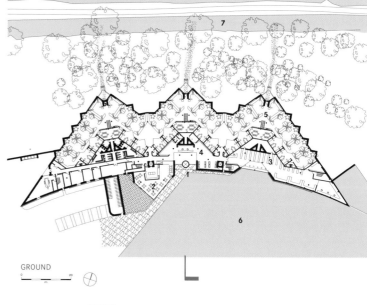

A second competition in 2004 presented the opportunity of designing a new headquarters for Scottish Natural Heritage (SNH), who were relocating to Inverness. (11–15) The competition was complicated by being a developer/architect selection with each team proposing a different site. This site was on a flood plain between a disused log float pond and the River Ness on the southern edge of the city. Sustainability was obviously a key factor, but more interesting was that the SNH had a very specific brief describing a hierarchy of teams, managers and staff and some unusual requirements, such as map storage chests and outsize desks.

Instead of asking what was the most *efficient* space in which to work, the practice chose to avoid the possibly anonymous space that might be created and asked the question—what would be the most *delightful* place in which to work and how could the teams and hierarchies find architectural expression within it? Looking north from the site through the birch trees towards the River Ness, the idea of the wonderful north-facing gallery against woodland at the Burrell Collection in Glasgow came to mind and with it the potential for every worker to have a desk against a woodland view. (10)

The stepped section was developed so that two-storey spaces interlocked and stepped down towards the Ness. (13, 15) All offices would have looked north through the trees to avoid solar glare.

Single-storey offices deeper in the plan were reserved for managers and meetings rooms. The building was then manipulated in plan to ensure the maximum amount of external area to the landscape taking on a distinctive 45 degree geometry which at the same time delineated different teams' territories. Along the south side would have been placed the unique events of the library, entrance area, sports building, cafeteria, etc., on a circulation spine which then in turn was bent into a gentle curve. The whole building was clad in green oak to the south and the log float lake was refilled with water so that it could be used for cooling purposes. (14) The building set out to achieve a BREEAM 'excellent' rating, but the competition entry was not successful.

1 ENTRANCE
2 CONFERENCE
3 LIBRARY
4 FOYER
5 OFFICES
6 LOG FLOAT POND
7 RIVER NESS

GROUND

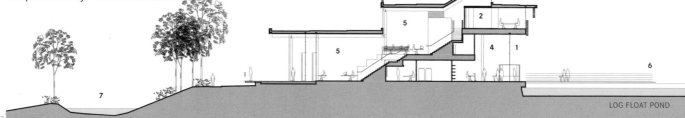

LOG FLOAT POND

RIVER NESS

OFFICE AND HOTEL JUSTICE MILL LANE

Aberdeen; completed 2011

A breakthrough was made in the practice's third and biggest office competition. The brief was for a very substantial office, hotel and housing development on Justice Mill Lane in Aberdeen. (17–34) The new site owners inherited a planning permission at the very high plot ratio of 1:4.7. The site was being used as a car park. Historically, Justice Mill Lane had developed as mostly the back extremities of properties on Union Street with which it runs parallel. (17, 18) There is a prominent urban corner with Hardgate and a considerable fall to a large social housing scheme to the south. Initially, the project was an exciting and unusual exercise in making a piece of city; and in particular, how to combine the three elements in a truly urban manner.

Developers rarely contemplate the horizontal layering of uses, so the competition adopted a French courtyard model, dividing the three uses vertically and arranging them around external spaces within the site. (16) Three courtyards, each connected by pends to Justice Mill Lane, were proposed, two of which led to three towers of apartments. (19) These took advantage of the southern aspect and single aspect flats could also extend down beneath courtyard level. The hotel was placed on the corner of the site and it had the dedicated use of the third courtyard. Offices spanned above the pends along most of the Justice Mill Lane facade. Upper floors on the street were set back above a significant projecting cornice line to diminish their impact on the lane itself. Beneath the accommodation a semi-underground car park was set into the natural sloping topography of the site.

1828

1866

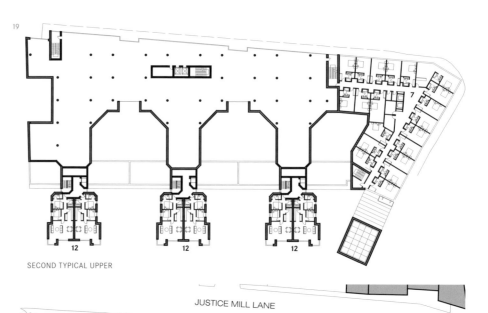

SECOND TYPICAL UPPER

JUSTICE MILL LANE

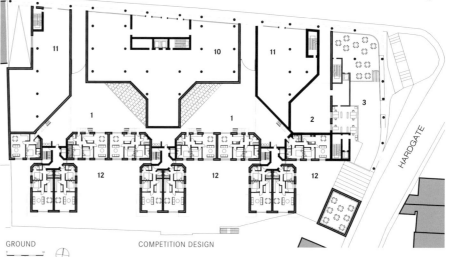

GROUND   COMPETITION DESIGN

1 RESIDENTIAL COURTYARD
2 HOTEL COURTYARD
3 HOTEL FOYER AND RECEPTION
4 HOTEL ENTRANCE
5 HOTEL DINING AND BAR
6 HOTEL FUNCTIONS
7 HOTEL ROOMS
8 GYM
9 OFFICE ENTRANCE
10 OFFICE FOYER AND RECEPTION
11 RETAIL
12 APARTMENTS

After winning the competition in 2006, the design progressed until the developer client decided that the housing element was uneconomical and this was deleted. The proposition of a hotel sitting on top of an office was advanced but was considered too financially risky for Aberdeen, so the design became two adjacent buildings linked but independent and needing to find some appropriate shared architectural expression. The two elements of the building were in themselves straightforward in plan. The hotel forms six floors of bedrooms ordered in an L-shape above a ground floor of public facilities arranged around a courtyard garden. Originally designed as a 160 room five star hotel the brief was amended to a 185 room three to four star Park Inn late in the design process. The practice planned the entire interior lay-out but its interior design has been carried out by others.

The office is designed over six storeys around a central atrium with floors retreating from both north and south elevations at upper levels creating external terraces for the topmost floors. The atrium is set into the section connecting only the lower four floors but filled with light from its south-facing roof. Inside the space is a spiral stair. Various sections were attempted, including one inspired by Asplund's stair inside the Gothenburg law courts extension, which disappears through a void in the ceiling, complete with hidden source of light, as if ascending to heaven. (22) Sadly, the client could not be persuaded to accept the additional cost and loss of floor space that this poetic development of the design would incur! (23)

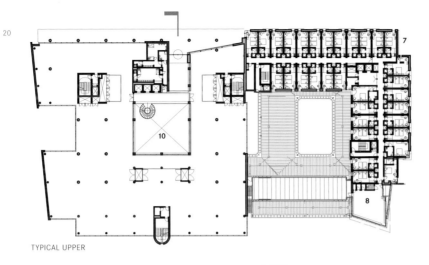

TYPICAL UPPER

JUSTICE MILL LANE

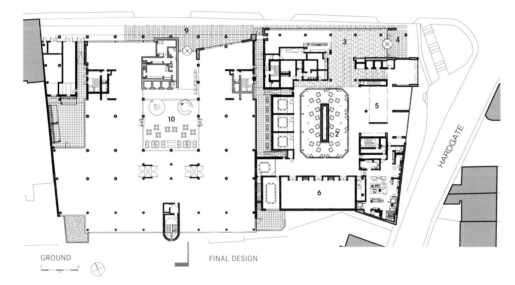

GROUND FINAL DESIGN

HARDGATE

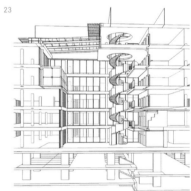

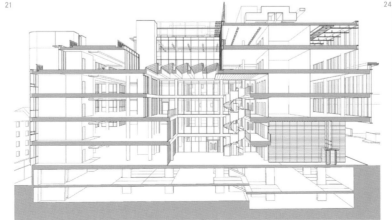

28

The offices have a gross/net ratio of 86 per cent and can be let as six individual floor plates or subdivided into up to three units per floor. The design set out to be a low energy solution from the outset and the environmental strategy is holistic, using exposed concrete soffits, under floor displacement ventilation systems and an environmental control strategy, which has delivered a building 30 per cent more energy efficient than current building regulations require.

Externally there is a clear differential between the two buildings which have, in any event, substantially different floor to floor heights. However, they are unified by the cornice retained from the competition scheme. (31) The hotel elevation, made of overlapping rain screen panels of render edged in steel, distinguishes the hotel from the fully glazed facade of the offices and disguises the variation in storey heights. (25)

The combined building was completed in 2010. Park Inn announced after their first year of trading that it was their most successful European hotel. A few months later the offices were let to two tenants, split at the third floor, for the highest office rents ever recorded in Scotland.

And in 2012 the British Council for Offices awarded it the best commercial office in Scotland award.

29

30

31

HAYMARKET

Edinburgh; unbuilt

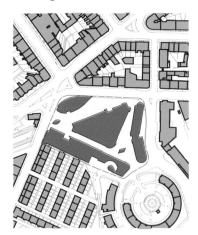

At the same time as the Justice Mill Lane project, the practice began a long involvement with a development site on the western edge of the Edinburgh New Town at the Haymarket. (35–51) Railway marshalling yards had been removed in the 1960s and since then the site has been subject to a number of planning applications, the last of which proposed covering it with a gigantic office development. The Haymarket site is adjacent to a complicated and poorly planned traffic interchange and is close to the city's second busiest railway station. Its main corner terminates the vista along Grosvenor Street, part of the later neoclassical extension of the New Town. Beside the southern boundary are the diminutively scaled parallel rows of 'colony' houses (see page 86) A further complication lies underground. Two major railway tunnels run tangentially across the eastern corner of the site and the engineering exigencies of building near or over them became a significant factor in the master plan.

The practice's master plan evolved with several objectives: key among these was the need to avoid a monoculture. Two hotels, one a major five star landmark, and three separate office buildings plus retail spaces and an underground car park were proposed (an element of housing was, sadly, rejected). Considerable 24-hour pedestrian public space should be included; the sensitive boundary with the colonies should be intelligently designed; and full cognisance was to be taken of the engineering issues presented by the presence of the railway tunnels. In addition, the design team were encouraged by planning authorities to think about the wider area, in particular the relationship with the station, although at the time there was no equivalent design team there with which to engage.

A major phenomenon of the site is the massive daily flow of commuters from the station, along Morrison Street and to the city's West End financial district. The master plan was determined to 'capture' these into a pedestrian boulevard which aligned with the tunnels and gave the commuters a short-cut to their destination. The master plan evolved so as to place two offices and the three star hotel around two edges of the site, a larger triangular-planned atrium office in the centre fronting the boulevard, reserving the site isolated between the boulevard and the Haymarket interchange for the five star hotel. The practice proposed that Sutherland Hussey Architects join the design team and they designed the three star hotel along the colonies boundary. Comprehensive Design Architects (CDA) advised on the internal office layouts and car-park.

1960

1 FIVE STAR HOTEL
2 HAYMARKET STATION
3 THREE STAR HOTEL
4 OFFICE BLOCK A
5 OFFICE BLOCK B
6 OFFICE BLOCK C
7 COLONY HOUSING

1836

1893

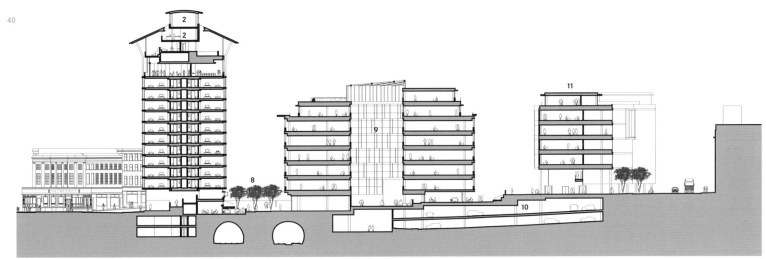

The five star hotel design quickly became the architectural focus of the entire project. The restricted site area and the area required for a 200 bed hotel with all the usual ancillary spaces translated into a tower of 17 storeys. It became symmetrical around its long axis, adopting a leaf shape plan which arose from the curve of the street frontage. The structure cantilevered from a double spine row of columns using bedroom party walls as the tension elements. In this way, one of the tunnels could be incorporated into the footprint. The top of the tower was developed as a sky bar, pool and spa with two mono-pitch copper-clad roofs to resonate with the copper-clad domes in the city.

In urban terms, the tower would have performed a variety of functions, both near and far. From Wester Coates (the main approach to the city centre from the west) it closed the vista and marked the beginning of the city centre. (39) Similarly when exiting the city along Morrison Street it presented a particularly dramatic farewell profile. (41, 43) It closed the New Town axis of Grosvenor Street in a typical New Town fashion with a major public building (albeit in this instance not a church). (42) The hotel also marked in a distinctive way what could have become a new sub-centre to the city. In the wider context, it would have taken its place with the other familiar landmarks in the city, in particular the Castle, but also the three spires of St Mary's Cathedral. Critically, however, neither of these was to have been obscured from any major vantage points.

The project became high profile, in every sense of the word. It was passed by the City Council's planning

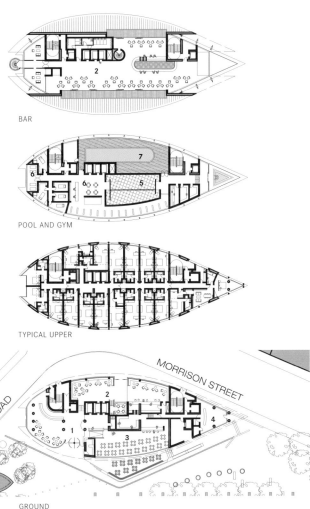

BAR

POOL AND GYM

TYPICAL UPPER

GROUND

1	ENTRANCE AND RECEPTION	7	POOL
2	BAR	8	BOULEVARD
3	CAFE	9	TRIANGULAR OFFICE ATRIUM
4	SHOP	10	CAR PARK
5	POOL CHANGING	11	OFFICE
6	BEAUTY AND GYM		

committee only to be called in by the Scottish Government. After a lengthy and hugely expensive public inquiry, the scheme was rejected, the height of the hotel and the 'interruption' of the skyline of Edinburgh being the main reasons given for this decision. Reading the inquiry report, the implication is clear; according to the report, 700 years of evolution of the Edinburgh skyline has now officially come to an end. No future 'interruptions' are to be permitted above a certain proscribed height. A former Civic Trust Secretary once said, referring to another project, that "Shortly, Edinburgh will be finished!" In terms of its skyline, it now is.

A second design was commissioned. (44–51) But, this time, against a background of recession a five star hotel was deemed uneconomic. A major office building was proposed in its place, the boulevard was narrowed and a small public square formed to front onto the crossing to Haymarket Station. The new office, again aligned with the tunnels, proposed two sections joined by a long narrow atrium. Our original proposal that this should have been a 'Jacob's ladder' staircase, which would also have increased the lettable area, was rejected by the developer in favour of a more conventional stair and atrium design. (48–50) The new design was only eight storeys in height and faced far less opposition as a result. Planning approval was granted in 2010.

42

44

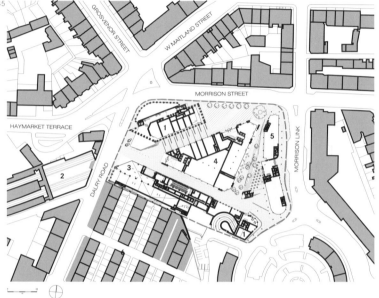

45

46

1 OFFICES
2 HAYMARKET STATION
3 THREE STAR HOTEL
4 OFFICES
5 OFFICES
6 COLONY HOUSING

47

1   ENTRANCE
2   FOYER RECEPTION
3   FEMALE WC
4   MALE WC
5   PLANT AND BICYCLES
6   OFFICE

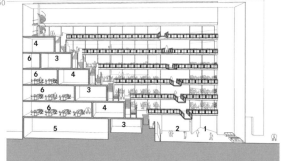

HAYMARKET STATION

Edinburgh, unbuilt

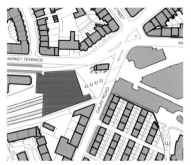

Frustration at having no 'partner' across the road at the station with which to engage on a wider master plan, proposals were produced speculatively to show how a new station might operate. (52–55) Haymarket is the third busiest station in Scotland and is projected to become much busier. It is woefully inadequate. In 1842 the existing building was briefly the western terminus for trains to Edinburgh. It is a Grade A listed building, being the oldest railway building in Scotland. Nearby "Ryries Bar", once a cattle drovers' watering hole, and now an isolated pub at the edge of the Haymarket junction is also listed.

The design suggested decking over the tracks to make an urban space which would have been a continuation of that already proposed on the other side of Dalry Road. The new station was defined by a floating horizontal roof and glazed facade and this would have extended around the original building so that it would have found itself entirely inside the new concourse; a museum piece now in a glass cabinet. Escalators connected to the platforms. The tram interchange became the termination to the north and commercial accommodation and taxis to the south.

The main facade would have orientated to the geometry of the boulevard across the road, so as to be its termination, and would have formed a new entrance portal into this part of the city.

Scotrail eventually produced an alternative design which orientated the station away from the Haymarket. After the many previous remonstrations from the planning department about 'joined up thinking', the Scotrail project exhibited no such ambitions but was granted planning permission at the first attempt.

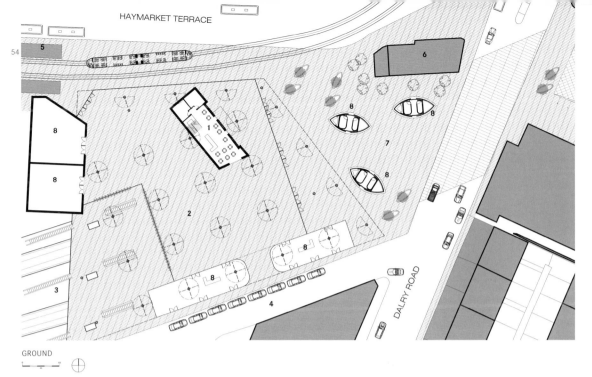

GROUND

1 HISTORIC STATION BUILDING
2 NEW STATION CONCOURSE
3 PLATFORMS
4 TAXIS
5 TRAMS
6 RYRIE'S BAR
7 STATION FORECOURT
8 COMMERCIAL

LANG-JIU WHISKY DISTILLERY

Sichuan, China; unbuilt

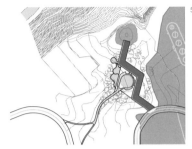

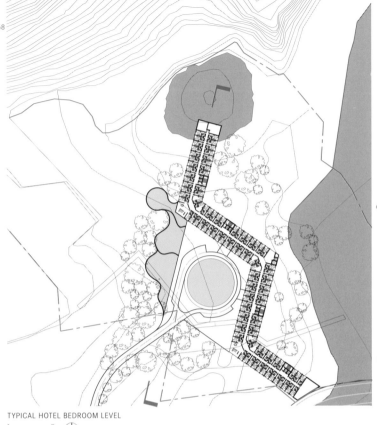

An invitation from China pitted the practice against two American studios in a highly unusual project: the Lang-jiu Whisky Distillery Company wished to build a new corporate headquarters, conference centre and hotel in the small distilling town of Erlang, in a remote corner of Sichuan Province. (56–62) This area is the 'Speyside' of China, although the product bears little similarity to its Scottish namesake. The site was spectacular. On the edge of the town, it spanned from the main road to a raised knoll at the edge of a breathtaking cliff down to the gorge of the Red River. The two extremes of the site sat at the same level but with a significant hollow between them which gave rise to the idea of the building as a dam or bridge between the two. The conference centre and hotel would have occupied opposite ends of a long walled building, which divides the site between the public and private spaces for both facilities. On the roof, level with the main road, would have been roof gardens and tea houses, but also a road to the corporate headquarters at the far end. This element, trapezoid in elevation, cantilevered out over the gorge to maximise the drama of the site. (62) Internally, offices were arranged around an atrium and a 'Jacob's ladder' staircase (61) with the managing director at its apex.

The plan form of the building, being effectively a bridge from the main road to the edge of the gorge, took the form of the traditional Chinese landscape zigzag bridges found at all scales in Chinese gardens. (56)

The materials of the main part of the building were proposed to be a stone base with horizontal bands of vertical timber louvres to bedroom windows, a palette borrowed from traditional houses in the Old Town of Erlang. (57) The corporate headquarters was designed to be seen as an object in its own right, particularly from a distance from the town and from across the gorge, so it was to be clad in gold coloured anodised aluminium— the panels to glint in the sunlight. The competition was narrowly lost to a Californian architect.

TYPICAL HOTEL BEDROOM LEVEL

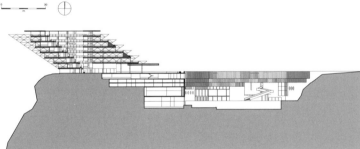

INVEREWE GARDENS RESTAURANT
unbuilt

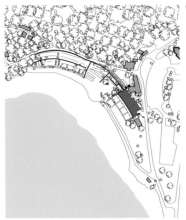

The practice began its life with an open competition win for a restaurant at Inverewe Gardens in Wester Ross in 1991. (63–69) This remote sub-tropical garden, warmed by the gulf stream, is over 100 years old and is now managed by the National Trust for Scotland. The existing route to the house and garden sits above two walled gardens which follow the curve of the shore and the fall of the land. The new restaurant design on the adjacent site to the walled gardens would have become a piece of constructed landscape. The curve was to continue into a curved building, itself being a sequence of four 50-seat cafes (the size of a pre-booked bus party), which could be progressively opened and closed as demand required. Each cafe opened onto its own new diminutive walled garden, which together would have made a sequence of seven gardens each to be planted with a different botanical regime.

GROUND

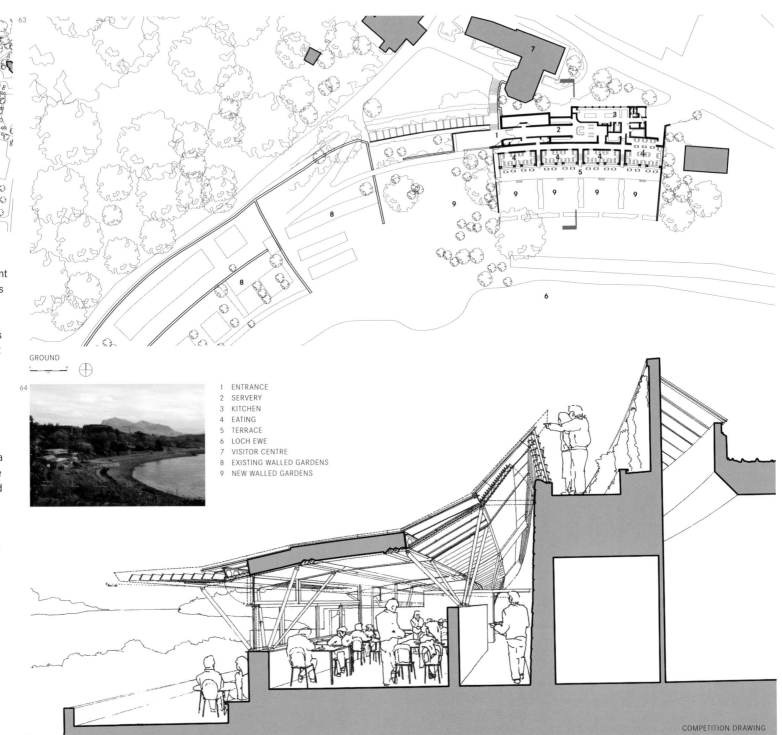

1 ENTRANCE
2 SERVERY
3 KITCHEN
4 EATING
5 TERRACE
6 LOCH EWE
7 VISITOR CENTRE
8 EXISTING WALLED GARDENS
9 NEW WALLED GARDENS

COMPETITION DRAWING

FINAL DESIGN DRAWING

The servery was to become a self-service grotto in the hillside and the restaurant would have appeared as a glasshouse with a canopy supported on delicate steel trees.

The environmental strategy circulated warmed air around the building and placed the cafes themselves in dappled light, as if in a woodland setting. (67) The project was cancelled a week before construction was due to begin.

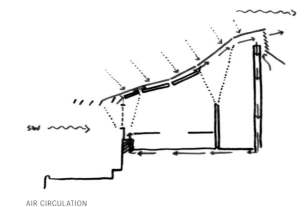

AIR CIRCULATION

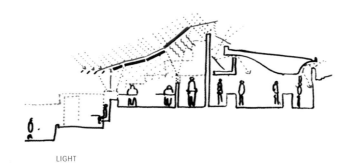

LIGHT

OLOROSO RESTAURANT

Edinburgh; completed 2001

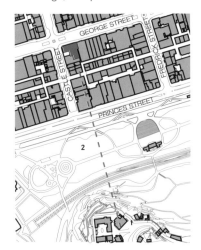

1 EDINBURGH CASTLE
2 PRINCES STREET GARDENS

Many years after the Inverewe project the practice did get the unusual project for the roof top restaurant, Oloroso in Edinburgh. (70–73) A commercial building on a New Town Corner was being completely renovated by CDA Architects. The top two floors were reserved for an exclusive restaurant. Eventually, the site retreated to the top floor only and the restaurant element benefited from full-height glazing to the north and west with an extensive terrace beyond. At first sight, a north-facing terrace might seem strange, but for after-work drinkers, this is where the sun comes from on a Scottish summer's evening. The west terrace and a private dining room focus on the nearby Castle. There are now three roof top restaurants in Edinburgh, but it is astonishing how the amazing possibilities of roof top inhabitations for all functions of building in this most topographical of cities are rarely exploited. On this occasion, the practice had the unusual and pleasurable experience of being the subject of food critics, as opposed to their

architectural colleagues. Reviewing the restaurant, Gillian Glover of the *Scotsman* wrote—"Amid the grumbles, gripes and bellyaching bills of the New Year; a little oasis of elegant calm has emerged in the capital. Poised high above Castle Street in a stunning development devised by the prince of organic architecture, Richard Murphy. Deep charcoal carpet absorbs the clangour of the restaurant, while sweeps of yellow and white compliment the stunning roof top vista. The result is serene and beguiling, I wasn't sure I cared about the food."
Joanna Blythman of the *Sunday Herald* wrote—"Oloroso, the new rooftop restaurant in Edinburgh's Castle Terrace is the first significantly designed restaurant in Edinburgh. It has benefited from the attention of Edinburgh's most interesting architect, Richard Murphy; better known for his conversions of Dundee Contemporary Arts Centre and Edinburgh's Fruitmarket Gallery. Oloroso is another demonstration of Murphy's ability to be radical but harmonious with tradition. Window-doors which draw light into darker zones while identifying and opening up outside views and vistas and the trick of somehow drawing the outside in, are just a few of his strengths."

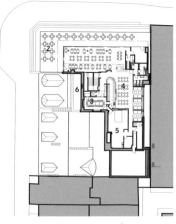

1 RESTAURANT
2 EXTERNAL TERRACE
3 PRIVATE DINING
4 BAR
5 KITCHEN
6 ENTRANCE (FLOOR BELOW)

RESTAURANT PLAN

EDINBURGH SPORTS CLUB
unbuilt

1 EDINBURGH SPORTS CLUB
2 PROPOSED HOUSING
3 TENNIS COURTS

LOWER GROUND

UPPER GROUND

FIRST

1 ENTRANCE
2 RECEPTION/FOYER
3 CHAMPIONSHIP SQUASH COURT
4 SQUASH COURTS
5 DOUBLES COURT
6 GYM
7 CHANGING
8 RESTAURANT
9 TERRACE

Finally, despite the presence of some fanatical sportsmen, the practice's only venture into the world of sport has been an unbuilt tennis and squash club for the exclusive Edinburgh Sports Club. (74–75) The existing building sits on an island in the Water of Leith and is a typical agglomeration of original building and unfortunate ad hoc extensions. The proposal was for a partnership with a developer in which the latter would secure the site for 24 luxury flats by constructing a new building for the club.

Squash courts are notoriously dumb boxes so these were used to build up a two-storey plinth, slightly set into the ground so entrance level could be located at first floor with changing below. All the social facilities of club room, restaurant, viewing terrace and gym and fitness rooms were to be arranged as glazed pavilions on the roof. A cleft down the centre of the plan organised the circulation and connected the entrance to the riverside, where an 'exhibition' squash court and audience were to be placed. Negotiations between club and developer collapsed and in the absence of another bidder the project was abandoned.

British High Commission, Sri Lanka

Two Embassies

"A BRIDGE BETWEEN TWO COUNTRIES"

BRITISH HIGH COMMISSION

Sri Lanka; completed 2008

Historically, as a type the embassy was the house of the ambassador. Gradually the convention was established that the ground on which it stood became the territory of that government. When the number of employees increased, the embassy and the residence often became two different buildings but with the embassy remaining sovereign. The recent developments of security have returned the residence as the primary location for entertaining, leaving the function of the embassy as largely bureaucratic. Within an embassy there are the offices of the ambassador, his deputy and occasionally a military *attaché* all located within a secure inner sanctum; a visa issuing office; a consulate mostly for the use of UK citizens abroad; and then a range of different organisations including trade promotion, sometimes the Department for International Development, sometimes an immigration office and then the management office charged with maintaining the estate itself, which can consist of a considerable number of houses in addition to the embassy. These departments can wax and wane quite rapidly so it is essential that office space remains flexible. And since building alterations within an existing building are a security problem, there is an understandable but unspoken tendency to future-proof new buildings and make them a bit bigger than they actually need to be.

Security for embassies used to be mostly about espionage, making sure no bugs could be planted during the construction process and that the building could not be burgled. Demonstrations outside the compound wall were to be expected and some minor damage accepted, but the advent of the massive explosive delivered by lorry totally changed thinking. The aftermath of 9/11 made all embassies potential targets, but this was made very real by the bombing of the British Consulate in Istanbul in 2005.

The American solution has been to turn the United States' embassies into mini-fortresses and to relocate from city centres. They also have standard designs that are parachuted into diverse countries and climates all over the world. By contrast, the British Government is determined to maintain an almost impossible balancing act of being on the one hand secure with a serious duty of care to their employees but on the other open and welcoming to visitors. The Scandinavians partially solved this conundrum in Berlin by neatly placing the five national embassies which need security in a combined walled compound, with a sixth entertainment and cultural building placed outside but also acting as a gatehouse.

In Sri Lanka the previous British High Commission (a High Commission is an embassy to a fellow commonwealth country) was located in the centre of Colombo. It was a five storey concrete clad slab block which while well located and in generous grounds had severe environmental and maintenance problems. (1)

1 WESTMINSTER HOUSE
2 SRI LANKAN METEOROLOGICAL INSTITUTE
3 NEW HIGH COMMISSION

The decision was made to sell the site and a new and undeveloped corner site within the diplomatic suburb of Cinnamon Gardens was purchased. Winning the competition for the new High Commission was a major coup for the practice. (3–32) It was one of the rare occasions that the Foreign & Commonwealth Office (FCO) has ventured outside London for their architect and certainly no Scottish practice has been commissioned in modern times. A later discovery and a happy coincidence was that the British colonial development in Sri Lanka (then Ceylon) had in fact been largely Scottish; all the tea plantations bearing Scottish names to this day.

The pre-eminent architect of twentieth century Sri Lanka is, of course, Geoffrey Bawa, whose many buildings on the island reworked traditional Sri Lankan roofs, spaces, gardens, patterns of light, etc.. His own office, now converted into a delightful restaurant in Colombo, demonstrates a superb working environment.

In a photograph, Bawa is seen in shaded space next to a garden, space flows from one to another, a breeze blows through and the sound of water in a fountain emanates from the garden. (2)

Seeing this space on a visit during the competition process, Richard Murphy was determined to make equivalent working conditions in the embassy. A single-storey building was conceived, organised around a series of courtyards, each with different manifestations of water. This idea coincided with the idea of empowering the office workers to switch off air-conditioning when humidity levels allowed, open windows to the courtyards and induce a breeze through their offices by a thermal chimney operating down to the middle of each 'leg' of the design. (19, 20) The section shows this arrangement. (6) The chimney takes the form of a glass lantern and heats up air expelled through rotating ventilators. An internal glazed panel can be raised and immediately an updraft is created within the office below. The glazed chimney also reflects light up onto the polished concrete vault in the manner of Kahn's Kimbell Gallery.

Externally, the building is clad in the local materials of granite, coconut wood and Sri Lankan terra cotta tiles. The glass thermal chimneys return as lanterns at each gable (where the air conditioning plant for each wing is also located) and three of the gables extend across the 'stand-off' zone to engage with the perimeter wall.

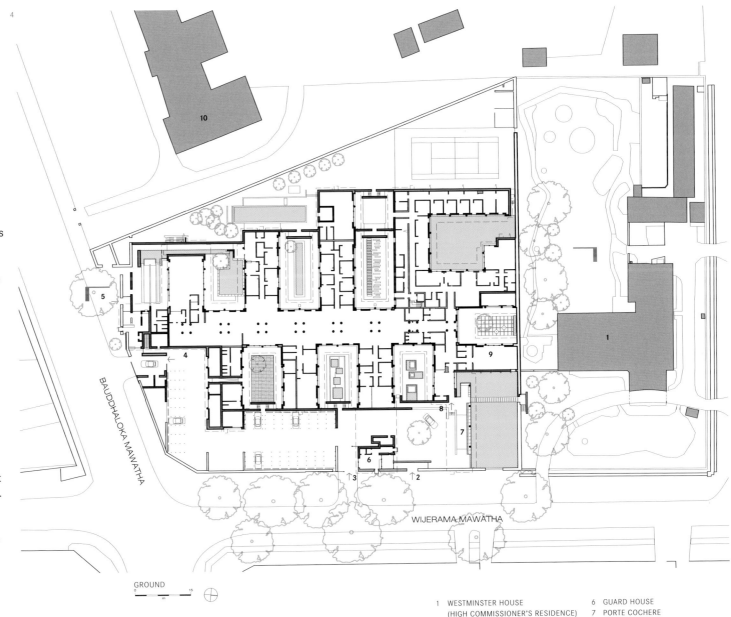

GROUND

1 WESTMINSTER HOUSE (HIGH COMMISSIONER'S RESIDENCE)
2 PEDESTRIAN ENTRANCE
3 VEHICLE ENTRANCE
4 VEHICLE EXIT
5 CONSULAR AND VISA ENTRANCE
6 GUARD HOUSE
7 PORTE COCHERE
8 MAIN ENTRANCE
9 EXHIBITION/CONFERENCE ROOM
10 SRI LANKAN METEOROLOGICAL INSTITUTE

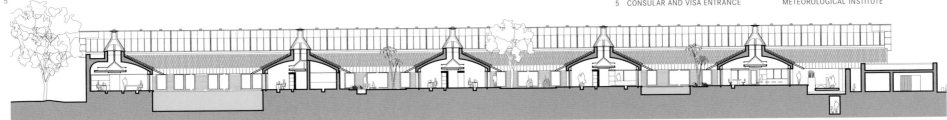

There are three entrances: a vehicle and main pedestrian entrance on Wijerama Mawatha with a separate visa and consular entrance on Bauddhaloka Mawatha where the only mature tree of the site was preserved and incorporated into the design.

The site is approximately trapezoid shaped and forms an informal boundary with the British High Commissioner's existing residence (Westminster House) and garden, and a private route was opened for his use, celebrated by stepping stones across an entrance lake. (10) All other embassies within Sri Lanka are surrounded by high security walls and the UK High Commission was

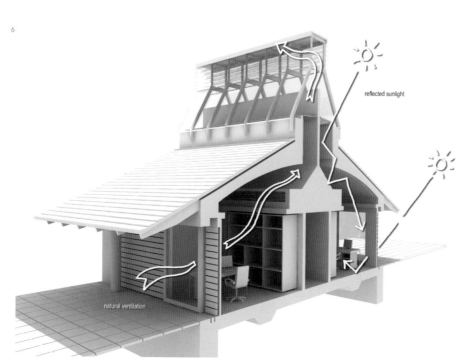

reflected sunlight

natural ventilation

no exception. Nonetheless, the FCO was persuaded to insert a window from the exterior to the entrance lake and this one gesture has to a degree demystified a building which only a few will ever actually visit. (22) The fourth boundary has been devoted to the High Commission Club, complete with swimming pool. (15, 16) Walls are painted single blocks of colour both as a homage to local colourfulness but also to the Mexican architect, Baragan.

Peter Hayes writes:

Embassies are more than bricks and mortar (and concrete, steel and glass). They are more than a functional place of work. They are, in a very physical sense, our representatives abroad. Ambassadors and High Commissioners may come and go, and some may have a high profile locally. But the building remains as an enduring presence. In many capital cities of the world, the British Embassy will be known to the local population. It will be a landmark. Whether intentional or not, the building says something about who we are, and about our relationship with that country.

Our aim, in commissioning the design for a new High Commission building in Colombo, was to meet not just the challenges of a modern office building in a tropical country that was, at that time, beset by terrorism. Our hope was for a design that also said something about modern Britain: innovative without being frivolous, functional without being stolid, secure without being forbidding.

Importantly, the building had to have a connection to the country in which it sits, rather than something that could have been lifted out of London or Edinburgh and dropped down in the tropics. Embassies and High Commissions, at their best, should be a bridge between the two countries, rather than an alien implant from one to the other. The new High Commission building fulfils that role admirably. The use of water and local materials, courtyards and overhanging eaves are all characteristically Sri Lankan, yet the building is quite unlike anything else on the island, and retains an air of British practicality and functionality, without being austere.

I was delighted to be the first High Commissioner to occupy the building. Despite the disruption of moving a busy operation across town, and the inevitable challenges of a new building, the High Commission team was genuinely excited by the prospect of the move. It helped that the building, even before we moved in, had become a landmark and a talking point around town. One of the most compelling parts of the design is the large window between the entrance courtyard and the street. With security concerns meaning that many Embassies and High Commissions look more like fortresses (or prisons), this window was a powerful symbol of the openness we sought to project.

The new building also forced us to behave differently as an organisation. The previous five-storey office building, whilst dramatically sited opposite the President's House and facing the Indian Ocean, was not well-suited to a modern, flexible, collegiate operation. The inevitable split of the High Commission team between offices and between floors served to separate and isolate our component parts.

The new, single-storey building has teams in a largely open-plan environment, with each team arranged around one of the beautiful courtyards. This provides teams with a sense of identity and place within the building, whilst ensuring they are each open and accessible to others. The central communication spine through the building allows for a natural flow and interaction between the occupants.

We were honoured to have HRH the Duke of Gloucester open the building in 2008, in the 60th anniversary year of Sri Lankan independence. His father as Duke of Gloucester had represented the King at the independence celebrations 60 years earlier. At the opening ceremony, I quoted the architect Cedric Price, who could not have put it better: "The reason for architecture is to encourage people to behave, physically and mentally, in ways they had previously thought impossible."

Dr Peter Hayes was British High Commissioner to Sri Lanka and the Maldives from 2008–2010.

22

BRITISH EMBASSY
FYR Macedonia; completed 2006

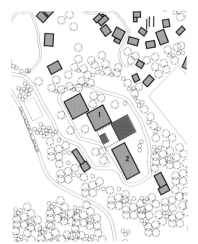

1 FRENCH EMBASSY
2 SEISMIC INSTITUTE

around which all departments of the new embassy are now organised.

The project brief was a very different one to the BHC in Colombo and required the quick, clear and concise identification of achievable design and technical goals within a very tight programme. The aim of the project was to create a publicly accessible building and interior that was more akin to an art gallery than a government building and in doing so challenge the preconceptions of what an embassy should be.

The building was completed in December 2005, just nine months after the initial briefing.

GROUND
0   15
        m

1 ENTRANCE
2 RECEPTION

In a lull in the design process, for Colombo the FCO in 2005 appointed the same design team to convert an existing building, part of a former Seismic Institute, in the Macedonian capital of Skopje. (32–39)

The project involved the complete internal re-organisation and restructuring of a two-storey building, housed on a shared compound (along with the Macedonian Seismic Institute and the French Embassy housed within an identical neighbouring building) and included also the design of a guardhouse, common gatehouse and external/security works for the entire compound.

Internally, the building was effectively dismantled with various original structural features, previously hidden, exposed and subsequently exploited in the new design. This included the original poured concrete "honey comb" ceilings throughout and the structure of the central top-lit atrium skylight,

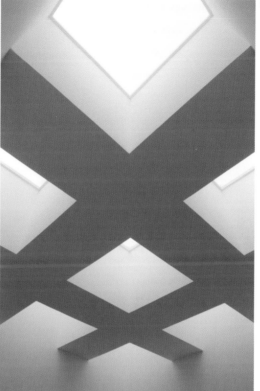

Building for Art

"ACE CAFE WITH A QUITE NICE MUSEUM ATTACHED"

THE FRUITMARKET GALLERY
Edinburgh; completed 1993

The lottery has led to a boom in cultural building of which art galleries, arts centres, visitor centres and museums are a major part. Often seen as a means of regenerating local economies, sometimes the building itself becomes the prime attraction. They can be precarious adventures. An ambitious business plan is easy to write, frequently problematic to fulfil. There have been some embarrassing lottery 'turkeys' with well known cultural buildings opening to great fanfare, but quietly closing a few months later.

At the height of the 1980s, the V&A Museum outraged the arts world with their poster strap-line "Ace cafe with a quite nice museum attached". It seemed to some the ultimate Thatcherite dumbing-down of a great international cultural institution. In reality, however, the advertising studio had cleverly observed a dramatic change in the function of galleries and museums. 40 years ago one visited a gallery and, if there was time, visited the cafe; today the sequence is often reversed. Arts Centres have become social meeting places and if there is time, an exhibition might be visited.

In such a way, the threshold can be dissolved between the public and what is, for many, the rather esoteric world of modern art.

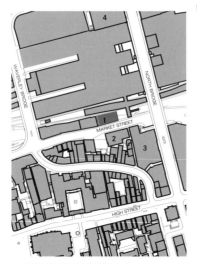

1 FRUITMARKET GALLERY
2 CITY ART CENTRE
3 SCOTSMAN HOTEL
4 BALMORAL HOTEL

The Fruitmarket Gallery was a pre-lottery project; indeed, from the perspective of projects undertaken since 1993, the total building budget of £300,000 for the complete reconstruction of a substantial gallery seems today absurd. (1–12) The original building arose from a typical Edinburgh topographical phenomenon; what appears to be ground floor at street level is in fact a bridge. Old railway tracks below facilitated the arrival of foodstuff which was hoisted up to be sold at Market Street level or stored on the first floor. (6) A 1979 'conversion' had done little other than moved art in where there had been fruit. (5) A cafe had been established at first floor level where no-one could see it, neither gallery had natural light, the upstairs ceiling was very low, two fire escapes were the only connections between the levels so that visitors often didn't realise that there was an upstairs. Added to

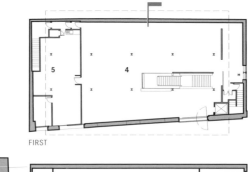

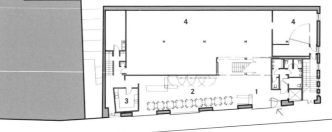

FIRST

GROUND

MARKET STREET

1 ENTRANCE
2 CAFE/BOOKSHOP
3 KITCHEN
4 GALLERY
5 OFFICES

that, the exterior appeared to be a bunker. And this was the Scottish Arts Council's "flagship gallery"!

By happy chance, although very undistinguished itself, the gallery's location at the heart of the central valley of Edinburgh, places it among the city's monuments: the City Art Centre and Scotsman buildings immediately across the street, the spans of the North Bridge nearby and further afield, the Balmoral Hotel and Scott Monument. The renovation gave birth to the idea that these permanent and familiar monuments, or significant recognisable fragments of them, might be drawn into the changing exhibitions within.

With the miniscule funding, three ambitious main moves were proposed: a new roof, a new stair and a new facade. The most dramatic was the roof. The low parapet flat roof was replaced with a winged roof that sailed above the parapet with a glazed clerestory between so that it appeared to float. At a stroke, the hanging height of the upper gallery was dramatically increased.

The new roof, rectangular in geometry, overlays the trapezoidal plan of the original building so that it has a dynamic relationship with the street facade and cantilevers, at its greatest point, over the new entrance. At the same time, two longitudinal roof-lights were inserted either side of a central light reflector which houses the new air extract system. The whole assemblage appears to fly off new double-pinned internal steel columns.

A new staircase connecting the floors was placed beneath the new roof-light. The lower section pivots like a New York fire escape in reverse to permit large objects to enter the rear ground floor gallery. (8, 9)

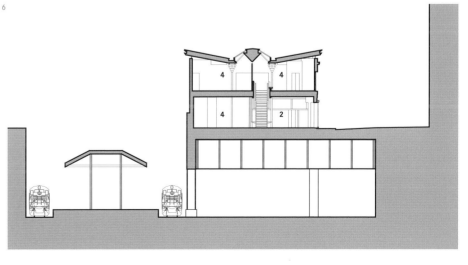

The facade was opened up at ground floor to make a street cafe. A complete vertical slice of facade was removed to form the entrance and a window to the first floor gallery slides aside to allow a permanent crane to hoist objects into the upper gallery. The theme of sliding was continued on the facade where panels of rusticated stone were removed and screens of lead panels and glass blocks were inserted and detailed so that they appear to slide behind the stone (an idea freely lifted from the main facade of Scarpa's work at Castelvecchio).

From the street, a hidden source of sunlight illuminates an upper wall and tempts visitors up the stair. In the upper gallery, as no funding was available to filter light, it was simply admitted. (12) Interestingly, during the first ten years of the gallery's rejuvenation, there were few shows where this proved problematic and exhibition visitors were able to remain in touch with the ever changing Scottish light and at the same time have subliminal views of the city all around through the clerestories and roof-lights. The reception desk and cafe were designed by the office, but the bookshop which was an integral part of the design was never constructed.

In 2003 a change of gallery director led to all gallery windows being blocked up obliterating views of the city. The roof-light was amended to diffuse light so that the upper gallery appears now to be four white walls with diffuse top light, another version of the standard gallery found all over the world. One day these changes might be reversed.

DUNDEE CONTEMPORARY ARTS CENTRE
completed 1999

The experience of the Fruitmarket Gallery led directly to a much larger and more complex project. Dundee Contemporary Arts (DCA) was won in limited competition against major London and Scottish practices. (13–31) To the practice, this project became a 'rite of passage' testing the office both architecturally and managerially at a much larger scale than hitherto.

DCA forms a major part of the re-establishment of the cultural identity of the City of Dundee. It has succeeded in making a public arts venue, which is inclusive and enticing and encourages interaction between the public and many forms of visual arts. To quote the *Sunday Times* (7 March 1999) "It is one of the most satisfying, sublime and stylish public buildings opened in years." It is certainly the most successful arts venue in Scotland in terms of visitor numbers, a

remarkable feat since Dundee is only Scotland's fourth largest city.

The competition was won in July 1996. From the outset, the aim of the scheme was to group all activities, galleries, cinemas, print workshops, shop and research facilities around a central social space and cafe. (19) The point of putting many different functions within one building must surely be the possibility of interaction between them and their respective audiences. The design partially re-uses the brick warehouse of the former Maclean's garage and forms an L-shaped plan on a site which falls three storeys from front to back. The cafe and foyer sit at the internal corner of this L and are, therefore, at the heart of the building, both in plan and section.

Unlike the Fruitmarket Gallery, which could present its activities to the street, this site has a very narrow street frontage between the Roman Catholic Cathedral and a Georgian house occupied by the Clydesdale Bank. In order to draw visitors into the building, the foyer was aligned on South Tay Street opposite so that it might form an extension of that street into the building: the entrance was pulled back and placed below a dramatic canopy and beside the shop (the commercial reality of the arts activities within) to give a breathing space to the street edge and a presence to the approach and reduce the extent of the foyer within. Use was made of continuous roof-lights to cast sunlight and shadow across the internal walls of the foyer, drawing the eye to the furthest part of the plan. It was an essential objective of the

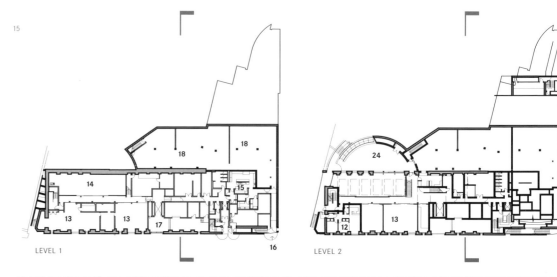

LEVEL 1

LEVEL 2

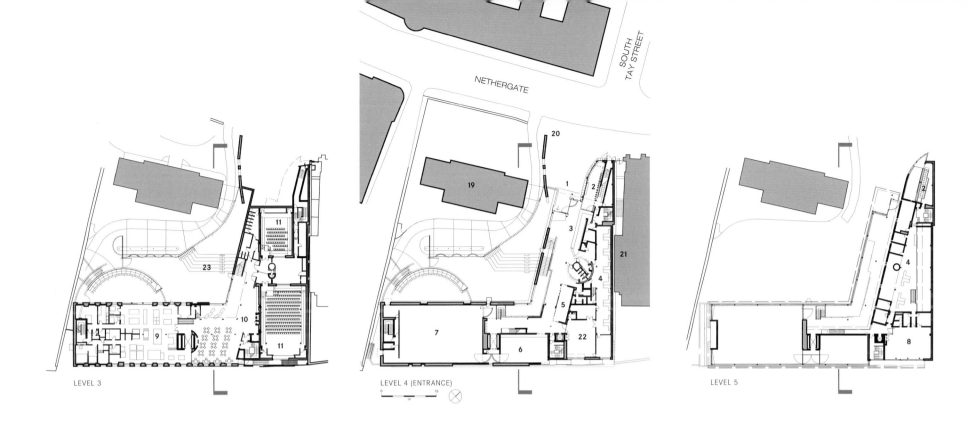

SOUTH TAY STREET

NETHERGATE

LEVEL 3

LEVEL 4 (ENTRANCE)

LEVEL 5

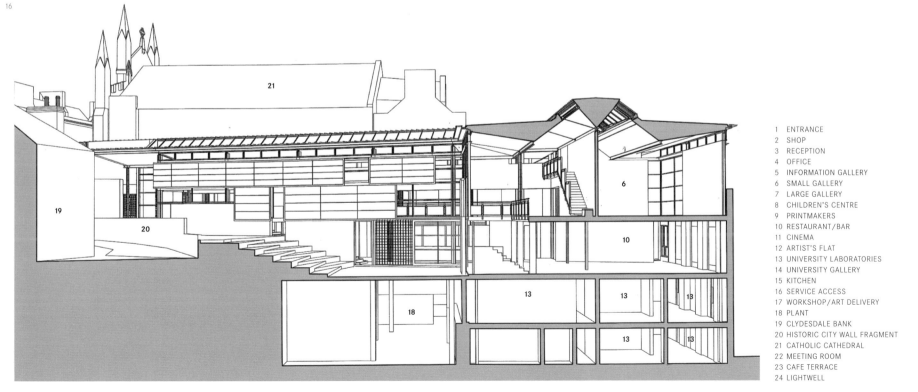

1 ENTRANCE
2 SHOP
3 RECEPTION
4 OFFICE
5 INFORMATION GALLERY
6 SMALL GALLERY
7 LARGE GALLERY
8 CHILDREN'S CENTRE
9 PRINTMAKERS
10 RESTAURANT/BAR
11 CINEMA
12 ARTIST'S FLAT
13 UNIVERSITY LABORATORIES
14 UNIVERSITY GALLERY
15 KITCHEN
16 SERVICE ACCESS
17 WORKSHOP/ART DELIVERY
18 PLANT
19 CLYDESDALE BANK
20 HISTORIC CITY WALL FRAGMENT
21 CATHOLIC CATHEDRAL
22 MEETING ROOM
23 CAFE TERRACE
24 LIGHTWELL

design that everyone should have an instant grasp of the geography of the building; there should be no 'Barbican' problem (the London complex of cultural facilities with a notoriously disorientating circulation system).

The building has particular visual connections between inside and outside or between significant interior spaces. Windows are placed to give glimpses of the Tay Estuary to the south and also between foyer and cafe and galleries and cinemas. The aim was to entice the visitor to see an exhibition or film when they might have come only for a coffee, to draw them in without their feeling the need to specifically come for a show. Even the main cinema has a large window below the screen inviting the audience to be connected to Dundee before and after the film and allow the external world a glimpse of the interior at the same time. (20) This was part of the idea started at the Fruitmarket Gallery, that an arts building should be connected to the city in which it finds itself, unlike, for example, the National Gallery of Scotland on the Mound where one enters a completely detached interior world. All the activities of the Centre are visible from either the internal street or the cafe/bar. This street is supported by the necessary ancillary facilities within a colonnade and behind the scenes by a double-height office space. Adjacent to the cafe and visible from it is the world of the printmakers, placed there as an enticement to participate whilst beneath is the two-storey 'engine room' of the university facilities grouped around a double-height experimental gallery. Both are directly accessed from

the cafe making this the pivotal space in the whole conception.

The language of the building grew out of the idea of inserting the new facilities within the eroded shell of the former brick warehouse. The new building of copper sheet and steel windows slips past the formalised ruin of brickwork in a series of planar elements. (14, 28, 29) These planes then became the language of the new wing beneath a single unifying roof profile.

Internally, the galleries have a family resemblance to the Fruitmarket Gallery, particularly in the section, using toplight and clerestories. Here, however, funds allowed alternative sun shading and blackout blinds and the roof shape conceals full flow and return air-conditioning routes. Although not part of the brick warehouse, the cinemas were clad internally in brick, like those used in the early days of Soviet factory cinema performances. Slots from the cafe bar give glimpses of the film being shown within. A secondary entrance was formed by a staircase from the carpark which climbs up the exterior entering the central level in the cafe, thereby obviating the need for a second entry desk. The cafe bar, (19) successful beyond the wildest of expectations, spills out in summer to an external terrace which catches all the afternoon sun. (28)

Clive Gillman writes:

Over the past 20 years, some of the most exciting and adventurous building projects in the UK have involved the creation of new spaces for the presentation of art. The introduction of the National Lottery in 1994 and the consequent creation of the Arts Lottery Capital Fund led to a boom in the creation of a whole new generation of galleries, theatres, concert halls and production facilities, many of which offered the opportunity for architects to create public projects on a scale that previously would not have been possible outside of the relatively prescribed environments of health and education.

The process of creating these new arts buildings sometimes involved a reappraisal of the syntax of space, using the opportunity of a naive or willing client to re-invent and rewire the habits people employ when seeking comfort or security in the built environment. In many cases this was a useful challenge to the blandly homogenised urban environment in which these buildings were often located, but in other cases it led to the creation of vain and hostile spaces—spaces which did little to counter the worst of what surrounds us. However, getting it right—creating a space which could offer comfort and engagement, while also providing stimulus and delight and a home for effective engagement—is no small feat. This is especially the case when creating buildings for the presentation and production of contemporary culture, an area where effective engagement is always a challenge.

Having been the custodian of the Dundee Contemporary Arts building for the past seven years, I would argue that this building succeeds in a way which I have not encountered elsewhere. The building, which is the home to a diverse range of cultural functions as well as a shop and a bar and restaurant, is an attractive and hospitable environment. It works on a human scale with texture, colour, transparency and pattern linking together the suite of spaces designed for specific technical functions (galleries, cinemas, print studio), while consistently placing people at the centre of its life. When in use (and it is open 14 hours a day, seven days a week) it feels populated and sociable and offers delight (that wonderful concept that dates back to Vitruvius) to many people in many places and in many different ways. And this is one of its greatest successes, a building which is lived in and loved by over 300,000 people each year, located in a city which, when the project was conceived, was considered by many to be a place that did not deserve such ambition.

Over the past 13 years the DCA building has become the city's front room, the place where the rich mix of city life plays out amidst an uncompromising attitude to intelligent culture and the pleasure of socialising. It has been a game-changer for this city because of a successful alliance of vision, sustained quality of experience and a very well designed environment, and deserves to be the model for any city with ambitions for a rich cultural life for its citizens.

Clive Gillman has been Director of DCA since 2005.

31

CENTRE FOR CONTEMPORARY ART AND THE NATURAL WORLD

Poltimore House, near Exeter; unbuilt

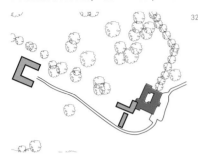

GROUND

FIRST

1 ENTRANCE
2 BOOKSHOP
3 INFORMATION
4 CONFERENCE
5 COURTYARD
6 NEW GALLERY
7 GALLERY

■ DEMOLITIONS
(ACTUAL AND
PROPOSED)

Although the Fruitmarket Gallery and DCA had been radical alterations of formalised ruins of existing buildings, both had been previously robust industrial structures. Not until the project at Poltimore House was the practice able to engage with a listed building of some pre-existing historical complexity. (32–39) Indeed, Poltimore's growth from Tudor, with eighteenth, nineteenth and twentieth century additions and reorientations had massive resonance with the history of Castelvecchio in Verona. Like Scarpa, the wish was not simply to add new architecture or re-inhabit a previous structure, but rather to make quasi-archaeological demolitions so that previous eras might once again be displayed. The diagrams show the growth of the original house and its complete reorientation from a northern to southern approach with the original L-shaped Tudor house and its beautiful stair downgraded to servants' accommodation serving the new eighteenth century wing.

The project involved a number of radical demolitions, as eventually agreed with English Heritage, mostly of the nineteenth century alterations to the house: principally, the demolition of an already fire gutted and ineptly designed ballroom wing, the removal of the west wing and complete removal of a much vandalised grand staircase in the centre of the building. The result was a courtyard building where the original Tudor facade, including its stair tower, would have been once again visible for the first time in 200 years. The courtyard went on to act as a visual heart but also a social organiser for the whole building.

Late sixteenth century

Early nineteenth century

1831

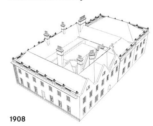
1908

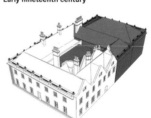
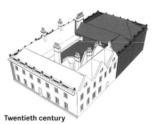

Twentieth century

Proposed

1 THE TUDOR HOUSE
2 THE EIGHTEENTH CENTURY FACADE
3 THE EIGHTEENTH CENTURY FACADE
WITH ROMANTIC LANDSCAPE
4 THE CLASSICAL CONVERSION
OF ONE OF THE TUDOR FACADES
5 THE ENTRANCE FACADE TODAY
6 THE TUDOR STAIRCASE AS WAS
7 THE TUDOR STAIR TODAY
8 THE GRAND STAIRCASE AS WAS
9 THE QUEEN ANNE ROOM

1

2

3

4

5

6

7

8

9

The major proposal was the construction of a new west wing of galleries on the ground and first floor. These would have been large white rooms, characterised by a series of sliding walls on opposite sides of the gallery, one facing the wider landscape, one the courtyard. (36) Three sliding surfaces of white plasterboard, translucent glass and clear glass sat behind each other on opposite elevations so that a variety of wall conditions could be selected by the Gallery Curator. In each gallery, between the four wall conditions available and the two opposite walls, there would have been 16 different combinations of space available. Galleries would look into the courtyard or look out to the landscape or do both, or neither on ground and first floor. The roof of the upper gallery formed a new gable of the same pitch, and adjacent to, the three surviving Tudor gables. So, the exterior would have moved clockwise from century to century; sixteenth century, then eighteenth, nineteenth and finally twenty-first and back to sixteenth again.

In the basement a cafe/restaurant was to be constructed into a lowered garden whilst in the attic space, office accommodation for the building and a caretaker's flat were inserted. The remainder of the house was to have been converted into galleries, bookshop and study centre and education facilities with the major historic room "The Queen Ann Room" (described by Prevsner as "one of the finest rooms in Devon") being restored as a small conference facility. The project failed in its bid to obtain significant lottery funding.

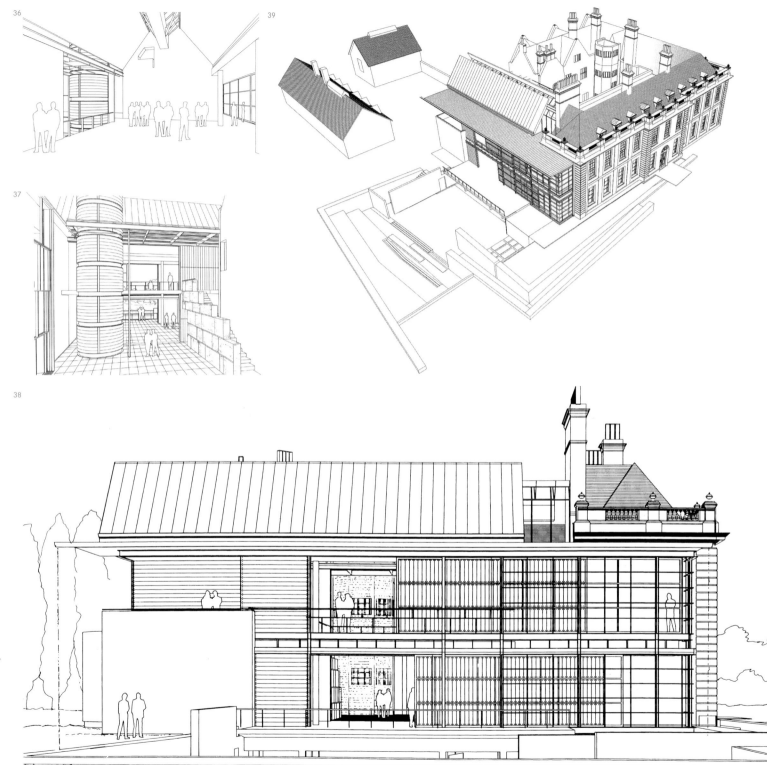

BRANDHORST ART GALLERY
Munich; unbuilt

The architecture of galleries for changing exhibitions can be controversial. Curators will always tend towards gallery neutrality—four white walls and diffuse top light and the maximum of flexibility. Although an understandable approach, the practice's attitude is to try to make a memorable space in itself and to then facilitate many different variations within it. Poltimore House developed the concept of changeable sliding walls and in an invited competition in Munich this idea became a major element of the design. (39–43) The project sat on the edge of a museum park alongside the Alte Pinakothek Gallery which, after the war, had been cleverly rescued, but not restored, by German architect, Dollgast, so that the bomb damage remained evident. (41) Internally, he developed a stunning symmetrical arrangement of two cascade staircases which instantly sets up an obvious circulation diagram. (40) The submitted design adopted the same idea and would have created a chasm of top-lit space through the length of the building which would have extended out as upper lookouts in the parkland landscape at either end. Galleries consisted of two storeys of connected rooms

between this space and the facade. Like Poltimore, the elevation would have been made of sliding panels both glazed and solid, with internal walls clad externally in copper, so that the variations in the galleries on the interior from one show to another would have been reflected in a constantly changing exterior facade. The plan was simple. A series of parallel galleries were to be placed alongside the double staircase chasm. These galleries would have been lit from the kinetic facade and from the top-lit staircase. Balancing the galleries on the other side of the stair were the gallery cafe and a special top-lit gallery where Cy Twombly's 12 painting collection *The Battle of Lepanto* was to have been displayed.

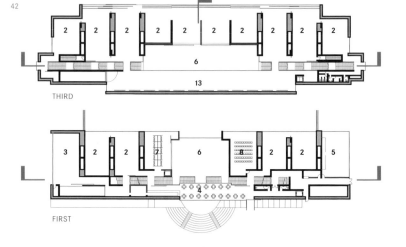

THIRD

FIRST

GROUND

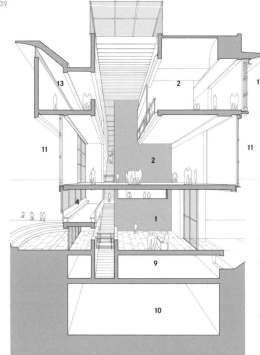

1 ENTRANCE FOYER
2 EXHIBITION SPACE/GALLERY
3 DELIVERY
4 CAFE
5 RESTORATION STUDIO
6 VOID
7 LIBRARY
8 CINEMA/LECTURE THEATRE
9 STAFF
10 PLANT
11 VARIABLE FACADE
12 FIRE ESCAPE
13 TWOMBLY GALLERY

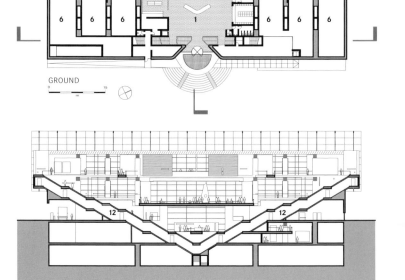

JOHN MUIR BIRTHPLACE TRUST VISITOR CENTRE

Dunbar; completed 2003

The opportunity to create galleries around permanent collections is rare and the project for the John Muir Birthplace (45–50) represents a tiny example.

The John Muir Birthplace Trust bought the house in the High Street of Dunbar, where John Muir, the famous conservationist, visionary and founder of the American National Park System, was born in 1838. Although he lived only two years there, the house had become something of a shrine for the environmental movement, in particular for American tourists. The building had been a laundrette before the Trust purchased it in the 1970s, when it was completely gutted with a small exhibition constructed on ground floor level, a rented flat at first floor level and at the top floor a recreation of what the inside might have been like at the time of Muir's birth.

The project was to make a tiny museum with a permanent exhibition with the idea that the house should be divided into "John Muir in Dunbar" on the ground floor, "John Muir's Travels" above it and finally "John Muir's message to today" on the top floor. To do this it was proposed to remove the entire 1960s interior and create a three-storey free-standing tower within and to exhibit the four walls of the house and its roof as the remaining historic fabric.

Mostly timber in construction, the exhibition and architecture are indivisible. In a way the whole three-storey tower is a giant exhibit, a huge piece of furniture within the four walls of the original house.

Through massive misreporting in the press the project hit enormous numbers of objections (over 4,000 from the American Sierra Club) and front page coverage in the *Los Angeles Times*. Once the sense of the project was widely understood the objectors became supporters and planning permission and funding was achieved. Since the museum opened in August 2003, a record number of visitors have been through the doors and the reaction has been universally favourable.

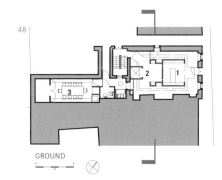

GROUND   FIRST   SECOND

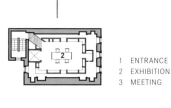

1 ENTRANCE
2 EXHIBITION
3 MEETING

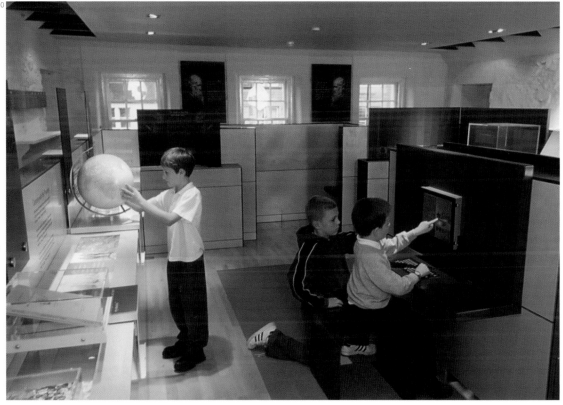

SHERWOOD FOREST VISITOR CENTRE
Nottinghamshire; unbuilt

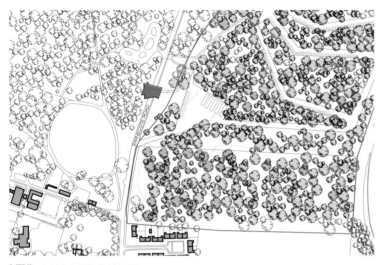

52

CURRENT OPEN GRASSLAND
(PROPOSED CARPARK AND FOREST)

The visitor centre as a type is now ubiquitous thanks to the lottery. Curiously, regardless of location or purpose the brief generally remains the same: exhibition, cafe, shop, auditorium, children's centre, offices or some combination of these. Sherwood Forest today is a tiny fraction of its former extent and notwithstanding a famous oak (reputed to have been Robin Hood's hiding place) is a relatively small forest. It is also a site of special scientific interest. An extremely large Visitor Centre was proposed for a field adjacent to a busy road over which it would have been necessary for visitors to cross to enter the forest. The practice's design rejected the site and put forward instead an 11-storey tower (and consequently a tiny footprint) which would have spanned the road. (51–56) Visitors would have ramped up from the carpark, through the centre and continue onto a treetop aerial walkway in a way that would have made the road itself invisible.

The design develops upwards in a non-repetitive way to conclude in a three-storey high exhibition space and look-out. Clad in Corten steel externally, with its natural rusted patina and lined in timber internally, the tower drew its influences from forest fire look-out towers, tree houses, nearby pit winding gear and gatehouse entrances, allowing the viewer to rise above the trees so that the whole of Nottinghamshire and the distant extent of both the existing and former forest could have been seen.

51

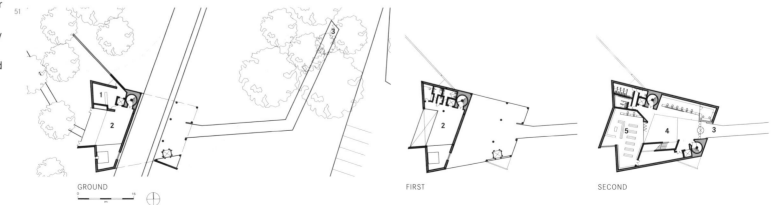

GROUND

FIRST

SECOND

53

54

55

56

1 CYCLE HIRE
2 DISCOVERY EXHIBITION
3 ENTRANCE RAMP
4 ENTRANCE AND TICKETS
5 SHOP
6 AUDITORIUM
7 GALLERY
8 TERRACE
9 ADMINISTRATION
10 CONFERENCE BREAK-OUT
11 SELF-SERVICE DINING
12 RESTAURANT/BAR
13 INTERPRETATION LEVEL
14 ROOF TERRACE

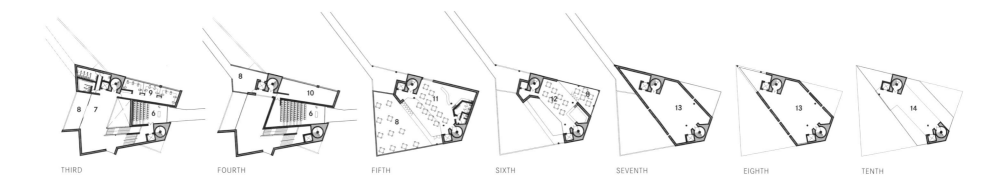

THIRD   FOURTH   FIFTH   SIXTH   SEVENTH   EIGHTH   TENTH

DUNFERMLINE MUSEUM AND GALLERY
projected completion 2016

1 CITY CHAMBERS
2 ABBOT'S HOUSE
3 DUNFERMLINE ABBEY

In 2007 in Dunfermline, the practice won a competition for a new museum and visual arts centre to be sited alongside the world's first Andrew Carnegie Library, Dunfermline, being the great philanthropist's birthplace. (57–65) The site looks over the graveyard to the remains of the celebrated Romanesque Dunfermline Abbey—only the nave survives—which is almost a three quarters scaled version of Durham Cathedral. (57)

Beside this is the restored Mediaeval Abbot's House, (58) run independently as a museum and in the distance the romantic turrets of James C Walker's City Chambers. Like the Fruitmarket Gallery an aspiration in the design was to draw all of these remarkable nearby buildings into the experience of the museum. However, the problem with the site was how to enter what is effectively a land-locked space with a Grade B listed disused bank between it and

the main street, Abbot Street. The practice's solution was to propose hinging a substantial section of the listed bank facade so that it opens in the morning and closes each evening returning the facade to its original state. (59) This would have led to an internal street beside the library and around which all the facilities are organised, exiting at the furthest end into the Abbey graveyard. (61)

1 MAIN ENTRANCE
2 ENTRANCE FROM ABBOT'S HOUSE
3 ENTRANCE ABBEY
4 RECEPTION/TOURIST INFORMATION
5 EXHIBITION/GALLERY
6 EXISTING LIBRARY
7 OFFICES AND RESEARCH
8 STAFF ROOM
9 EVENTS AND LECTURES
10 CAFE
11 KITCHEN
12 PRIVATE DINING
13 TERRACE
14 CHILDREN'S LIBRARY
15 LOCAL HISTORY ARCHIVE ROOM
16 RETAIL

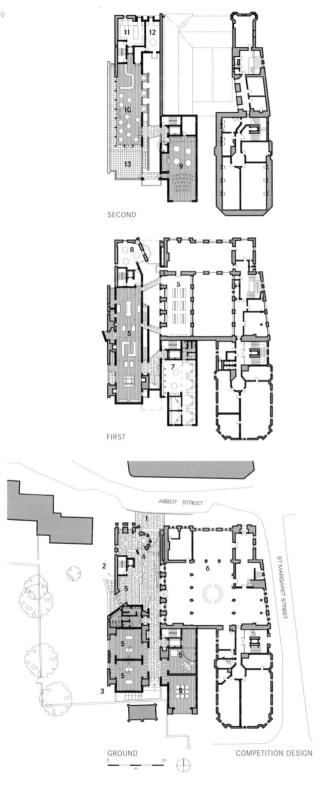

60

SECOND

FIRST

ABBOT STREET

ST MARGARET STREET

GROUND

COMPETITION DESIGN

0   15

m

61

Historic Scotland were the sole objectors to the pivoting facade idea (local Councillors were particularly enthusiastic, one even describing it as Dunfermline's equivalent to the Buckingham Palace daily changing of the guard), but this was enough to veto the progress of the entire project and threaten its funding. Eventually consultations with the Trustees of Abbot's House Museum led to the purchase of the adjacent carpark and this allowed a relocation of the entrance and also the creation of a walled garden alongside the centre. (62, 65) The amended design, which has been able to take advantage of the new entrance otherwise follows the competition design street concept. (64) A local history archive room has been elaborated into an Aalto-like cascade section, a children's library opens direct onto the garden, a cafe sits with terrace facing the abbey and the vertical journey concludes with both the galleries and the museum space at the same level. The route concludes with a connection to two historic rooms in the library, which will be converted into reception room and functions/lecture theatre.

GROUND   REVISED DESIGN

Theatre Buildings

BUILDING AS THEATRE

TOLBOOTH THEATRE
Stirling; completed 2001

Like in the visual arts, the years since the launch of the national lottery have seen a boom in the construction of performance spaces of all types. The practice has completed three theatres: a 200-seat conversion of the grade A listed Tolbooth in the Old Town of Stirling; a 250-seat conversion of a disused grade B listed church in Peebles, now called The Eastgate Theatre; and "Galeri", a new 400-seat arts and business centre in the Welsh speaking town of Caernarfon in North Wales. A fourth project, the restoration and extension of the historic Perth Theatre is, at the time of writing, progressing through a lengthy funding cycle. Stirling Tolbooth was a competition win, but there have been competition disappointments too: the "Byre" Theatre in St Andrews; an Arts Centre in Hamilton; and an invited competition in Augsburg, Bavaria for a 400-seat theatre were all unsuccessful. Frustratingly, a competition for a music centre in the Shetland Isles was won on design but lost to the second placed competitor on the basis of their fee quotation.

All these auditoria are at the smaller end of the scale (with the exception of the unrealised projects for the Queen's Hall and the Sean Connery Filmhouse in Edinburgh which are featured below). A small theatre space, especially one in a relatively small town, needs to work very hard to survive. As well as the usual variety of theatre configurations (from proscenium to theatre in the round) a facility needs to be immensely flexible, both functionally and acoustically, to accommodate music, conference, dance and

even cinema. To go from cinema to music is to go from one extreme of reverberation time to another.

In order to achieve this flexibility, retractable seating is virtually the default. This can have the unfortunate consequence of forcing the plan into the straight jacket of orthogonal 'lecture theatre' style seating. Only recently has curved retractable seating been invented and at considerable extra cost. In these projects the only exception to this was the invited competition design for the theatre in Augsburg, which requested fixed theatre seating for a single theatrical function.

Two projects where orthogonal auditoria were inserted into listed buildings were Stirling Tolbooth, (1–15) and the Eastgate Theatre in Peebles. (16–28)

A tolbooth is a unique Scottish building type. In Stirling it represented a complex of buildings dating from the seventeenth century onwards, combining town council, courthouse and town jail. In 1997 Stirling Council held an invited competition to renovate the building as a music focused arts venue.

The existing building formed a U-shape in plan with the three wings having been built at different times and to different sections. The floor levels were also all different. The only major space, the court house, occupied the central section at first floor with a vaulted undercroft and cells beneath. It sits between the two main parallel streets on the approach to Stirling Castle. As part of the competition design, the practice suggested that the connecting street of Jail Wynd should be closed and pedestrianised and it is here a new entrance was made, utilising one of the vaulted cells as a new entrance.

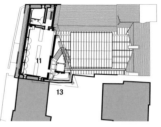

FOURTH

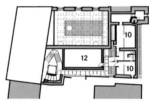

THIRD

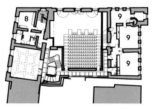

SECOND

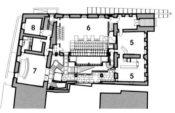

FIRST

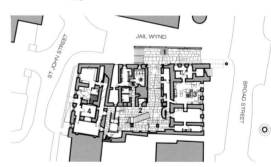

GROUND

1 ENTRANCE
2 RECEPTION
3 KITCHEN
4 RECORDING STUDIO
5 RESTAURANT
6 THEATRE
7 BAR
8 CHANGING
9 MEETING ROOM
10 OFFICES
11 DANCE STUDIO
12 PLANT
13 VIEWING BALCONY

The three public facades of this grade A listed existing building could not be altered and apart from the formation of the new entrance these were simply restored. Similarly the finest rooms within retain their character and can be enjoyed as 'the old Tolbooth'. Special interiors were reserved for special uses within the new building; the old courtroom is reused as the main performance space, the judges' robing room became a grand bar and the old council chamber, a restaurant.

On this very restricted site, all the major interventions necessary to achieve the brief were located in the only empty space available, a narrow courtyard to the rear of the building set tight against a back green belonging to the adjacent residential tenements. Within this space was created the foyer and circulation system of the building rising

vertically to connect six different floor levels. Over-hanging it is a new "backpack" containing the extension to the courtroom which created the auditorium and, above it, the air handling plant. (2) The sloping soffit of the raked seating is expressed to signal to visitors where to find the auditorium. (6–8) The court house originally sat about 100; by rotating the theatre's axis through 90 degrees and adding the new back-pack, this was doubled. The audience sits half in the old building, half in the new. (12) The seats can be retracted and a screen pulled across so that the original volume of the courtroom can be recreated.

In reality, the real foyer is the vertical circulation, which is the main drama of the building. Rising against a backdrop of the new rear glass wall and flooded with light, a stair collects visitors from the foyer and takes them to a sequence of three hanging stairs. (9, 10) These, all different from each other, are suspended from a single pole which connects to an expressed double beam spanning between the original structure and the new exterior wall.

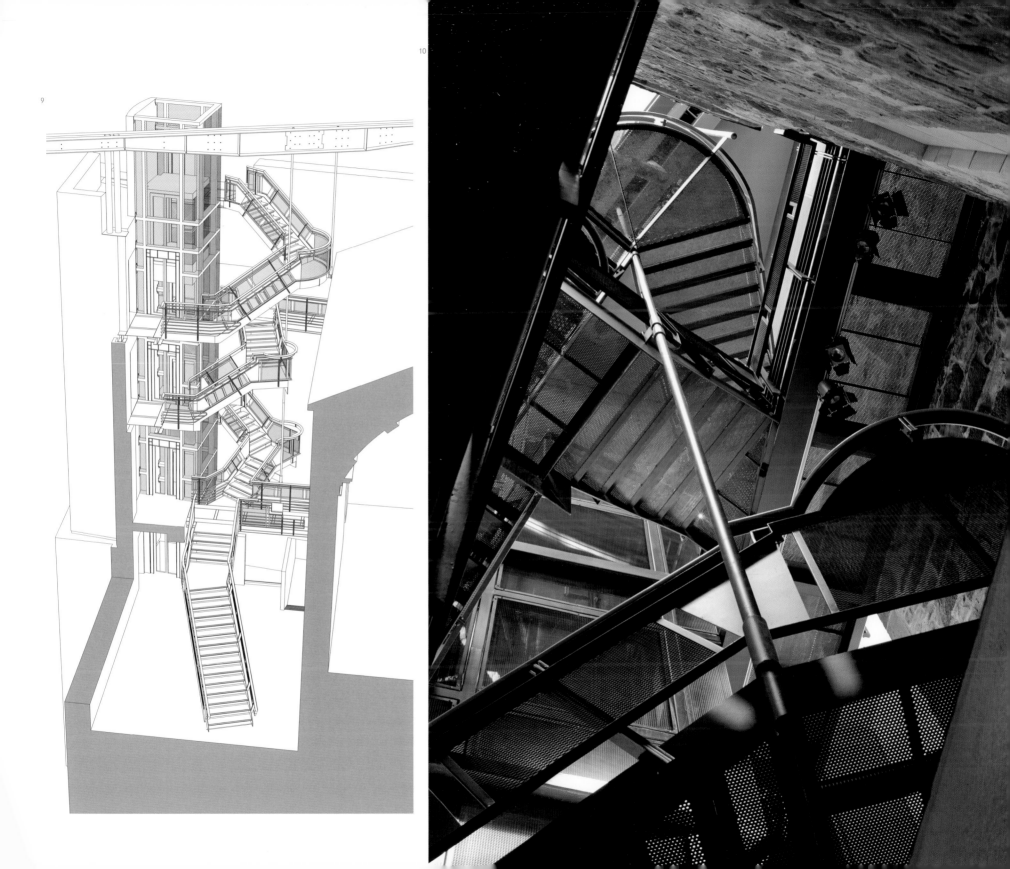

This wall was 'hollowed out' to form stairways at the three levels so that the upward journey around the lift continually oscillates between stairway and staircase, stairway defined by space and staircase as object. Both stair and lift mediate the existing disparate floor levels on either side of the existing building.

At the top is found a dance space in the attic, (11) an external viewing balcony from which to see the whole town and an opportunity to view the clock tower crown at close quarters. (14) A moment of anarchy occurs when a new glass roof meets the original and parts of the original slated roof find themselves in the new interior of the building. (15)

13

14

15

EASTGATE THEATRE

Peebles; completed 2004

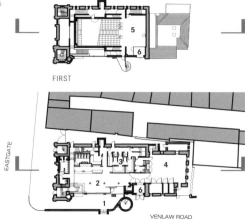

FIRST

EASTGATE

VENLAW ROAD

GROUND

1 ENTRANCE
2 FOYER AND CAFE
3 CHANGING
4 SECONDARY PERFORMANCE
  SPACE/GALLERY/CHANGING
5 AUDITORIUM
6 SCENERY LIFT
7 PLANT

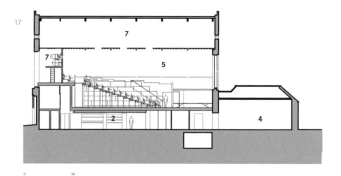

The project for the community theatre for the Borders town of Peebles (population 12,000) was very ambitious. (16–26) Independent of the local authority, it was promoted by an alliance of arts organisations in the town. The brief asked for a 250-seat flexible auditorium which could be used for professional and amateur music, theatre, cinema and flat floor events. This was to be supported by a rehearsal room (doubling as an exhibition space), the necessary ancillary accommodation of green room, changing rooms for artists, a small catering facility and cafe/bar and offices.

The 1871 United Free Church, grade B listed for its townscape value, presented its spire and main front to the town's High Street, but a relatively blank wall to a side street which was used by pedestrians to access the main town carpark. The conversion of a disused church to a non-religious function is a common project, but generally the new function is only grasped when entering, since a church will always register as such through the power of its architectural rhetoric. External signage is usually the only indication of the new use within.

The design was developed in the strong belief that the presence of the theatre should be evident from the exterior rather than simply discovered on the inside of an otherwise unchanged church exterior. A decision was made to create a building with two different faces. The main 'ecclesiastical' Gothic facade remains virtually untouched, but the side elevation is completely removed and substituted by a new glazed entrance elevation revealing the foyer and theatre within.

The existing ground floor level was lowered and a new floor was inserted into the church hall so as to accommodate the theatre, above which appears to be a 'theatre in the roof', the only internal original element of any architectural significance. (25) The theatre is essentially a proscenium arrangement with a flat floor and flexible seating. Fixed side galleries give additional seats and aim to counter the 'lecture hall' problem inherent with retractable seat systems.

In this way, the developing history of the building can be understood, and both eras of its construction can sit in harmonious but contrasting juxtaposition with each other. The former church hall works hard at the ground floor level, primarily as exhibition space flowing direct from the foyer but also as a separate small performance venue and as a mass changing facility for the Christmas Panto and other amateur performances, where large numbers of players are required. Within the foyer, professional changing rooms, box office, office and cafe are all tightly planned.

At the practice's suggestion the street became partially traffic calmed. An external lowered cafe terrace is connected to the foyer by a giant retractable glazed screen and this has become a great success, capturing the passing shoppers between the carpark and High Street. (23) The fire escape from the auditorium was designed as a metal clad tower and glass canopy and sits on the pavement announcing the presence of the theatre on the street.

BYRE THEATRE

St Andrews; unbuilt

Three projects which represent significant urban interventions are two unsuccessful limited competition entries; one for the Byre Theatre in St Andrews and the other for the Hamilton Arts Centre and Library; together with the stalled proposal for a Sir Sean Connery Filmhouse in Edinburgh.

Both of these theatre projects, along with proposals for theatres in Augsburg and Shetland and the completed theatre in Caernarfon, exhibit an obsession with the idea of expressing the semi-circular plan form of the auditorium within the foyer; that is, a building within a building. The idea has a lineage which can be traced through Aalto's early project for a theatre in Jyväskylä (27) all the way back to Palladio's auditorium for the Teatro Olympia, Vicenza, (28) or indeed, Piero della Francesca's 'Ideal City'. (29)

In both St Andrews and Hamilton the foyer would have become by default an internal piece of city as they would have been urban shortcuts, an idea revived later in the project for Perth Theatre (see pages 282–283).

The Byre Theatre in St Andrews had grown, as the name suggested, from a converted farm shed. (30–31) Its front-of-house was located off one of St Andrews' many pedestrian wynds, but with stage access from a larger street to the side. Our proposal turned the auditorium through 90 degrees, conceiving it as an object building with a ground floor colonnade and a surrounding halo of light from a perimeter roof-light. (31) The new foyer naturally flowed between the two front doors and around this new focal point connecting the theatre to both sides of the town.

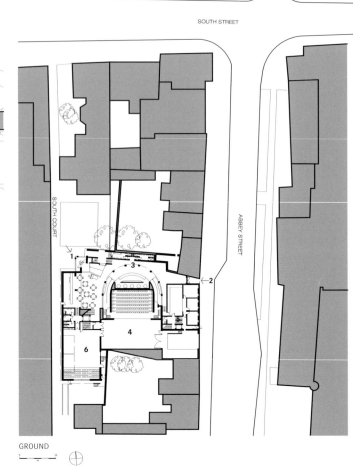

1 MAIN ENTRANCE FROM PEDESTRIAN WYND
2 SECOND ENTRANCE FROM ABBEY STREET
3 FOYER/RECEPTION
4 THEATRE/AUDITORIUM
5 STAGE ENTRANCE/ACCESS
6 STUDIO THEATRE

GROUND

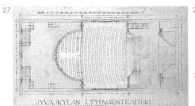

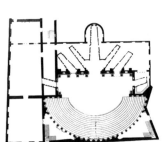

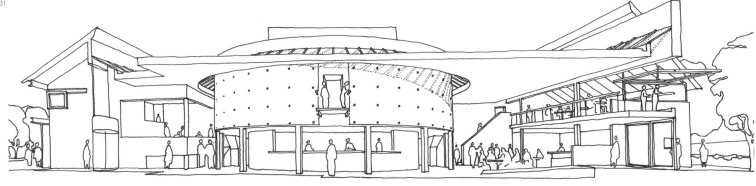

ARTS CENTRE
Hamilton; unbuilt

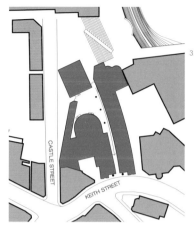

In 1997 the practice was invited to enter a limited competition for a new arts centre in the centre of Hamilton. (32–35) The previous year a competition had been held for the formation of a new town square and this building linked the proposed square to the existing centre of the town. The retention of the grade B listed facade of the former Phoenix Theatre on Keith Street was a requirement of the competition.

The brief was complex, requiring a new town library, a fully functioning theatre space and a series of smaller events rooms and a major new 'town room'. Instead of creating a single complex, the proposal expressed the main functions of library, theatre and town room as distinct buildings linked by a public internal arcade. (34) The theatre used a familiar semi-circular form. The library was to be a long wall of books on three retracting levels of galleries. The town room would have taken the form of a town house or a moot hall on the new square with a large first floor opening onto the square and a cafe at ground floor level.

The restored Phoenix Theatre facade was to have led to an arcade between the library and the theatre and leading to the internal town square created in the atrium between the three main buildings. Light was to be admitted through this arcade, along its entire length, and there would have been views of the activities of the library, in particular the great ascending cascade of library terraces (inspired obviously by Asplund's great cascade of books at the central library in Stockholm) which it was proposed to make a form of town wall against the Clyde Valley landscape. (33) The 'cascade' library concept has since been revisited for an unsuccessful competition project in Hereford and in proposals for the University of East London (see page 186).

1 MAIN ENTRANCE FROM TOWN SQUARE
2 SECONDARY ENTRANCE
3 'TOWN ROOM'
4 LIBRARY
5 THEATRE
6 INTERNAL SQUARE
7 LISTED PHOENIX THEATRE FACADE

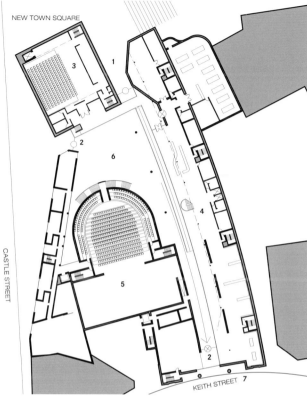

FIRST

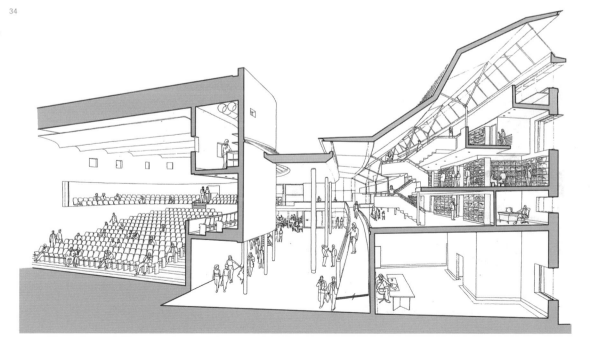

THEATRE
Augsburg, Bavaria; unbuilt

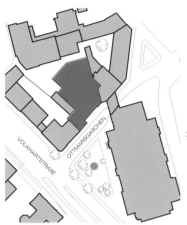

The practice was invited to participate in a limited competition in the Bavarian town of Augsburg. (37–39) The brief was unusual; a fixed seat proscenium theatre with no flexibility and no alternative functions! The site was a small gap site alongside the surprisingly large existing Neo-Classical opera house (sic: this in a city the size of Dundee). Back stage had already been designed for competitors to incorporate so that it linked through to the back stage of the opera. An onion domed church spire looked down on the site. (37)

Once again, the auditoria was expressed as a semi-circular building wrapped by the foyer and viewed through a mostly glazed facade from the street. The foyer was extended to be a vertical event as a cascade of steps (inspired by those found leading to the chapter house at Wells Cathedral) (36) and this would have continued up the side of the auditorium giving access to all levels and all other public facilities. A sight line organised to be viewed when climbing the stairs focused on the onion dome through a circular oculus roof-light.

1 MAIN ENTRANCE
2 FOYER / RECEPTION
3 THEATRE / AUDITORIUM

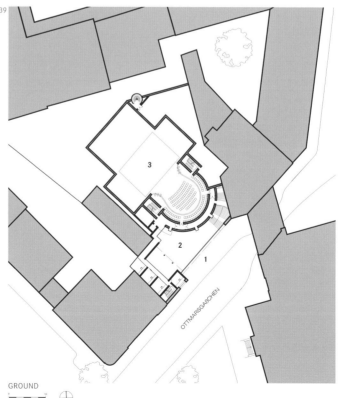

GROUND

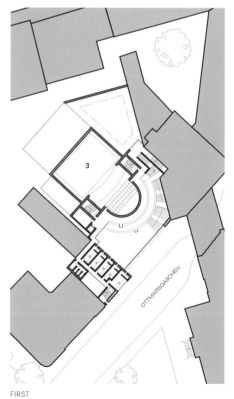

FIRST

MUSIC CENTRE
Shetland Isles; unbuilt

From the centre of Europe, to the very fringe, where the practice was invited to compete for a music theatre in Lerwick in the Shetland Isles. (41–44) The site alongside the recently completed museum was prominent from the water and from the ferry, but hidden from the centre of Lerwick. To ensure that the building would become a destination, not just for locals but for visitors too, it was thought important for it to be a highly distinctive and recognisable shape, but one which had some resonance with the windswept landscape. Although the imagery of an upturned boat has been somewhat hijacked by Miralles' self-confessed inspiration for the Scottish Parliament, on this occasion it was considered that this would be a highly appropriate starting point for creating a distinctive shaped building. There are many in the Shetland landscape. (40) The proposed building would have had a bright green copper roof pulled down low against the wind and sitting above a local landscape of dry-stone walls taking their cue from the many examples on the islands. This single form would have covered both theatres and tapered in plan and section towards the two respective auditoria stages.

The entrance would have been immediately obvious on approach and the building was to become a route from the land to the water. The two main public spaces of theatre/cinema and cinema were to be placed back to back sharing a projection suite. The boat-like structure seen first as a copper object from outside would reveal itself as an all-encompassing double-walled timber structure from the inside. From the central foyer the revelation of the main theatre space would be as if a building were standing within this overall timber structure, like a number of other theatre designs, already mentioned. A cafe would have sat at first floor level enjoying views of the harbour and a window behind the stage of the main auditorium would focus on the ferry terminal on the opposite side of the bay. (41) Although the jury placed this design first, the bid was also a fee competition and the practice was undercut by a competitor to finish overall in second place.

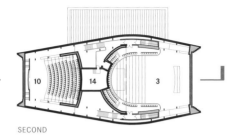

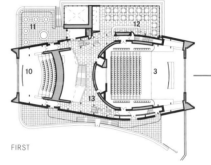

43

SECOND

FIRST

1 ENTRANCE
2 FOYER/RECEPTION
3 MAIN AUDITORIUM
4 OFFICE/ADMINISTRATION
5 REHEARSAL STUDIO
6 SERVICE YARD
7 PLANT
8 KITCHEN/STORES
9 CHANGING
10 CINEMA
11 ROOF TERRACE
12 CAFE
13 FIRST FLOOR FOYER
14 PROJECTION ROOM

GROUND

SEAN CONNERY FILMHOUSE
Edinburgh; unbuilt

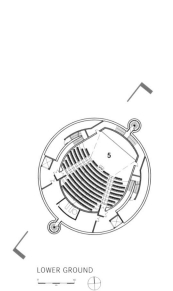

1   SHERATON HOTEL
2   USHER HALL

Two larger projects in Edinburgh both progressed considerably further than their original feasibility briefs; and both remain in limbo.

The idea of a new home for both the Filmhouse, Edinburgh's premier art-house cinema, sitting currently uncomfortably in a converted church, and the Film Festival, the world's longest running Film Festival, was the brainchild of Scottish filmmaker Murray Grigor. (45-49) His vision for what he coined a 'kineopolis' would rightly put film on the same urban footing as the other arts in the city. Just as painting has the National Gallery and the Royal Scottish Academy, music the Usher Hall, artefacts the Royal Scottish Museum, film would also have its equivalent temple in the city. The first proposal was presented to the public at the conclusion of the 2004 International Film Festival and received much publicity. (45)

The ambitious project included cafe, restaurant, filmhouse and festival offices, a museum and six auditoria. The design has been exhibited at the Venice Biennale in 2004 but later the brief was expanded and the building redesigned to

include a 600 seat festival auditorium, a museum and offices for film production companies. The design has a circular plan in a great historical tradition of circular buildings sitting in open spaces—Bramante's Tempietto in Rome or the Oxford Radcliffe Camera being the most obvious examples. (46) Following on from the design for the cinema at Dundee Contemporary Arts, most of the auditoria had the facility to connect with the outside world before and after a film through a variety of hinged and sliding panels giving the exterior a constantly kinetic quality and anchoring the experience of seeing a film into that of being in Edinburgh. In addition, vertical circulation would have been visible on the exterior and giant external cinema screens advertising trailers of films during both day and night. This was to have been a building with a single ever changing elevation.

The site of Festival Square was controversial. The square master planned by Sir Terry Farrell, but surrounded by undistinguished offices and the exceptionally mundane Sheraton Hotel facade, despite expensive re-landscaping, has been an urban design failure.

A Filmhouse operating from mid-morning to late night, is one of the few cultural buildings that could have populated this otherwise deserted place.

Sir Sean Connery, born half a mile away, and undoubtedly the most high profile Scottish personality on the world stage, enthusiastically agreed

to allow his name be attached to the project. Fundraisers immediately declared that, while Sir Sean remained with us, professional fundraising, particularly in the United States, would have been an exceptionally easy task. But, neither the Filmhouse nor the City Council has ever risen to the challenge.

1   FOYER
2   CAFE
3   SHOP
4   BOX OFFICE
5   300 SEAT AUDITORIUM
6   150 SEAT AUDITORIUM
7   75 SEAT AUDITORIUM
8   600 SEAT AUDITORIUM
9   FUNCTIONS
10 OFFICES
11 FILM PRODUCTION COMPANIES
12 RESTAURANT AND TERRACE
13 SHERATON HOTEL

48

LOWER GROUND

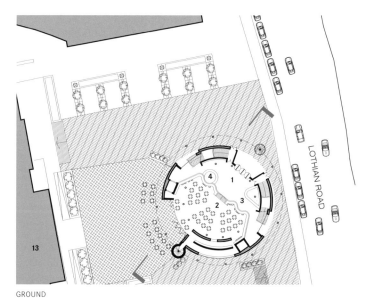

GROUND

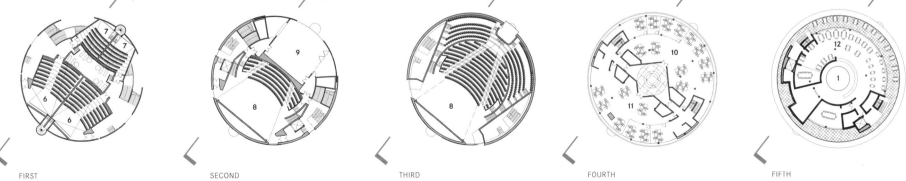

FIRST

SECOND

THIRD

FOURTH

FIFTH

NEW QUEEN'S HALL

Edinburgh; unbuilt

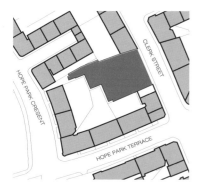

The Usher Hall provides Edinburgh with a 2,500 seat concert venue but the City lacks a 1,200 seat music venue, the equivalent of the City Hall in Glasgow. In the 1970s a disused church dating from 1840 was pressed into service as a concert hall and as the rehearsal base for the internationally renowned Scottish Chamber Orchestra. The Queen's Hall auditorium can seat a maximum of 800 but 200 of these seats have very restricted views and if the orchestra is joined by the choir many further seats have to be removed reducing this number to something closer to 500. (50–54) Foyer, circulation, toilets and backstage are all seriously overcrowded.

The brief for a new hall was to place, on the same site, an auditorium of 1,200 seats (capable of being reduced in number and converted for flat floor events), to increase reverberation time, to double the size of the foyer, to vastly improve the backstage facilities while preserving the service entry from the rear, and also to make the building more easily accessible from the street.

The design proposed the demolition of the majority of the building with the exception of the steeple and pedimented facade to Clerk Street. The argument was successfully advanced that, for those nostalgic for the 1840 listed church interior, there is an almost identical design of the same vintage still in use as a church in the centre of the New Town's Bellevue Terrace. The new auditorium not only would have had more seats but was also substantially larger in volume per person to improve the acoustic performance. This would have been achieved by occupying the entire width of the site, by excavation and by raising the height of the roof. In addition, the auditorium was to be turned through 180 degrees so that the apse and the staircases currently at the rear of the church and forming an integral part of the plan of the entrance would have become the back drop to the stage of the new concert hall. To further enhance this marriage of new and old a semi-oculus roof window was proposed so that the presence of the spire, floodlit at night, would have been visible from within the auditorium during performances. (54) Both the ceiling and the auditorium floor were intended to be adjustable to change the format, character and scale of the space for more intimate events. The space underneath the raked auditorium was to be developed as a new foyer wrapped around the performance space and flowing into

1   ENTRANCE
2   FOYER
3   AUDITORIUM
4   CAFE
5   GARDEN
6   BACKSTAGE FACILITIES
7   SERVICE ENTRANCE
8   BOX OFFICE

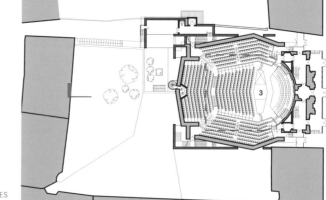

FIRST

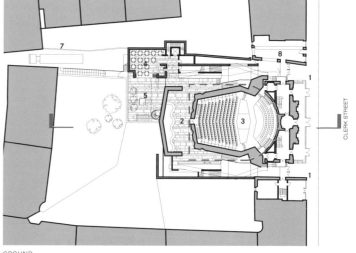

GROUND

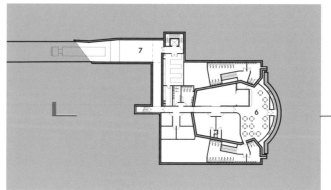

LOWER GROUND

the area currently occupied by the existing bar, itself a conversion of the former church hall. So extensive was the space which would have been released by this plan, it was felt possible to develop a small garden at the centre of this new foyer. Underneath both the foyer and the auditorium was to be a complete new floor of backstage facilities accessed directly by a ramp from the rear service lane and allowing the stage to be serviced independently of the auditorium.

The search for a 'perfect' site for a new 1,200 seat concert hall continues while this very feasible proposal languishes. The Queen's Hall itself continues to struggle with its operational and financial difficulties.

54

53

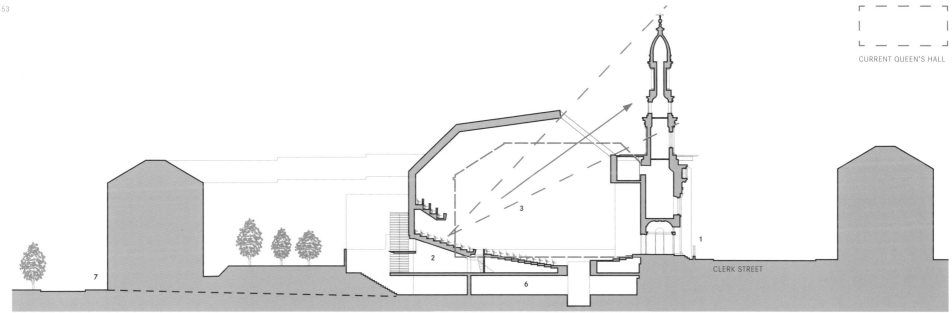

CURRENT QUEEN'S HALL

CLERK STREET

THEATRE

Perth; projected completion 2014

1 PERTH THEATRE CONCERT HALL

Another project working with a listed building is the restoration and redevelopment of Perth Theatre's historic category B listed Edwardian auditorium. Perth Theatre is one of Scotland's oldest repertory theatres. (55–59) The building itself was constructed in 1900 but it is part of a much longer history of theatre in Perth dating back to 1589. The need to repair and restore the theatre proved the catalyst for a more ambitious plan to address not only all the accessibility and practical needs of a theatre in the twenty first century but also to provide for the aspirations of a producing company by creating new performance, social and workshop spaces.

The existing theatre is an elegant 450 seat Edwardian proscenium theatre with a horseshoe plan but is hidden in the backland behind the High Street. Its entrance is from a narrow doorway and a flight of stairs to the first floor. To the rear a studio space, workshops and dressing rooms had been built in the 1980s but these had limited connections to the rest of the building. Perth's new concert hall, which is also run by the client team, is nearby on Mill street to the rear of the theatre.

The design proposes the demolition of all the additions built to the east of the original theatre and the creation of a new triple-height foyer space which links all levels of the existing and new facilities and contains the bar, restaurant, box office and all social facilities.

The new studio theatre is located at first floor level above the Mill Street entrance. Its reflective metal and glass exterior will be lit to form the principal facade of the new theatre. The intention is that this becomes the main facade while preserving the High Street entrance. A third new entrance is formed from the adjacent Cutlog Vennel. (59) In this way, it is hoped that the foyer will become a genuine 'shortcut' urban route.

Three new workshop/performance rooms are arranged over three floors to the east of the foyer and beneath the studio. These provide multi-purpose rooms for rehearsal and for the thriving youth theatre and community programme.

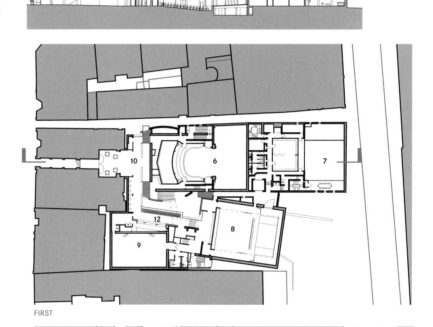

56

FIRST

55

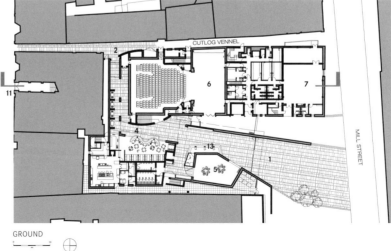

GROUND

1   MAIN ENTRANCE
2   SECOND ENTRANCE
3   FOYER
4   RESTAURANT/BAR
5   YOUTH THEATRE/
    COMMUNITY ROOM
6   EXISTING AUDITORIUM
7   BACK OF HOUSE
8   STUDIO THEATRE
9   YOUTH THEATRE
10 FIRST FLOOR FOYER
11 ENTRANCE FROM HIGH STREET
12 BAR
13 BOX OFFICE

57

59

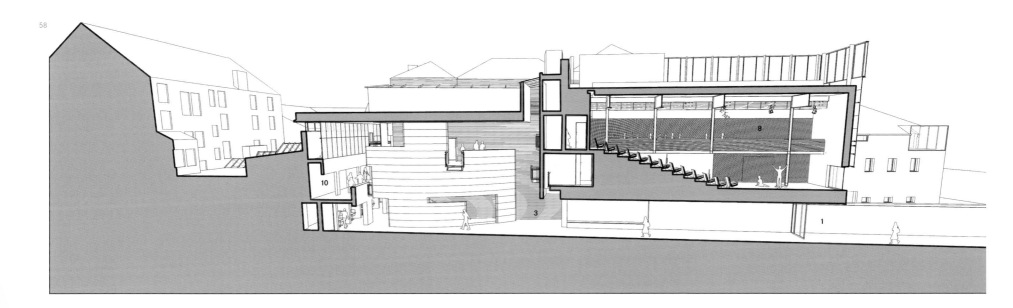

58

GALERI THEATRE
Caernarfon; completed 2005

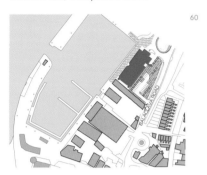

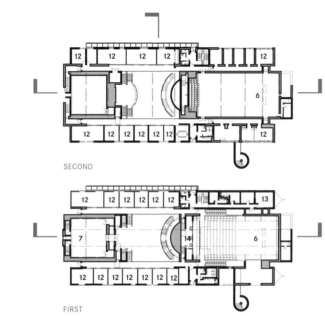

SECOND

FIRST

1 MAIN ENTRANCE
2 SECOND ENTRANCE
3 RECEPTION
4 FOYER/BAR
5 EXHIBITION
6 AUDITORIUM
7 REHEARSAL STUDIO
8 CAFE
9 ADMINISTRATION
10 BACKSTAGE
11 VICTORIA DOCK
12 CREATIVE ENTERPRISE/
   OFFICE/REHEARSAL
13 CHANGING
14 CONTROL ROOM
15 SOUND REFLECTOR/
   CINEMA SCREEN

The practice's only completed
'new build' theatre is the Creative
Enterprise Centre or "Galeri" in
Caernarfon, North Wales. (60–72) This
was a project which arose from the
resurgence in this area of the creative
industries and the Welsh language,
together with a perception of a need
for a contemporary, flexible and
medium sized performance space in
the town. The building is effectively
a hybrid between theatre/rehearsal
spaces and 30 small office spaces
aimed at young creative Welsh-
speaking companies. The essence
of the design idea was that whilst
theatres generally spring to life in the
evenings, the office life of the building
is a daytime activity, and that putting
these two functions together, both
of which involve creative people, will
ensure a building that has an intensity
of use all day and into the evening.
At the heart of the building must be
the idea of communication between
those working there, both amongst
themselves and between themselves
and visitors.

The diagram was inspired by its
location on the dock. Its warehouse-
like construction, takes the form
of three parallel sheds, a central
shed containing the large volumes,
requiring large span structures,
flanked on either side by small or
more domestic scaled structural

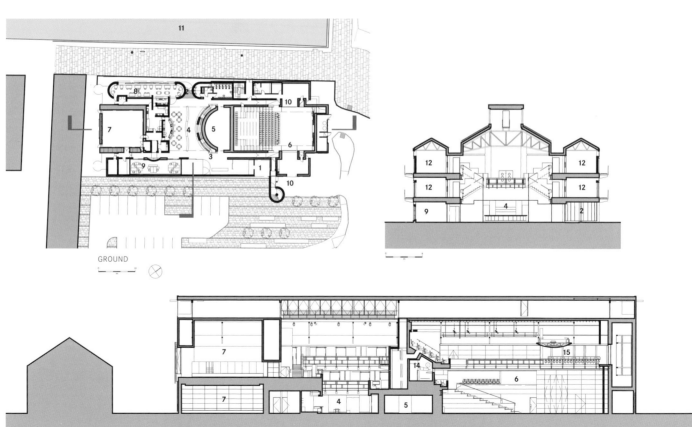

GROUND

sheds of individual office rooms. The
inner shed has the theatre at one
end and two rehearsal rooms one on
top of the other at the other, with a
large atrium foyer space at the centre
which links all the spaces and houses
the bar.

The objective of the design has
been to attempt to ensure that all the
office spaces are located on the first
and second floors and give directly
onto walkways in this atrium space so
that their activities and their presence
are visible to everybody entering the
building. (65) There are no corridors.
The idea of this space is further
strengthened with the presence of
both theatre on one side and the
rehearsal room on the other side
as curved objects inserted into the
orthogonal warehouse shape of
the building. (70–72)

The main theatre seats 400 and
has three tiers with the stalls
retractable for flat floor events, but
with side galleries ensuring a sense
of gathering. The auditorium can
be converted for cinema, conference,
theatre and music use and internal
wall curtains and drapes in the roof
vary the acoustic accordingly. A convex
sound reflector was invented and this
is suspended over an orchestra, but
can be hoisted vertically and reversed
to reveal a fully stretched cinema
screen on its rear face.

The exterior of the building is muted, formed of a steel frame and western red cedar boarding. (63) This forms a natural weathered grey patina over the years and acts as a rain screen to the building. The interior of the building is filled with coloured polished plasterwork as a contrast to the relatively monochrome exterior.

At the time of writing, designs are progressing to add more lettable offices and a new 100 seat cinema.

63

Gwyn Roberts writes:

The artistic vision for Galeri was of a centre that would be alive with professional and community activities put together through creative partnerships with a range of organisations and individuals. It was to be a theatre but also, in order to ensure financial and creative sustainability, a hub for the arts and the creative industries in northwest Wales. Rentable studio and meeting spaces were additional in-built revenue generators as was the cafe and bar areas. The latter also being a vital element in the perception of Galeri as an informal social space open to all. As Richard Murphy keeps on reminding me whenever we meet, it was an unusual brief to which he responded with an appropriately elegant architectural solution. I am glad to admit that he was right about that. We had already been through a lengthy period of looking at various design options, with a variety of other architects, before Richard came on board, and none seemed to get it quite right. I have still got Richard's initial designs for Galeri because those few lines on paper, for the first time, put physical form to a concept that I had been carrying around in my head for several years.

The design just felt right from the start and basing an opinion on instinct is as good as anything else.

Having said that, I really don't know why I selected him to do the job in the first place. His was one of six architectural practices on a shortlist that had been whittled down from around 50 initial applications. All the other practices came to the interview with pre-prepared drawings of the proposed building and some well defined ideas about the form and functionality of the Centre. Richard ambled in without so much as a newspaper under his arm and proceeded to engage us in an extremely well informed discussion—on his part—around general town planning principles and whether we had really considered all our options regarding the most appropriate location for Galeri in Caernarfon.

In the event, it was the right location, but I'm glad that we had the discussion and I'm glad that he became an integral part of that discussion and subsequent development. His commitment to our project, and the commitment of all the staff that we worked with from Richard Murphy Architects, went above and beyond the call of duty, and the building he created is a joy to work and perform in and a pleasure to visit.

Since the original building opened in 2005, we have employed Richard Murphy Architects to successfully extend our theatre space in 2010 and we are currently employing them to design a 1,500 square metres extension to Galeri. I think it must mean that we enjoy working with them.

Gwyn Roberts is Chief Executive of Galeri Caernarfon.

70

72

71

A BUILDER'S TALE
Steve Evans

Almost 20 years ago, a slightly forlorn Richard Murphy sat at our dining table. The sea was proving unboatworthy and an unappreciated and impatient architect was considering his options.

My own business, Inscape Joinery began its life in the Orwellian dawn of 1984. There was no plan, no vision... not even a little white van. It was just a case of doing something which seemed to come naturally to me, something I always felt I had an affinity for. My mother once told me, many years ago, that I was never happier than when I had a mash hammer in my hand. She could have been right, mothers usually are.

Having graduated from Edinburgh University with an MA in Sociology, my gravitation back to the building trade was in part driven by the need to supplement an inadequate student income. The Thatcher years had eroded the value of the student grant, even for a mature student and I started helping out a plumbing and heating engineer in Edinburgh. From this association, Inscape Plumbing and Joinery was established which quite quickly became Inscape Joinery as I set out alone; a stranger in a strange city.

The business grew modestly but organically. Inscape took on its first employee, Donald McLean Logan, and we acquired our first workshop in the form of Donald's oversized, but amply equipped garage. On a personal level, my family was also growing as my wife Gail, gave birth to our first child, Jason and the small flat where we lived in Maryfield suddenly seemed insufficient. All of this led to my first meeting with Richard Murphy.

Before we could sell the flat, it was necessary to have the Edinburgh Council Building Department grant a retrospective building warrant. I had demolished an internal wall in the flat with my trusty mash hammer and you are meant to ask their permission to do that. Donald had an architect producing designs for his Colony House and, by coincidence, the architect was a neighbour of mine in Maryfield. So it was then that Richard Murphy, with his student apostle, tenant and future junior partner at Richard Murphy Architects, came around to do the most mundane of architectural tasks. He and Graeme Montgommery surveyed the flat and put forward the application for a retrospective building warrant.

At the same time, Inscape was working for Marion Blythman, doing some minor internal work in her flat in Zetland Place in Edinburgh. Marion had plans to move back into her former home on Inverleith Row which had been rented since the passing of her husband some years before. She wanted the house upgraded and had a vision of creating a garden room to improve her contact with a beautiful Japanese styled garden. One day, she asked me if I knew an architect "with a bit of imagination". I told her that I thought I did and apparently added, "He's a bit quirky like you, I think you'll get on well."

Richard designed the ground-breaking and multi award winning 'Garden Room' extension for Marion and curiously he convinced her to build it on the first floor level. He asked me if Inscape would like to build it, which we did. So it began and 21 years later in a sense, we are still building it.

Inverleith Gardens was to be our first serious building project, it was full of shadow gaps, expressed steelwork and trademark disappearing corners. The ground rules from the very beginning made the unusual the norm and, as a result we never saw a problem in a lateral building concept. We tried to pride ourselves on the premise that we wouldn't make a problem out of an idea and we adopted the Lennonesque motto, "There are no problems, only solutions." The work of Richard Murphy Architects has tested this intent to its limit and beyond. Often technically very difficult and complex, every project also has the constraints of time and budget, but always with the insistence of quality. Against this, a business has to make profit to be viable. These would be the most testing of circumstances for any kind of relationship and yet the collaboration between Inscape Joinery and Richard Murphy has lasted over the course of these years with only the occasional and very minor hiccup. This may surprise some, but Richard Murphy is not a difficult man to deal with and although his dedication to his special skill is well known, he is not so blindly led by self belief that he fails to see the sometimes conflicting needs of the builder or the client.

Some architects will insist that the drawings are religiously adhered to, even if the detail sometimes needs to be inferred. In Richard's case, he will work closely with the builder and is aware of the constraints of budget that we face. Jobs are often competitively tendered and costs are cut to the bone, mistakes on either side can ruin a budget, but mistakes are made from time to time. A detail can sometimes be misinterpreted, drawings cannot map every facet of a job and very occasionally, with the best intention, what is built isn't exactly what was intended. In all these circumstances, Richard Murphy has never shown himself to be so precious as to demand his version of things to the exclusion of all else. There is a genuine professional relationship and respect in the process and for our part we also try to be proactive in that process. If we think a detail may be improved or that something won't work or has been wrongly specified, we try to pin that down before it's been built. We have often been told by young architects in the practice that there is a sense of relief when they know we are to be the builders for those very reasons. A successful project is in everybody's interest, and, for us, successful does not just mean profitable.

Sitting around the dinner table that night, Gail and I tried to offer Richard some advice. The building trade is a tough place for self employed architects, no less than self employed builders. We had eeked out a living over the first few years and tried to build up a loyal client base. Richard wasn't as patient, he wanted to move quicker, but patience and resolve was all we could offer. I seem to remember telling him to "be thorough" and not to give "them" the excuse. 21 years later and the

task is no easier, the next job has to be won, critics have to be answered, wages and bills have to be paid. Architectural ability alone is not enough. There are so many other skills required in business, but where the business focuses on an individual's gift, then the demand and the pressure is more intense and it is the way of things in such a jealously practiced discipline, that success tends to be measured against failure. In this context, 21 years of practice is no easy achievement. The body of work produced, as well as dozens of new young architects given the confidence and experience to step out into architectural practice on their own, needs to be admired and applauded.

All these years later, and with so many projects between and behind us, the next prospective RMA project is still as exciting and still has the same sense of anticipation as the others had. As I write, we have just handed over the completed second extension and renovation of Ivy Bank House in Dirleton for RMA and the sense of having achieved something special is again present in this project. We work for many of the best architects in this city and it is genuinely an honour to be sought out by them, but an RMA project often has that extra spark to it... an excitement. Some tiny piece of elegant simplicity in the design, maybe a touch of genius, who knows, but the finished result can be breathtaking. For me as the builder of these little crafted edifices, they are part of my claim to the future, my small piece of immortality. I imagine my great-grandchildren visiting them and telling their children who it was that built them. What more could a man want than a claim to the future? I have Richard to thank for that.

Steve Evans is the Managing Director of Inscape Joinery. Inscape have constructed over 40 of the practice's projects as well as the Breakfast Mission, Richard Murphy Architects' office since 2001. Inscape are currently building Richard Murphy's new house (see pages 45–47).

1 BLYTHEMAN HOUSE, EDINBURGH (SEE PAGES 16–17)
2 FRANCIS HOUSE, EDINBURGH (SEE PAGES 18–19)
3 PALMER HOUSE, EDINBURGH (SEE PAGES 20–21)
4 GOUGH/DENT HOUSE, EDINBURGH
5 MORRISON/GAIT HOUSE, DIRLETON (SEE PAGES 22–23)
6 LUDLAM HOUSE, EDINBURGH
7 KNOX HOUSE, EDINBURGH (SEE PAGES 36–37)
8 FINEGAN HOUSE 1, EDINBURGH (SEE PAGE 37)
9 STRATHEARN ROAD, EDINBURGH
10 COLBURN HOUSES 1 AND 2 (SEE PAGES 31–34)
11 HARRISON HOUSE, EDINBURGH (SEE PAGES 24–25)
12 BAR AT DUNDEE CONTEMPORARY
   ARTS CENTRE (SEE PAGES 246–251)
13 THE BREAKFAST MISSION, EDINBURGH

    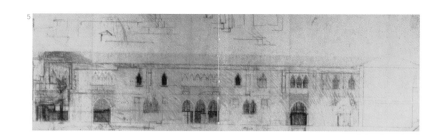

POSTSCRIPT; RICHARD MURPHY

In 2001 I contributed to our previous publication *Richard Murphy Architects, Ten Years of Practice* with a postscript called "a moment of introspection". Re-reading this over a decade later, I can see that although the scope, geographical spread, size and number of projects have all increased dramatically in that period, our core objectives have remained virtually unchanged. Indeed, the title of this publication, *Architecture of Its Time and Place* is found within that essay. It is a title I give to lectures about our work and so it seemed appropriate that it should also be the title for this book.

In a way, the title is explained by our location between two opposite points of view. Ten years ago I acknowledged, without apology, that there was little in our work that might be called avant-garde and that remains the case. We do not subscribe to the high octane world of the international 'starchitects' depositing iconic (the very word makes me wince) buildings in different cultures around the world, which whilst having some superficial photo-journalistic value, rarely in my opinion repay close inspection. These buildings and the reputations of the architects who produce them seem to be sustained by a small coterie of architectural journalists whose 'theories' I find usually amount to little more than fashion statements. On a visit to our office the celebrated Australian architect Glen Murcutt told me in a wonderful reference to a famous Monty Python sketch that he describes this world as the Ministry for Silly Buildings. Perhaps we are considered old fashioned, but we try to make buildings which are predominantly rooted to the place in which they are located, rather than being about the architect who has made them.

The other position is represented by the society in which we are working, namely Edinburgh in particular, but also elsewhere in the UK. To be frank, this is a city where many citizens wish that the modern era had never occurred. Modern architecture, it seems to be universally agreed, has spoilt the view. There is a particular British antipathy towards contemporary architecture, in extremis in Edinburgh with its understandably cherished and jealously guarded status as a World Heritage Site. But even historic cities need to be constantly renewing themselves otherwise, as a well-known former Edinburgh Civic Trust secretary once said "Edinburgh will shortly be finished." He meant of course 'complete' whereas in reality 'dead' would have been a more appropriate interpretation. On countless occasions we have had to explain patiently to planning officers, buildings inspectors from Historic Scotland, residents' associations and irate neighbours that it is essential for the health of our culture that we make buildings which are recognisably of today so that in the future there will be some history from this era to preserve. Rooting recognisably new buildings into old places, or into particular landscapes, contributing towards, rather than damaging, their location, continuing, rather than fossilising, the history of a place have always been our objectives. We call it architecture of its time and place.

Whilst we are fascinated by many architects, both historic and contemporary, my academic studies of the works of Carlo Scarpa (1906–1978) have of course had a huge influence on the way we have worked with existing buildings. Scarpa's work is, in my opinion, a built interpretation of the theories of Morris and his manifesto for the Society for the Protection of Ancient Buildings which itself was grounded in the writings of Ruskin. Right from the beginning we have always had the objective of making the distinction between new and old absolutely clear so there is no ambiguity and indeed so that the two elements can enjoy their mutual juxtaposition and continue to tell a story about the development of a building. Like Scarpa, we also think of partial demolition as part of a creative process, often so that previous eras of construction can be examined in an archaeological way as well as given clarity.

The early house extensions are treated as additions to elements of the house, parts of which have been conceptually "ruined". The contrast of the thick stone walls of Edinburgh Edwardian villas and the flying structures, thin roofs and tectonic elements of the new enclosures sets up an enjoyable contrast of opposites. [1] This game has continued into the idea of 're-lining' facades, sometimes described as the strategy of placing a new building demonstrably inside an existing structure and enjoying the syncopations set up between the two. Early examples of this approach are the facades to the first mews house in Royal Terrace Mews, [2] Maggie's Centre, [3] the Fruitmarket Gallery [4] and then, at a much larger scale, the major 'ruinations' of the facade of the Grade B listed Church converted to the Eastgate Theatre in Peebles and the existing warehouse converted into DCA in Dundee. All these moves come from the extraordinary games that Scarpa set in motion when remodelling the French nineteenth century barracks facade found within the Mediaeval Castelvecchio Museum in Verona, which itself is of course dramatically "ruined" to create the great space around the equestrian statue of Cangrande. [5, 6] That game was repeated by Scarpa at the nearby Banca Populare but this time in the context of a completely new building. And as in Scarpa's work, ensuring that the moment of junction between old and new is obscured is essential for the illusion to be successful. In our case, shadow gaps and mirrors are utilised to this end.

We have also had the opportunity of working with two important historic buildings. The Grade A listed Tolbooth at Stirling, like Castelvecchio, was already an accumulation of many eras of history. In a rare moment of indulgence, Historic Scotland allowed us to inject a contemporary era (although typically only at the back and out of sight!) and internally there is a constant oscillation between new and old which gets more intense the further one progresses in the vertical journey up the building. In this instance the opportunity for creative demolition was minimal, but in the unbuilt project for the conversion into a contemporary art centre of the Grade 1 listed Poltimore House we were able to persuade English Heritage to contemplate major demolitions. These recreated a central courtyard and then added back in a new wing of galleries to complete the building. From the exterior the architecture passed, like a baton, from Tudor to eighteenth century to twentieth century and back to Tudor and is the closest we have come to our objective of a serious fully Scarpa-esque engagement with an historic building. [7]

Reading the history of a site or understanding the historic growth patterns of a city is our usual starting point for understanding how to make buildings that are rooted to their place. In Edinburgh, two housing projects in particular at Dublin Street Lane and Old Fishmarket Close, (8) are both predicated on the idea of rebuilding a pre-existing historic pattern of development; in one case building on the footprint of the pre-New Town village, in the other, rediscovering and reconstructing the extended kipper bone plan of the Old Town. (9) Similarly in St Andrews with our unrealised project for the University we were able to produce a design which both extended the rigg pattern of the historic town centre, but at the same time made a new courtyard which defined this particular university faculty. Again, the two proposals for Jesus College, both unbuilt, refer directly to the 500-year-old development of three-sided courts which confront the extensive landscape of the College by simply continuing that pattern but at different scales.

The language of architecture can also make historical references without tipping over into the abyss of planner-friendly pastiche. Our project for housing at the Canongate, Edinburgh, (10) is a reworking of Mediaeval themes found elsewhere in the Old Town but achieving modern lighting and privacy requirements. (11) In Ireland our houses take the language of the undulating dry-stone walls of the Co. Galway landscape and the simple forms of agricultural shed roofs and marry them to make an architecture which we hope is read as inseparable from its landscape. (12) Locking projects into a wider landscape is also an objective of "rooting" the building. For example, the project for Wells Cathedral School, and housing at Westport in Ireland both have strong connections to distant landscape phenomena. At Wells the auditorium focuses on the distant tower of the cathedral behind the performance whilst at Westport, the site plan is entirely predicated on the idea of a 'gun site' framed view of the distant but highly distinctive pilgrimage mountain, Croagh Patrick.

From time to time the planning system obliges us to propose what we call "stealth projects"; buildings which appear not to exist. This tendency is becoming more prevalent as planners are become increasingly risk-averse and lack the imagination to conceive of an alternative approach. House designs at Colinton in Edinburgh, North Berwick, Guildford and Earlston are all representative of this approach. More positive engagements with landscapes however are our various "longhouse" proposals and sadly unrealised attempts to build towers in the landscape in the time-honoured Scottish tradition at Inverness and Seil Island. Undoubtedly, however, our most complex reinterpretation of a landscape, was our first project, the design for a new glasshouse restaurant at Inverewe Gardens. There we simply extended a pattern of curved sloping walled gardens, reproducing these in miniature and then covering them with a canopy of glass and steel. The garden theme was continued with the servery taking the form of a top-lit grotto.

Working abroad is fraught with the danger of 'architectural imperialism'; of ignoring local traditions, materials or climate. In Sri Lanka with the design of the High Commission of the former colonial power this was, of course, a particularly sensitive issue. The High Commission design based on courtyards, water pools, sequences of intense light and shade and the merging of building and landscape is a reinterpretation of the Sri Lankan tradition learnt from Geoffrey Bawa, Sri Lanka's most celebrated architect, and at the same time was able to include Western environmental innovation. (13, 14) In Malta, the dry-stone walled terraced landscape of small fields was the very starting point for the competition entry design, (like Inverewe, a piece of constructed landscape), and in both projects using exclusively local materials helps to bed the buildings into their respective surroundings. In China, where the host country seem to be in a headlong rush to become "Western", I recall how bemused my hosts were when I asked to visit the semi-derelict and deserted original village of Erlang. They could not understand why I was interested in these old buildings. But the massive stone base and timber louvered top of our conference and hotel building was a direct consequence of that visit, attempting again to root this large project into the origins of the nearby settlement. (15) At the same time the overall form of building, acting as a bridge from the main road to the edge of the gorge, was deliberately connected to the Chinese landscape tradition of zigzag bridges.

The integration of external place-making into our planning has always been a major feature of our work. At a domestic scale, courtyard houses at Earlston, North Berwick and Guildford present relatively blank elevations to the outside world but are open to courtyard gardens conceived as external rooms. Our two pioneering suburban projects at Cramond and Harlow both attempted to square the circle of combining the suburban dream of the detached house into groups to make walled courtyards or lanes; external spaces formed by buildings rather than buildings sitting surrounded by generalised space. (16) Higher density housing projects, such as those at Ferry Road and the former Royal Infirmary in Edinburgh and at Graham Square and Moore Street in Glasgow, revive the ideas of shared private courtyards or gardens, often as the means of accessing apartments. (17) The housing projects at Dublin Street Lane, Edinburgh and at Westport in Ireland have both created little pieces of urbanity with their own paved spaces between the housing.

Academic institutions have also been organised around the idea of courtyards with a particularly successful example being the development of the University of East London Stratford Campus. There we were able to counter the prevailing tendency to build isolated object buildings surrounded by unplanned and meaningless external space. The unrealised project for a circular cloister at the heart of the Merchiston Campus of Edinburgh Napier University would have effected a similar total transformation of the perception of that Campus. At a smaller scale the arrangement of Harmeny School focuses on a controlled garden and in Malta the school is organised as a town square leading to covered external streets of classrooms.

Almost all the projects for health buildings have set out to create courtyard gardens adjacent to which the circulation has been organised to avoid the phenomenon of the internal corridor. And finally, our High Commission in Sri Lanka, epitomises this approach. Embassy buildings today are almost universally isolated object buildings surrounded by space, if for no other reason than security. The Colombo project has turned this concept inside out; the seven courtyard gardens have become 'rooms' that are almost more important than the offices adjacent. And instead of the building sitting as an "object" it can only now be understood as a journey from one space to another. At an urban scale we believe the city needs fortifying by continuing urban patterns rather than the invention of new models. At Edinburgh's Haymarket the proposal is as much about the urban spaces and thoroughfare as it is about the five buildings on the site.

The manipulation of light is a continuing theme. It is also a factor which subliminally connects buildings to their Scottish location. At this latitude the changes in light from mid-summer to mid-winter become dramatic with almost continual daylight on 21 June and total darkness by 3.00 pm by 21 December. In domestic architecture, this has produced a theme of opening and closing external skins, where summer time buildings can be extrovert to adjacent landscape and by the use of sliding and pivoting shutters the same spaces can become introvert in wintertime or at night: the opposite poles of the human psyche finding seasonal architectural expression in the same space. The Palmer House extension with its complex system of shutters pioneered this idea and this was then transferred to the house at Milldale, and to some of the mews houses, and will form a major feature of my own house at Hart Street. (19–22) The concept of shutters is not merely about saving energy in the winter; it is also responding to a deeper psychological requirement to close down the relationship with the outside and to create a wintertime cocoon. This is expressed by the idea that the section might contract in various ways between summer and winter and or between day and night. The Harrison House, my own house in Hart Street and the unbuilt house in Inverness each illustrate the concept, wonderfully encapsulated by Mary Harrison's remark that "at night it is like living inside a cigar box".

Toplight in Scotland produces six times the equivalent illumination generated by side light and so can be a very powerful tool. Hidden sources of light falling on wall planes, inspired mostly from Sir John Soane's house in Lincoln Inn Fields, feature in almost all the houses and house extensions. South-facing houses often with a roof pitch which admits low winter light but shades in the summer have their internal north elevations articulated and enlivened by the admission of toplight along the northern boundary wall so that light appears to be coming from the two long sides of the plan. By contrast, the mews houses use ridge roof-lighting which has the opposite effect of introducing a sundial-like beam of sunlight, which moves around the space during the course of the day. To extend these domestic spaces visually, mirrors have often been inserted into the gables under the roof-light and these have the secondary effect of sending a further beam of light in the opposite direction.

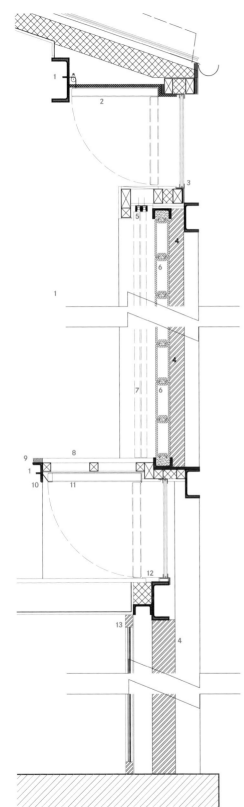

Colburn House 2, pages 33–34

CONSTRUCTION SECTION 1:20

1 SHUTTER WIRE PULLEYS
2 BEECH VENEERED PIVOT SHUTTER IN OPEN POSITION
3 BESPOKE STEEL FRAMED WINDOWS FORMED WITH STANDARD ANGLE SECTIONS
4 SLIDING DOOR GEAR TO SHUTTERS
5 MIRROR
6 GLASS BLOCK WALLING
7 BEECH VENEERED SLIDING SHUTTERS
8 BEECH FACED SURFACE
9 50x25 mm SOLID BEECH NOSING
10 100x50x8 RSA
11 SHUTTER IN OPEN POSITION
12 REMOVABLE BEECH VENEERED MDF FOR GLASS REPLACEMENT
13 MAIN ENTRANCE DOOR

In both Stratheden projects, light was deliberately admitted from two opposite sides of each individual bedroom since the movement of natural light is believed to be a stimulus to those with dementia. Reflected light is used at both the Jack Kilby Computer Centre at Edinburgh Napier University (18) and the Colombo High Commission building, each situation resulting in light bouncing up into a barrel vault and then down into the main space, obviously inspired by Kahn's Kimbell Gallery.

Perhaps most controversial are the lighting arrangements to the Fruitmarket and DCA galleries. With the former, the budget allowed for no lighting controls, and for the first ten years of the Gallery's life, natural light was admitted. One of the most memorable experiences of visiting was to see how changing Scottish light animated the space, transmitting itself dramatically to the interior. At DCA the arrangement was repeated, but this time the budget allowed for both complete blackout blinds and light-diffusing blinds used as and when required. Light as an inducement to enter is also used in both galleries. At the Fruitmarket Gallery, from the adjacent street, a hidden source of light casts patterns on an upper wall seen (until recently closed) through the prominent first floor window and subliminally invites visitors to enter. (23) At DCA a roof-light runs the entire length of the two-storey foyer wall forming patterns of light which again subliminally draw visitors into the depth of the building and deliver them to the galleries at the far end. (24) Our experience is that, like moths, humans are drawn to sources of light, particularly where the source itself is concealed, so in both the Edinburgh and Dundee galleries light in the far corners from a hidden source induces the visitor to promenade through what is otherwise a dead-end space (although in the Fruitmarket's case this has been blocked up) and thereby engage with the exhibition. (25, 26)

Closely allied to the manipulation of light are considerations of energy and sustainability. These issues are now of enormous importance and we like to think that they can become a springboard for making expressive architectural form and not just be about reducing the gas bill. At a small scale, the various mechanisms of shutters have already been explained, but in the proposals for my own house, there is a further experiment with the concept of generating heat through a glass roof and ducting it to a rock store in the basement to allow for evening time re-use. Heavyweight buildings induce a time lag to diurnal changes in temperature. Malta is an example but more ambitiously are our two unbuilt auditoria at Wells and Jesus College Cambridge which both anticipated using environmental strategies of heavy construction and natural ventilation (in the case of Jesus College induced through glass topped chimneys), obviating the need for mechanical cooling. Undoubtedly, the High Commission in Sri Lanka has been the most ambitious project to generate its overall design form from its energy agenda. Here the objective is to give the individual office workers the facility to switch off their air-conditioning and rely, when not too humid, on natural cooling. By sliding open their windows they can also have the sensation of working on a deep veranda adjacent to a garden and within earshot of moving water. (13) Air circulation is induced through a glass "thermal chimney" which forms the ridge

to all the roofs and generates the necessary warm updraft but also gives the building a distinctive lantern-like silhouette. (14) Within the chimney flaps can be opened and large windows to each office slid back to adjacent courtyards so that air cooled over water ponds flows across the space.

Sir Richard MacCormac has observed that our 'DNA' as a practice comes from the Arts and Crafts tradition through offices such as his own or Ted Cullinan's. The latter described the elaboration of construction as "the celebration of necessity" and as a practice we strive hard to continue our design into all aspects of detailing, interiors and if possible even furniture too. We rarely employ technicians as we believe that there is no such thing as a "standard" detail. I am always sympathising with students, who of course rarely build their design projects, that they miss out on half of the exciting part of designing a building; namely, the investigation of the structural and constructional logic of the building and its role in gradually enriching the original idea. Expressing, or indeed over-expressing, how the building is made we believe gives a visual richness at a local scale that can so often be missing in many contemporary buildings. Whilst we never let structure dominate the design at the same time we like it to be elegantly resolved and often expressed as a separate entity from the enclosing elements of the building. The early house extensions all revelled in the idea of expressive steel structures holding roofs free of the previous stone walls and thereby allowing the intervening elements complete freedom to slide, pivot, etc.. In the larger projects, we concentrate the detail into crucial moments of intensity and we have continued the idea of roofs that float and hover over the building with walls made of overlapping tectonic elements. DCA is a particularly interesting example. (27–29) Half the building is in a re-inhabited warehouse, the other half an entirely new construction. The planes of copper and steel framed windows which appear as a new inner lining behind the formalised ruin of the brick warehouse reappear in the new wing as their own architecture of overlapping planes. The whole composition shelters under a hovering datum-like roof.

Most architects get uncomfortable with the word "style" and we are no exception. We prefer to think of the visual reality of our buildings arising predominantly from their programme and location and that elevations spring inescapably from plans and sections. But of course our own architectural predilections inevitably inform what we do. If we have a style, and some say we do, it comes from how we make the everyday elements of architecture. We have a tendency to manipulate roofs to be thin floating planes, flat, inclined or curved, and we have been called "roof architects" a phrase to which I have no objection although I would prefer the more generalised acknowledgement of an overactive interest in manipulating the section. (30) In the unavoidable task of composing elevations, windows are made, where possible, not as holes in walls but rather as apertures formed by the overlapping of planes and the demonstrable layering of materials. In the spirit of free space we tend to avoid structure at corners and have a predilection for steel, in particular enjoying the expression of the thinness of the flanges of rolled steel elements and how light falls on these whether they

be structure, balustrade, etc.. Making staircases we enjoy the expression of the "stepped-ness" of balustrade planes, which I acknowledge has become something of a signature. (31) We move with caution to investigate the nature of materials, rarely experimenting with more than one unfamiliar material per project. Some, such as panels clad in lead, internal shadow gap detailed beech plywood and the three-dimensional expression of glass block panels have become favourite elements which tend to be repeated. Illusions often using mirrors are used both internally and externally using tricks learnt in the Soane Museum. As has already been alluded to, the fourth dimension, time, is something that intrigues us. Buildings that open and close their skins and internally have a variety of spatial arrangements have become a major feature of our designs and the expression of these moving parts (and sometimes the illusion of stationary elements that look as if they might slide) has become part of our language. I've heard architects and others use the word "Murphy-esque" describing one of our projects or indeed sometimes buildings by other architects. It's one of the aspects of architecture that it can be at one and the same time rooted to a particular place and yet still be recognisably by a particular architect; a balancing act, one of many of what my mentor the late Isi Metzstein called the "negotiations within architecture" which makes its practice so intriguing.

In a conversation I had once with our client for the Maggie's Centre and architectural critic, Charles Jencks, we discussed our nominations for the single most important book of theory for the second half of the twentieth century. Unsurprisingly, Jencks' candidate was Venturi's critique of what he understands to be modernism in his ground-breaking book, *Complexity and Contradiction in Architecture*, published in 1966. In response, my nomination was the *Pattern Language* by Christopher Alexander published 11 years later. To me this is an inspiring and wonderful reassertion of the human values of architecture, the activities and human relationships that can be facilitated (or indeed prevented) by certain types of architectural form or ways of planning cities. I find myself mentally reaching for this book at the inception of a project almost by default. That in itself is a confirmation that whilst we see architecture as a visual art, as a piece of continuing cultural history, as having environmental, structural and constructional responsibilities, above all these, it is primarily viewed in this practice as a social art and it is no accident that almost all the projects in this book are described explicitly in these terms.

For example, a house extension to an Edwardian house is described around the necessity of making a series of spaces and relationships which allow a modern family to live a modern family life in contrast to that of their Edwardian predecessors. Similarly, our individual new houses tend to focus on the idea of a large combined family, eating, entertaining, relaxing and cooking in a single space at the heart of the house (the kitchen as "cockpit"), expressing the reality of the contemporary family's communal lifestyle. (32) External staircases to apartments provide semi-private inhabitation (in complete contrast to their internal alternative) and thereby opportunities to engender neighbourly sociability such as

in the private housing projects in Dublin Street Lane or Westport, the two social housing projects in Glasgow, (33) or our forthcoming student housing project in Belfast. Using the staircase becomes a little piece of theatre. Similarly the idea of the sociability of a kitchen in a shared student flat and the potential for interaction from flat to flat via their respective kitchens were generators for the designs for both Jesus College and Warwick University.

In his 2012 RIBA Gold Medal Lecture, Herman Hertzberger mentioned that he had spent his entire life crusading against corridors. I had already chosen that sub-title for our chapter on health buildings when I read his lecture, and in our own way we have had exactly the same objective, in particular in educational and health buildings, the two types where the dreary internal corridor is most prevalent. Every health building design in this book places circulation around the edge of the enclosure rather than as a corridor down the centre, often using courtyard gardens as orientation devices. (34) This is relatively easy in a building such as a doctors' surgery where the waiting 'room' is transformed into the open heart of the building, but we have also proved that it is still possible to maintain the idea in the relatively complex and large programme of a whole hospital at St Andrews. At Harmeny School, a facility for emotionally behaved children, circulation is largely through an open cloister. (35) It was interesting that, in a filmed interview, the Principal, Patrick Webb, said that a great deal of the school's "business" between an individual child and a teacher was not concluded in the classroom but rather done sitting on the low wall in the cloister. Again in the nursery school of Edinburgh Academy, it was the non-educational space of the entrance which we observed as the most critical; namely the place where children and parents are parted. Indeed, the elaboration of circulation space into places for informal meetings and occasional inhabitation also exists in all the health buildings, whether it be an individual seat on a half-landing in the Maggie Centre (so that an individual might have their own space and yet be on the edge of others' activities) or a lay-by seat in the Stratheden courtyard circulation system.

The Jack Kilby Computing Centre at Edinburgh Napier University had a brief which was astonishingly short, namely 500 computer stations. Our immediate response was to think of the psychological impact such a large number of computers in one space would have on students and we set about discovering a way using the section, structure, circulation and toplight to divide and define a series of much smaller units of 25, so that this gigantic space could be broken down into routes and places which could be grasped on entry; in other words to give it a human scale. That idea has been continued at the University of East London Computing Library. Also at UEL, we had the intriguing problem of trying to ensure patient privacy in their podiatry booths solving it with a two-storey 'opera box' model, a type which had never been tried before and has proved hugely successful. In our arts buildings, the social success of the building seems to us to be paramount. If the bar/cafe is a success, the building's success will usually follow. Contemporary art is not a mainstream activity and so our

objective has always been to maximise the number of visitors to the exhibitions by tempting them into the building and dissolving the threshold between street and gallery. Placing the cafe on the street in the Fruitmarket Gallery was an early direct example of this strategy. Having smelt the coffee visitors find themselves in an exhibition and visitor numbers quadrupled as a result. Following on from that, the bar and restaurant at DCA (36, 37) is deliberately placed at the heart of the activity, an intermediate meeting ground between all the destinations of art galleries, cinemas, the printmakers workshop and the University facilities. All of these are organised to be seen as glimpses from the cafe, enticing the visitor further into the activities of the building. On this awkward site, the front entrance is pulled back as far as possible, to reduce the internal circulation but mostly to make the presence of the bar/cafe immediately visible on entry. There is no question to my mind that the massive success of this building is because it has become a busy and attractive place to meet friends and enjoy the atmosphere even without necessarily visiting the other facilities on offer. In that respect its instructive to think how the building might have fared with a different competition design; for example, one architect of international stature placed the cafe remotely on the roof. At a smaller scale the trick was repeated by placing the cafe as an invitation on the street in the Eastgate Theatre in Peebles and we hope the cafe in the museum in Dunfermline sitting as part of the entrance experience will play a similar role. (38)

And finally at Caenarfon where the building's site has to a degree divorced it from the life of the town centre we began the design with the concept that the two unusually combined functions, lettable offices and theatre-going, should be combined to be mutually supportive so that the building became socially self-sufficient. The dramatic foyer in the centre of the plan connects all spaces and puts the activities of the offices on full view through glazed walls. (39) As at the University of East London Education Department this device makes "everything available": the activities of the offices are on display to visitors and the foyer becomes the social heart for office workers by day as well as a "see and be seen" foyer by night for the theatre goers.

I like to return to buildings and observe how they are being used and inhabited. It's always a didactic experience. Buildings are a little like children; they have to be let go to lead their own life. Sometimes they misbehave but on the whole we have been blessed with marvellous clients who genuinely seem to appreciate what we have achieved on their behalf. In addition I have had the moving experience of receiving letters from total strangers who have used the Maggie's Centre in Edinburgh telling me how much they have appreciated the building and the atmosphere we have created there. Teachers tell me that the buildings we have created at Harmeny School have made the transformation of the lives of seriously disadvantaged children so much easier to achieve. To complete not just three interesting buildings but also a whole new campus atmosphere (unrequested by the client!) from highly unpromising beginnings at the University of East London and then watch how the students have taken the place over, and to heart, is hugely satisfying. (40) At the opening ceremony the head of the

Education faculty singled us out and said our best quality was that we were very good listeners. That means more to me than any number of complimentary magazine articles or awards. The latter are of course always welcome and good for morale, but the best feeling is to sit anonymously (and one quickly becomes anonymous) in, say, the cafe at DCA and just watch the building in use all around.

On occasional visits to China my hosts usually ask me just one question—"what is your speciality?" This question has always baffled me as I find all building types interesting and have an ambition to be good at everything and not to get pigeon-holed. I hope that this book demonstrates an impressive record of architectural versatility; certainly that's borne out by our list of RIBA and other awards (more RIBA awards than any other Scottish practice in the same period). Indeed, looking back over 21 years, I see that some of our best designs and most heavily awarded buildings are for building types that at that time we had never attempted before. We believe passionately that a good architect is akin to a good barrister; able to pick up any brief and master it. It's frustrating that the opposite opinion tends to hold sway in most selection processes.

On one of our practice excursions we visited the beautiful small Baroque town of Eichstatt outside Munich specifically to see the work of the German architect Karl-Josef Schattner (1924–2012). (41–43) Massively influenced by Scarpa, for his whole life he was employed direct by the local Bishop and for the Catholic University in the town. His projects whether they be new build extensions or reworking of historic structures are all impeccably detailed, beautifully built, radical where they need to be but always respectful too. They are also all very well cared for by very proud clients. In a phrase which chimes exactly with my own approach, Schattner said to me that "I do the opposite of the original in order to give the history of the building a future." As well as admiration for both the man and his work I have to admit a slight twinge of jealousy as to his working milieu. It may surprise some but, like Schattner, I have no ambition to build all over the world, to have a large office and huge projects, rather if possible I prefer to build locally and for clients whose company we enjoy and whose projects we find stimulating and to have an office which is small enough so that I know what's going on but large enough to have a diversity of skills.

Isi Metzstein once said that the definition of an artist is that they are "driven"; they have something inside which needs to keep finding expression. Real artists just keep going and personally I have no intention of retiring. As I write I am just about to start building a house for myself. This is possibly the most difficult project of all; as everyone in the office knows with this project, my indecision is final! An ambition to create a museum is being fulfilled at Dunfermline and we are now looking at urban projects which allow us not just to make buildings but also to make pieces of city too. The number of universities commissioning us continues to grow and after two false starts in Cambridge we are now about to build there. We are building on our expertise in the health sector, in particular in mental health and for the care of patients with dementia. We continue to make well-crafted private houses. In the arts we are looking forward to developing our plans for Perth Theatre and returning to build on the success of Galeri at Caernarfon by constructing a substantial extension there.

Remaining ambitions are of course many. One day we may be lucky enough to build a substantial public building in Edinburgh. I would like to build a hospital if only to prove that they can be designed intelligently and humanely. Similarly it would fascinate me to design a school. Another Embassy would be fun. Building on my experience of working in Sir Richard MacCormac's office I would love one day to be invited to build within the hallowed grounds of an Oxford or Cambridge College. I remain fascinated by the possibility of a major opportunity to engage creatively with a historic building or to place a significant new building in a historic place. But even if none of these things happen my hope is that we continue to maintain the quality of work that has brought us 21 RIBA or RIAI awards in as many years, and continue to attract more wonderful clients and talented colleagues with whom to work on the enjoyable day-to-day challenge of making buildings together. Architecture is an endlessly fascinating "negotiation", as Isi Metzstein used to put it and every project is a fresh and unique challenge. I couldn't possibly imagine doing anything else.

THE PRACTICE

The practice enjoys or has enjoyed contributions from:

Alex Abbey; Usama Al Kindi; Clive Albert; Roger Alexander; Craig Amy; Graeme Armet; Duncan Bain;
Patrick Bankhead; Tim Bayman; Tina Bergman; Peter Besley; Lorraine Beveridge; Bill Black; Robert Black;
Matthew Blair; Adrian Boot; Matt Bremner; Cathy Brick; Michael Brookman Amissah; Andrew Brown;
Edward Burgess; Adam Burgess; Joe Carnegie; Phil Catchside; Oliver Chapman; Aaron Coates;
James Cockburn; Rebecca Crabtree; Robbie Cullen; Graham Currie; Francesco De Domenico; Lesley Dell;
Arnaud Demarque; Sean Douglas; Heather Duffy; Alan Dunsmore; Christian Erdrich; Michael Evans;
Daniel Fairbairn; James Falconer; Patrick Fallis; Justine Fernandes; Jose Fernandez; Tom Fitzgerald;
Mark Floate; Catriona Forbes; Colin Foster; Tom Fotheringham; Richard Foxley; Steven Fraser; Tom Fuggle;
Claire Gaffney; Dominik George; Hamish Ginn; Marcelo Gomes; Kris Grant; Allan Gray; Karol Grec;
Hamish Gunns; Peter Guthrie; Ian Hall; Lee Hallman; Josh Hampton; Scott Harrison; Fraser Hay;
Thomas Held; Fiona Henderson; Andre Henkamp; Lee Hentze; Carsten Hermann; Ed Hollis; Louis Hudson;
Dominic Humphrey; Peter Hunt; Klas Hyllen; Gareth Jones; Kathy Jowett; Christopher Kelly; Joanne Kelly;
Zoltan Kiraly; Piotr Kmiotczyk; Martin Lambie; John Leetch; Stephen Leonard; Michelle Leonard; Iain Levens;
Scott Licznerski; Ashley Little; Matt Loader; Riaan Louw; John Lyons; Chris Lowry; Tersius Maass;
Ewan MacDonald; Louise MacFarlane; Chris Malcolm; Isabelle Malecot; James Mason; James Mate;
Manfred Mattersberger; Alistair McAuslan; Andy McAvoy; Wattie McCallum; Jamie McCutcheon;
Calum McDonald; Euan McDonald; Ryan McGee; Rob McGill; Sarah McInenry; Ian McIntosh;
Guido McLellan; Ian McMurray; David McPeak; James Millar; David Milne; Graeme Mitchell; Patrick Mitchell;
Graeme Montgomery; Sam Moran; David Morris; Ray Muldoon; Stephen Mulhall; Richard Murphy;
James Nelmes; Graham Nottle; John O'Brien; Joe O'Sullivan; William Ould; Tim Parker; Paul Pattinson;
Daniel Plunkett; Gareth Pugh; Peter Quinger; Brent Railton; Gerard Reinmuth; Chris Rhodes; Jonathan Riddle;
Daryl Robbins; Chris Rogers; Keith Ross; Matthew Rourke; Jordi Sanahuja; Heilwig Schomecker;
Holger Schwarz; Guy Scott; Jie Shen; Rachel Simmonds; Neil Simpson; Bradley Slaughter; Richard Smith;
James Smith; Matthew Smith; Stewart Stevenson; Ian Strakis; David Stronge; Ryan Sylvester; Arai Tadashi;
Hugo Target; James Taylor; Marco Terranova; Alex Thurman; Brian Tobin; Will Tunnell; Iolanda Veziano;
John Walker; Neil Wallace; Laura Wardrop; Henrietta Warwick; Matthew Waterfall; Sarah Watt;
Adrian Welch; Nicola Wessels; Christian Wessolowski; Jo White; Louise Williamson; Ben Wilson.

CLIENTS

AMA (New Town) Ltd
Anglia Ruskin University
Argent Group
Belfast Health and Social Care Trust
Biggar Theatre Workshop
Borders 1996, Peebles
Brandhorst Foundation, Munich
Buredi Ltd
CALA Ltd
Cardonald College
Castle Rock Housing Association
Coatbridge College of Further Education
Cwmni Tref Caernarfon
Dundee City Council
Dunton Property Trust
East Devon District Council
East Dunbartonshire Council
Strathkelvin Development Company
East Lothian Council
Edinburgh Academy
Edinburgh Filmhouse
and Edinburgh International Film Festival
Edinburgh Napier University
Fife Council
Foreign and Commonwealth Office
Formby Land Trust
Foundation for Tomorrow's Schools, Malta
Frank Spratt Ltd
Fruitmarket Gallery Board
Gladedale Capital
Glasgow Housing Association
Glenmorison Group
Grampian Housing Association
and NHS Grampian
Harmeny Education Trust Ltd
Hazledene Estates Ltd
Highland Housing Alliance
Hillcrest Housing Association
Horsecross Arts Ltd
Inpartnership and The Burrell Company
Iwate Council, Japan
James Sankey and Tony Singh (Oloroso)
Jesus College Cambridge
John Muir Birthplace Trust
Kilmartin Property Group
Lang-Jiu Whisky Distillers
Leicester City Council
Maggie Keswick Jencks Cancer Caring Trust
Magnus Homes
Miller Developments
Molendinar Park Housing Association

National Galleries of Scotland
National Trust for Scotland
New Edinburgh Ltd
Newhall Projects Ltd
NHS Fife
Nottinghamshire County Council
Old Town Housing Association
Quartermile Ltd
Queen's Hall Board
Queen's University Belfast
Railtrack
RBS/Dunedin Properties
Rydens
Scottish Natural Heritage
South Lanarkshire District Council
Southside Capital Ltd
St Andrews University
Stirling Regional Council
Tiger Developments Ltd
Tom Joyce Ltd
Tourism Resources
Tyneside Building Preservation Trust
University of East London
University of Edinburgh
University of Warwick
Vejle Council, Denmark

Together with many private clients.

Richard Murphy Architects 2004—with special guest

SELECTED AWARDS

RIBA Award

2011 Stratheden 18 and 24 Bed Dementia and Mental Health Units
2011 Housing At Newhall, Harlow
2009 Housing Moore Street, Glasgow
2009 British High Commission, Colombo, Sri Lanka
2007 Mews House, 10a Circus Lane, Edinburgh
2005 Caernarfon Arts Centre, North Wales
2003 Computer Centre, Merchiston Campus, Napier University, Edinburgh
2002 Stirling Tolbooth Arts Centre
2002 Remodelled Flat, Edinburgh New Town
2001 Harmeny School, Balerno, Near Edinburgh
2000 Dundee Contemporary Arts
2000 Housing at Dublin Street Lane, Edinburgh
1999 Ivy Bank House, Dirleton
1998 7 Abbotsford Park, Edinburgh
1997 Maggie's Cancer Caring Centre, Edinburgh
1996 17 Royal Terrace Mews, Edinburgh
1995 49 Gilmour Road, Edinburgh
1993 Fruitmarket Gallery, Edinburgh
1992 29 Inverleith Gardens, Edinburgh

RIBA Stirling Shortlist

1997 Maggie's Cancer Caring Centre, Edinburgh
1996 17 Royal Terrace Mews, Edinburgh

RIBA Crown Estate Commission Conservation Award

2002 Stirling Tolbooth Arts Centre

RIBA Lubetkin Prize—Shortlisted

2009 British High Commission, Colombo, Sri Lanka

RIAI Regional Award

2006 Housing At Westport, County Mayo, The Republic Of Ireland.
1999 House At Killeenaran, County Galway, Ireland

Regeneration of Scotland Supreme Award

1999 Dundee Contemporary Arts
2001 Graham Square, Glasgow

Royal Scottish Academy Gold Medal for Architecture

1994 Experimental Energy Home
2004 British High Commission, Colombo, Sri Lanka

British Council for Offices—Scottish Awards—Best Commercial Office Award

2012 Justice Mill Lane Park Inn Hotel and Office Development, Aberdeen

Dundee Institute of Architects—Building of the Decade Award

2007 Dundee Contemporary Arts

EXHIBITIONS

1996 Transforming Architecture, Mathew Gallery Edinburgh
1998 Transforming Architecture, Providence, Rhode Island, USA
2001 Ten years of Practice, Fruitmarket Gallery, Edinburgh (1)
2002 Ten Years of Practice, RIBA London (2)
2002 Ti Ars Arbejder af Skotske Arkitekt, Aarhus and Copenhagen, Denmark
2004 The British Pavilion, Venice Architecture Biennale
2012 Of its Time and Place, RIBA London
2013 Of its Time and Place Royal Scottish Academy, Edinburgh

COMPETITIONS

1991 RIAS OPEN COMPETITION Inverewe Garden Restaurant WON
1992 RIAS OPEN COMPETITION Dundee Health Centre
1992 RIAS OPEN COMPETITION Highland swimming pool
1993 RIAS LIMITED COMPETITION Byre Theatre St Andrews
1993 RIAS OPEN COMPETITION Rural House West Lothian
1994 RIAS OPEN COMPETITION House for the future
1994 LIMITED COMPETITION Dubin St Lane Housing Edinburgh WON
1995 LIMITED COMPETITION Graham Square CONSOLATION PRIZE
1996 RIAS INVITED COMPETITION Glasgow Gallery of Scottish Art
1996 RIAS LIMITED COMPETITION Dundee Contemporary Arts WON
1997 LIMITED COMPETITION Jesus College Cambridge Student Accommodation
1997 RIAS LIMITED COMPETITION Stirling Tolbooth Theatre WON
1997 RIAS LIMITED COMPETITION Hamilton Arts Centre
1997 INVITED COMPETITION Bath Street Office foyer WON
1998 LIMITED COMPETITION Leicester Phoenix Arts Centre WON
1998 INVITED COMPETITION Housing Old Fishmarket Close Edinburgh WON
1999 LIMITED COMPETITION Queen's Gallery Holyrood Palace
2001 INVITED COMPETITION Brandhorst Galery Munich
2001 LIMITED COMPETITON Theatre Augsberg
2002 LIMITED COMPETITION British High Commission Colombo WON
2002 LIMITED COMPETITION SWIMMING Pool, Formby
2003 LIMITED COMPETTION Boys' School Malta WON
2002 INVITED COMPETITION Moore Street Housing Glasgow Master plan WON
2003 RIAS LIMITED COMPETITION Visitor Centre Botanic Gardens Edinburgh
2003 RIBA LIMITED COMPETITION Middlesborough Arts Centre
2004 INVITED COMPETITION Manchester Piccadilly master plan
2004 LIMITED DEVELOPER/ARCHITECT COMPETITION
Scottish Natural Heritage HQ Inverness
2005 INVITED COMPETITION Housing and Salvation Army,
Timmer Market Aberdeen WON
2005 RIBA LIMITED COMPETITION Castleford Museum and Library
2005 LIMITED COMPETITION Hadrian's wall visitor centre
2005 LIMITED COMPETITION George Square cafe, Glasgow
2006 INVITED COMPETITION Veile spinning Mills Art Centre, Denmark
2006 LIMITED COMPETITION PFI Bid for St Andrews hospital
2006 LIMITED COMPETITON Shetland Music Centre WON (design element)
2006 INVITED COMPETITION Mixed commercial development
Justice Mill Lane Aberdeen WON
2006 RIBA LIMITED COMPETITION Sherwood Forrest Visitor Centre
2007 RIBA OPEN COMPETITION Theatre Belfast
2007 INVITED COMPETITION Jesus College Cambridge auditorium hotel etc WON
2007 LIMITED COMPETITION Wells Cathedral School Auditorium
2007 RIAS LIMITED COMPETITION Dunfermline museum and arts centre WON
2007 OPEN COMPETITION Inverness Highland Housing. CO WINNER
2008 LIMITED COMPETITION Warwick University Student residences
2008 INVITED COMPETITION Old See House Belfast WON
2009 LIMITED COMPETITION Library Ledbury Herefordshire
2009 LIMITED COMPETITION Arts Centre Barnard Castle Co. Durham
2010 RIBA OPEN COMPETITION Whitehaven housing and offices WON
2010 LIMITED COMPETITION Edinburgh University postgraduate housing WON
2010 INVITED COMPETITION Whisky Centre China

Richard Murphy

OBE, BA (Hons), Dip Arch, RIBA, FRIAS, RSA, FRSA, FRSE

Richard Murphy was born and raised in Cheshire. He was educated at Newcastle and Edinburgh Universities and has worked in the West Indies, in London for MacCormac Jamieson and Prichard and in Edinburgh for Simpson and Brown and Alsop Lyall and Stormer. For four years he taught under Professor Isi Metzstein at Edinburgh University during which period he researched the work of the Venetian architect Carlo Scarpa at the Castelvecchio, Verona and subsequently mounted exhibitions in Edinburgh, London and Verona itself. He wrote the definitive book on the building and Scarpa's drawings (published by Butterworth Heinemann) and later wrote for Phaidon's *Architecture in Detail* series an analysis of Scarpa's work at the Querini Stampalia in Venice. He has also presented a film for Channel 4 on Scarpa's work and with Murray Grigor, the film's director, co-wrote *An Architect's Appreciation of Charles Rennie Mackintosh* for Bellew Publishing.

In October 1991 he founded the practice of Richard Murphy Architects. This book marks 21 years of that practice in which the practice has won 19 Royal Institute of British Architects Awards, one RIBA Crown Estate Commission Conservation Award, three Edinburgh Architectural Association Silver Medals, two Royal Incorporation of Architects in Scotland Regeneration of Scotland Supreme Awards, two Awards from the Royal Institute of Architects in Ireland and has twice been short-listed for the Stirling Prize and once for the RIBA Lubetkin Prize. His work has been extensively reviewed and he himself frequently contributes to architectural journals. He has lectured widely both on Scarpa and on his own work both at home and abroad.

Richard Murphy is an Academician of the Royal Scottish Academy, a Fellow of the Royal Society of Arts, of the Royal Society of Edinburgh, of the Royal Incorporation of Architects in Scotland and of Edinburgh Napier University, a Member of the Royal Institute of British Architects and a trustee of Turn End Charitable Trust. In 2006 he was voted Scottish Architect of the Year by readers of *Prospect Magazine* and in the Queen's Honours List 2007, he was awarded an OBE. In his spare moments he sings with the Chorus of the Scottish Chamber Orchestra and pilots his Microlight, *G-RIBA*, around the skies of Scotland and as far afield as Venice.

He lives in a house that he designed himself and is shortly to be moving to a second.

Sir Richard MacCormac

CBE MA PPRIBA RA

Richard MacCormac set up a consultancy in his own name in February 2011. Previously he was Chairman of MJP Architects which he co-founded in 1972. As well as being a committed practitioner working in historic contexts with projects in Bristol, Oxford, Cambridge, Durham and the City of London, Richard has taught and lectured widely and published numerous articles on urban issues, architectural theory and history. He has been an adviser to the City of Dublin where he was an adjudicator for selecting a new University College Dublin Master plan and he is currently adviser to the City of Bath.

He has an exceptional record for designing Collegiate buildings which include student residences for Trinity College, Trinity Hall and Fitzwilliam College, Cambridge, Worcester College, Wadham College, Balliol College and St John's College, Oxford. The most recent, 2011—Kendrew Quadrangle, St John's—is the most carbon neutral building in the City of Oxford.

Science and Education projects include the ongoing development of the Master plan for expanding the Physical Sciences for Cambridge University into West Cambridge, 1997–2012; an outline design for an auditorium for Trinity College Cambridge, 2006—commissioned by Martin Rees, Master of Trinity and President of the Royal Society; the Wellcome Wolfson building for the Science Museum, 2003; outline design for Entrepreneurship Centre, University of Cambridge, 2001; Library Plaza for the London School of Economics, 2001; the Wellcome Wing of the Science Museum, 2000; Lancaster University Library, 1996; Library and Auditorium, City of Durham, 1996; Ruskin Library, University of Lancaster, 1995; Cable and Wireless Training College, 1994.

Other major projects include the British Embassy, Bangkok, 2008; BBC Broadcasting House, Portland Place, 2006; Phoenix Initiative, a regeneration project for Coventry which won the Royal Town Planning Institute Planning Award in 2004; Building 1, Paternoster Square, 2003; London Jubilee Line Extension Station , Southwark, 2000, and the Wellcome Wing extension to the Science Museum, 2000.

Richard MacCormac is a Royal Academician, Honorary Fellow of Trinity College, Cambridge and Honorary Doctor of Science at Queen Mary University London.

PHOTO CREDITS

COLOPHON

Copyright 2012 Artifice books on architecture,
the authors, architects. All rights reserved.

Artifice books on architecture
10a Acton Street
London WC1X 9NG
United Kingdom

Tel: +44 (0)20 7713 5097
Fax: +44 (0)20 7713 8682
sales@artificebooksonline.com
www.artificebooksonline.com

British Library Cataloguing-in-Publication Data.
A CIP record for this book is available from the
British Library.

ISBN 978 1 907317 76 7

Artifice books on architecture is an environmentally
responsible company. *Of Its Time and Of Its Place:
The Work of Richard Murphy Architects* is printed using
sustainably sourced materials.

Designed by Stephen Leonard
with the assistance of Laura Varzgalyte.